Slices of Life

A Food Writer Cooks Through Many a Conundrum

by Leah Eskin

Illustrated by

Alison Seiffer Spacek

RUNNING PRESS

PHILADELPHIA · LONDON

For Aunt Ruth,
who taught me taste.

Published by Running Press,
A Member of the Perseus Books Group

All rights reserved under the Pan-American and International Copyright Conventions

Printed in China.

Books published by Running Press are available at special discounts for bulk purchases in the United States by corporations, institutions, and other organizations. For more information, please contact the Special Markets Department at the Perseus Books Group, 2300 Chestnut Street, Suite 200, Philadelphia, PA 19103, or call (800) 810-4145, ext. 5000, or e-mail special.markets@perseusbooks.com.

ISBN 978-0-7624-5270-5
Library of Congress Control Number: 2013950315

E-book ISBN 978-0-7624-5313-9

9   8   7   6   5   4   3   2   1
Digit on the right indicates the number of this printing

Designed by Frances J. Soo Ping Chow
Edited by Jennifer Kasius
Typography: Alana Pro, Avenir, Bookeyed Sadie, Bookeyed Suzanne, ITC Veljovic, Muncie, Samantha Ornaments, and Univers

Running Press Book Publishers
2300 Chestnut Street
Philadelphia, PA 19103-4371

Visit us on the web!
www.offthemenublog.com

Portions of this book first appeared in the *Chicago Tribune*.
They are reprinted by permission.

Table of Contents

Introduction

I write about food. People ask: Are you a chef? Are you critic? Do you eat out every night? I explain: No. I'm a columnist. I cook at home.

I chose my career the summer I turned seventeen. On a road trip, I drew up a list of all the jobs that seemed Important, then crossed off the ones that sounded boring. The only thing left was journalist. I spoke French. I liked to travel. Obviously, I'd sign on as a foreign correspondent, based in Paris. I'd write long, insightful stories about Injustice and Strife.

I stuck with the program: In college, I studied international relations. I spent my junior year in Paris. I went to journalism school and got a magazine job in New York. Nights, I read Janet Flanner's *Paris Journal*.

I moved on to freelancing and, weary of New York, moved to Chicago. On the job hunt, I arranged lunch with a reporter named Bob Blau. I fell for him before we met: I have a thing for double vowels.

Everything was new—new city, new boyfriend—and I tried writing about it in a new, personal, way. I sent a story to Alison True at the *Chicago Reader*. She liked it. And I liked her. I've kept the approach, and the friendship, since.

I always assumed I'd have to wait for marriage to get my Cuisinart, but when Bob bought me a white base model, it meant we could date indefinitely. We spent four years going out to dinner. One weekend we flew to Paris, split a platter of mussels and fries, and got engaged. At our wedding, I wore a veil that gathered into a silk-and-seed-pearl strawberry tart. The chocolate cake listed alarmingly, but tasted dreamy.

Two years into our married life, Bob was named a Nieman fellow. Before packing for Boston, I invited our friend Ann Marie Lipinski to brunch. She had been a fellow. Holding a drippy pear cobbler, I asked if the year away was good timing for a baby. "No," she said. "Wait until it's over." Ann Marie's a smart cookie. She would go on to edit the *Chicago Tribune* and run the Nieman Foundation. I do what she says. We thought up Hannah on the first day and delivered her on the last, after the graduation party.

Hannah grew, Noah arrived. I freelanced features, many for the *Tribune Sunday Magazine.* My editor brought me on staff and handed over the back page column. I named it "Sum of the Parts." I wrote about old shoes and new colors. I wrote about Gulf War stew and peaceful origami. I wrote about food.

When I was little we lived in Minneapolis; Dad worked in marketing at Pillsbury. Sometimes he'd bring home a new product. I felt special, being one of the first civilians to chew through a Space Food Stick. He took our critiques back to the test kitchen, which I pictured as NASA with ovens.

I took classes at the Minnesota Dance Theatre under the renowned Loyce Houlton. One year at the Nutcracker cast party, the principals staged a cheeky "Twelve Days of Christmas" where the men, as partridges, leapt into the arms of the women, as pear trees. I was four, little sister to a mouse. It took me all the French hens and golden rings to choose the stickiest chocolate cupcake. Finally the drummers drumming, pipers piping, and lords-a-leaping swept into a jubilant circle. Loyce Houlton held out a bony hand. To join the dance, I would have to drop the cupcake.

I stuck with the cupcake.

It was honest: I love food. And I love to cook. In grade school I dripped coffee for Mom and Dad. In junior high I foisted quiche on my brother Ben, bulking up for football. In high school I baked brownies to send to my brother Josh. I stir-fried tofu from a college closet and dragged clams up five flights for grad-school bouillabaisse. I cook for sustenance, for solace, and for joy.

So eventually my column became a food column. I started writing it when Hannah and Noah were small; now they're teenagers. I started writing it when we lived in Chicago; now we live in Baltimore. I started writing it when newspapers seemed solid; now they seem tenuous.

Over that time I wrote one column—an essay plus a recipe—almost every week. I liked that "essay" meant "try." I tried first person, second person, third person; I tried past, present, future; I tried, in a story on gnocchi, using every word that starts with gn. Those tries—reworked—became this book.

I write about food, so I write about home, about family, and about love. It's not always Strife or Injustice; it's rarely Paris. But it is, I'd say, Important.

Chapter 1: Fold

Growing up I read *Ms.* and marveled at the women who managed both career and family. Secretly I suspected career won and family lost. I worked out a workaround: Get rich and famous young. I became a mom at thirty-four. I'd been a stringer for *People*, and the editor of a magazine handed out in malls. Not rich, not famous, not young.

When Hannah was a few weeks old, Colman Andrews asked me to cover the Iowa State Fair for *Saveur*. Given my girlhood goat-tending, I felt qualified. Given my newborn, I declined. Colman countered with two gifts: He paid for a sitter. And he quoted editor Dorothy Kalins, back from a reporting trip in France: "They have babies there, too." Maybe I could both parent and work.

I did, from home, in yoga pants. Three years later, when Noah was almost one, I joined Bob on his daily drive to the *Tribune*. On the way I read him my stories, which he shredded. Bob paced his office in the fourth floor newsroom. I perched in a cubicle on five. Sometimes we managed lunch together. I loved Take Our Daughters (and later Sons) to Work Day. Watching Hannah and Noah page through the papers on my desk, I felt like some *Ms.* cover girl.

This chapter starts with a taste of lemon-tart romance. There's a bite of Hannah's first birthday cake and a sip of the day I explained Bob's work, editing a series on the death penalty. I helped Noah dig for fossils, endured Bob's bike obsession, and cringed through my first mammogram. And of course, we ate.

STARRY NIGHT

H ere's how to capture the mystery of the summer sky on a plastic fork: Choose a sultry evening. Clatter through the cupboards for a tart pan, 9 inches or so. Square is fine, but round suits the vaulted sky.

Consider filo with its connection, however flakey, to ancient Greece. Think constellations, celestial navigation, Odysseus returning from years at sea. In your own cluttered cupboards, the epic storyline has largely been lost. But you retain this definition of romance: The goddess Athena holding night still so that hero and heroine can whisper their secrets in the dark.

Remember that filo shatters, then sogs. That the home cook, like Odysseus, is mere mortal. Rely instead on tart pastry. Pat thin. Bake crisp. At sunset, as the air is turning thick and golden, pour in lemon curd. Steal a taste. It should be startling and sweet. A confidence at dusk.

Now the sky. Simmer blueberries thick and heap them over the tart. Nothing orderly; this is the cosmos in all its chaos. Turn your attention to the stars. Slice a ripe starfruit thinly crosswise. Scatter constellations over the blueberry blue-black. Think *Starry Night*.

Slice two wedges onto paper plates. Side by side with your sweetheart, stare up into the night. Spin the distant specks of light into a long and unlikely story, one compelling enough to postpone dawn.

Night Tart

Makes one 9-inch tart

1 9-inch fully baked
    Tart Shell (page 104)

2 cups Lemon Curd
    (page 262)

3 cups blueberries

¼ cup sugar

1 ripe starfruit, thinly
    sliced crosswise

1. Fill: Pour chilled lemon curd into cooled tart shell. Chill.

2. Thicken: Tumble half the blueberries and all the sugar into a medium saucepan. Cook over medium heat, mashing into a thick sauce, about 10 minutes. Pull off heat and stir in remaining blueberries, leaving these berries whole. Chill.

3. Decorate: Pour cooled berries over tart. Dot with starfruit. Enjoy.

ONE CANDLE

Hannah's birthday called for cake. Tiresome baby books recommended unsweetened carrot loaf, banana chunks, or cinnamon-sprinkled applesauce. This was my first baby's first birthday, the culmination of a year that had transformed her from blue-eyed stare to vibrant—and highly opinionated—Hannah. Cinnamon-sprinkled applesauce would not do.

My initial attempts to introduce Hannah to the joy of cooking had been rebuffed. Blended peas met with clamped baby lips and an outrage that asked, "Why poison?" Until I offered her my own spoon, heavy with tiramisu.

The modern baby is permitted so little variety. No cheese. No eggs. No sugar. No wheat. No cocoa. No coffee. No alcohol. Which are the ingredients of tiramisu. Hannah tasted. Then lunged for the bowl.

Another day she had come across an errant chocolate chip. I found her seated on the kitchen floor, smeared from cheek to cheek. Her blue eyes brimmed with one part joy, one part indignation. "Where," her thought-bubble read, "have you been stashing these?"

So, it was not as if I could shirk cake duty. I settled on a recipe: all chocolate. The day before the big day, I wrapped an apron around Hannah, twice. I sifted flour and sugar into a bowl; she scooped it out. Eventually we achieved a sticky mess of a batter. I baked the layers late, letting them cool in the darkened kitchen. I beat buttercream and thought about the night, a whole year earlier, when I had followed Julia Child's five-page recipe for braided apricot Danish, hoping its complexity would ease the longest wait I'd known.

In the morning I stacked and filled and leveled. By the time Hannah's baby guests were trudging down the hall, I hadn't managed a single rosette. Her cake, pure and smooth, was decorated with a single candle.

There was a round of "Happy Birthday." A toast. A puff of smoke. And a slice for everyone. Hannah liked hers. I can tell by the way she grins in the snapshot we took and by the way she's dressed—curls to toes—in chocolate.

Birthday Cake

Makes one 9-inch layer cake

2 cups sifted cake flour

¼ cup unsweetened cocoa ("natural" works best)

2 teaspoons baking soda

¼ teaspoon fine salt

12 tablespoons (1½ sticks) unsalted butter, softened

1½ cups sugar

3 eggs

4 ounces unsweetened chocolate, melted and cooled to room temperature

½ cup buttermilk

¾ cup hot water

Chocolate Buttercream (recipe follows)

1. Mix: In a medium bowl, whisk together flour, cocoa, soda, and salt.

2. Fluff: Using a stand mixer fitted with the paddle attachment, set on medium speed, beat butter and sugar fluffy, about 3 minutes. Add eggs, one at a time; beat fluffy after each. Scrape in chocolate, beat just to combine. Scoop in one-third of the flour mixture; mix on low. Pour in half the buttermilk; mix until just incorporated. Work in remaining doses of flour, buttermilk, flour. Thin with hot water. Scrape down sides of bowl and mix smooth.

3. Bake: Pour batter into two 9-inch cake pans, buttered and dusted with cocoa. Slide into a 350-degree oven and bake until center is springy, about 22 minutes. Let cakes cool in their pans, 10 minutes. Turn out on a rack and cool completely.

4. Frost: Smear a little buttercream on a cake plate, as glue. Set one cooled layer, bottom-side up, on the plate. Frost with one-third of the buttercream. Center the second layer on top, bottom-side up. Frost top and sides in big swooping swirls.

5. Serve: Chill. Bring cake to room temperature (about 1 hour). Slice, serve, celebrate.

Chocolate Buttercream

Makes about 1 quart

Slide 4 egg whites into the bowl of a stand mixer. Measure in 1 cup sugar. Set this bowl over a saucepan of simmering water. Whisk until foamy and 160 degrees, about 5 minutes. Return bowl to the mixer and whisk on high speed into fluffy, glossy peaks, about 5 minutes. Make sure bowl is no longer hot (rub the outside with an ice cube, if need be). Reduce speed to medium and add ¾ pound (3 sticks) unsalted butter, softened, a few tablespoons at a time, whisking constantly. Whisk in 5 ounces semisweet chocolate, melted and cooled to room temperature.

WINNOWER, MÉLANGEUR, AND CONCHE

Perhaps you are fond of chocolate. This does not make you special. It puts you squarely in the majority, along with the 52 percent of Americans who list chocolate as their favorite flavor. Many of them are people who let the flashy block grinning from a vending machine pass for chocolate. You know better. Chocolate can be beautiful, sensual, mysterious. Chocolate can be brownies.

You pity, of course, the dry square gasping in the bakery case. You believe you can do better. There will be research. Lab work. Disappointment. But you will persevere.

Initially, you perform a simple calculation: More = better. This leads you from two ounces of unsweetened chocolate to four. And, inevitably, to the day you empty the entire ten-ounce box into the double boiler. After which you try another approach.

You make predictable errors: You underbake, you reduce the flour to a spoonful. At some point, it occurs to you that an 8-inch-square pan is not the same as a 9-inch-square pan. You wonder why fudgy is achieved in tight confines and chewy under expansive conditions. You consider taking up physics.

Recipes that call for cocoa powder do not receive consideration. Likewise margarine. You ponder the mysteries of raw product. Instinct leads you to abandon the dull square of baking chocolate that has long been your traveling companion. You stride out of the aisle named, with apt urgency, "baking needs." You try imported candy bars. And then you notice that a revolution has taken place. While you were busy wondering if parchment paper is slicker than wax paper, better chocolate arrived.

The boxes have a noble look, flaunting chocolate content like a badge of honor: 56 percent, 71 percent, 99 percent. You read the details of production. How the cacao trees sun themselves only within ten degrees of the Equator. How the big bumpy pods are harvested and their beans are fermented. How the crunchy inner nibs are smoothed to silk by the roaster, winnower, mélangeur, and conche.

You read, with shock, a recipe that calls for chunks of unsweetened chocolate to languish in the batter. You dare to taste pure chocolate. It is a revelation.

Then, one night, you come across an unorthodox recipe. You try it; it works. Your brownies are dense and deeply chocolate. They are beautiful, sensuous, mysterious. You leave the recipe next to the empty 9-inch pan. And awake bereft: A helpful hand has cleared the counter. You may never reproduce the recipe. But trying will be 99 percent pleasure.

Encouraging Brownies

Makes 16 brownies

¼ pound (1 stick) unsalted butter

4 ounces unsweetened chocolate

1 cup sugar

2 eggs

½ cup sifted cake flour

½ teaspoon vanilla extract

1 pinch fine salt

1. Prep: Rub a little butter into the bottom of an 9-inch-square baking pan, as glue. Line the pan with two lengths of parchment paper, long enough for a couple inches overhang, crisscrossed.

2. Beat: Melt butter and chocolate in a medium saucepan. Pull pan off heat. Beat in, in order: sugar, eggs, flour, vanilla, and salt.

3. Bake: Scrape batter into pan and slide into a 350-degree oven. Bake until a toothpick poked in the center comes out flecked with crumbs, 18 to 20 minutes.

4. Slice: Cool completely. Lift out the brownie by grasping free ends of the parchment paper. Trim away the firm edges. These scraps are the cook's reward. Enjoy them while slicing the brownie into 16 small but highly effective squares.

TANGLED

In nine months of preparing for the arrival of my daughter, I made no provisions for hair. I imagined her serene and pink-cheeked and, as picture books had suggested, bald. Who knew she was devoting those months to developing hair? In abundance.

Hannah's strawberry curls gave her certain maturity, for an infant. But soon they required tending. Barrettes, then bands, then a hairdo. Which I did not. My own hair started at the top and descended, waving meekly along the way. I didn't like to interfere, for fear of further mortifying it.

But the girl with the Goldilocks complex needed intervention, and that's how I hired our babysitter, Sue Ann. Sue Ann had enthusiasm and, comb in hand, stone-cold confidence. Her first day on the job, she wrestled Hannah's tangle into two sleek pigtails. We gasped.

Sue Ann had practiced for years on Barbie. She could execute a tidy ponytail, the whale spout, piggy puffs. She took her time. Eventually, she took time off.

There were tearful tangled interludes during which I confronted some truths: A braid is not that complex. Asymmetry has its charms. Hair counts.

I committed myself to hair control with the same zeal I had already invested in wardrobe maintenance. Ever since knitting Hannah's first little bunny-buttoned dress, I had kept her in pin-tucked frocks, cable-knit tights and spotted rain boots. Despite the obvious: that the tools of toddlerhood—sandbox, gluestick, and finger paint—were best accommodated by the wash-and-wear simplicity of overalls. At the same time, the rigors of motherhood brought my own wardrobe to its shredded knees. Predictable. Pathetic.

These were worthy lessons for a new mother and they led me to wistful thoughts. I hoped that Hannah would fail to learn from my example. And I hoped for the speedy return of Sue Ann.

Angel-Hair Pasta

Angel-hair pasta cooks up so fine and tender, it's best simply tossed with butter and dusted with grated Parmesan. If you're up for something more complex, try this clam recipe. Also good with sturdier farro pasta.

Serves 4

24 clams, preferably Manila

3 tablespoons olive oil

4 cloves garlic, thinly sliced

1 cup dry white wine

2 tablespoons unsalted
butter, cubed

2 tablespoons chopped
fresh parsley

2 tablespoons chopped
fresh oregano

1 pinch dried red-pepper
flakes

Kosher salt and freshly
ground black pepper

½ pound angel-hair pasta

1. Clean: Scrub clams under cold water. Soak in several changes of cold water.

2. Crisp: Heat olive oil in a large skillet set over medium-high heat. Add garlic and crisp brown, 2 minutes. Use a slotted spoon to rescue garlic chips.

3. Steam: Add clams and wine to the pan. Cover and steam until clams open, about 5 minutes. Pull pan off heat. Stir in butter, herbs, and pepper flakes. Season with salt and pepper.

4. Boil: Meanwhile, cook the pasta, stopping 1 minute short of the recommended time. Scoop out ½ cup cooking water and set aside. Drain. Return pasta to the pot. Pour on the clam sauce and simmer 2 minutes. If pasta seems dry, add a spoonful of cooking water.

5. Serve: Tumble pasta onto a platter. Discard any unopened clams. Sprinkle with garlic chips. Enjoy hot.

PROVENANCE: *Adapted from a recipe by chef Tony Mantuano of Cafe Spiaggia, Chicago.*

AN ENDLESS CYCLE

Bob spent several hours a day cleated onto a fancy bike, sweating up and down the lakefront. It gave him a break from his hobby: bike maintenance, which seemed to involve finding and ordering and assembling and adjusting bike parts. Frankly, he'd been at loose ends since dropping his previous hobby: bike acquisition.

After he'd unpacked the black twig with the wheels, he spent a few days looking for a place to store it, settling on the room that served as his office, my office, and the television lair, at an angle that blocked doorway, filing cabinet, and closet. He seemed deflated. No more bike shopping.

Then he made a discovery: The stem—apparently a piece of the bike—came up short! Time to find and order and assemble and adjust some parts. He even whistled.

Bob's hobby claimed most of his waking hours and many of my sleeping ones. He would startle alert, snuggle close, and murmur: "I should measure my shoulder-to-elbow span again."

Not even dinner was safe. There we'd be, stabbing at Caesar salad. Bob would lean in and confide, "My knee-to-pedal cant is misaligned." I'd go on sponging up lemony anchovies, which he mistook for interest.

That's how I found myself steadying a pair of titanium handlebars while Bob, perched on the twig, affixed tape to his knee, a string to the tape, and a picture hook to the string. "See!" he enthused. "The plum line doesn't drop square with the axle!"

I knew what he meant: Time to order more parts.

Caesar Salad

Serves 4

2 eggs

2 lemons

1 clove garlic, mashed

1 teaspoon Dijon mustard

1 can anchovies, drained and chopped

3 tablespoons grated Parmesan cheese

½ cup olive oil

Freshly ground black pepper

2 heads romaine lettuce

1 loaf Italian or peasant bread

1. Boil: Settle eggs in a small saucepan. Cover with cold water. Bring to a boil. Pull pan off heat, cover and let rest 9 minutes. Run eggs under cool water. Peel and halve. Roll just-set yolks into a small mixing bowl. Snack on whites.

2. Mix: Zest and squeeze lemons. Add zest and 5 tablespoons juice to the bowl along with garlic, mustard, anchovies, and 2 tablespoons cheese. Whisk together. Drizzle in oil, whisking constantly. Season with pepper.

3. Trim: Remove and discard tough outer lettuce leaves. Slice each head in half the long way. Trim tough bottom, leaving enough stem to hold the leaves together. Brush cut sides with dressing. Slice 8 thick slices bread and brush both sides of each with dressing.

4. Grill: Prepare a hot grill (or use a ridged griddle over medium-high heat). Grill bread golden, about 2 minutes per side. Grill lettuce, cut-side down, until nicely tattooed, about 1 minute. Arrange lettuce and croutons on each of four plates. Sprinkle lettuce with remaining cheese. Serve with dressing, fork, and knife.

BAD NEWS

On the second day of preschool, that sunny Tuesday morning, students and parents, edgy with new-school anxiety, made play dough together. The somber science of heating flour and water and cream of tartar prevented us from gazing out the ivy-shaded windows. The new colleagues worked wooden puzzles, trying to fit house or dog into the empty space where a house or dog should stand. Four small engineers attempted to scrape the contents of the sandbox into a single, girl-high mound.

We emerged into a new world, one that looked eerily like the old. The clouds still drifted white and the leaves still shimmered yellow. But the sky was silent. Seven hundred miles away gaped an empty space where two skyscrapers were supposed to stand.

At home, we waited, diverting wide eyes from the fireball on the muted TV. Before we could compose an explanation, before we thought to offer blood or send boots, we made cookies.

We understood this effort to be futile. No cookie ever held an airplane aloft, nor a battle at bay. But the ritual offered solace.

Butter melds with sugar into grainy certainty, eggs always part with a satisfying crack. Flour, scooped and leveled, yields one cup, no more. Dusted in, it mollifies lumpy dough. Vanilla tints it warm, chocolate chips rain benevolence.

The mounds of batter look humble, huddled on their tray. In the oven, they never fail at their task: to scent the air with comfort.

The wave of warm brown sugar wandered through the house, through afternoons when the steady meter of measuring and mixing could temper a tantrum, coax a confidence, ease injustice. It trailed back through all the bold experiments—add oatmeal, suffer wheat germ, substitute chocolate chunks—to the earliest and truest recipe, one executed in play dough: Mix. Bake. Soothe.

Chocolate Chip Cookies

The chocolate chip cookie is the American cook's duty and honor. There are many variations, all of which are briefly amusing, quickly tiresome. Stick with a streamlined approach, heavily chipped. Commit this recipe to memory; it will serve as sturdy companion through disappointment, great and small.

Makes 36 3-inch cookies

Melt ½ pound (2 sticks) unsalted butter. Other recipes expect you to drum your nails on the countertop while butter comes to room temperature. Don't bother. Melting butter over low heat (or via a quick zap) is blasphemous but better. Add 1½ cups dark brown sugar. Standard practice calls for a mix of white and brown. Standard practice yields unyielding cookies. Unadulterated brown sugar makes cookies pliant and empathetic.

Crack in 2 eggs. Stir vigorously. Stir in 1 teaspoon salt, 1 teaspoon baking soda, and 1 teaspoon vanilla extract (2 if you're in need of extra encouragement). Sprinkle in 2¼ cups flour. Check that batter and bowl are cool. Rain down 12 ounces chocolate chips. Feel free to chop your own, but know that you'll end up with big chunks and small shards, not uniform chips.

Scoop the batter into balls using a two-tablespoon (1¾-inch diameter) ice cream scoop. Line up cookie balls shoulder to shoulder on a parchment-paper-lined baking sheet. Freeze solid. Drop into a zip-top bag and store in the freezer.

In troubled times, remove the requisite number, no more. Arrange about 3 inches apart on a parchment-paper-lined baking sheet (air-cushioned is especially comfy) and slide into a 325-degree oven. This stuns the frozen dough balls, allowing them no time to flatten out and go crispy. In about 14 minutes they'll firm into thick, chewy reassurance.

Blondies

Makes 16 bars

If bars are in order, follow this approach: Settle ½ pound (2 sticks) unsalted butter in a mixing bowl. Zap to melt. Stir in, in order: 1½ cups dark brown sugar, 2 eggs, 1 tablespoon instant espresso granules dissolved in 1 tablespoon brewed coffee, 2 teaspoons vanilla extract, ¾ teaspoon fine salt, 1 teaspoon baking soda, and 2¼ cups flour. Make sure batter and bowl are cool. Stir in 12 ounces semisweet chocolate chips or chunks. Scrape into a 13 x 9-inch baking pan lined with parchment paper. Sprinkle on 1 cup chopped and toasted pecans tossed with ¼ teaspoon flakey salt (such as Maldon). Slide into a 350-degree oven. Bake until browned and slightly puffed, about 30 minutes. Set pan on rack to cool completely. Grasp the parchment overhang and lift blondie block out and onto a cutting board. Slice into 16 bars, each about 3 x 2 inches.

A DUTIFUL DAUGHTER

Shortly after I got married, my parents replaced me with a dog. I should have seen it coming. My brothers and I had insisted on growing up. And Claude, as a committed black Lab, showed no propensity for that.

Claude was an easy child. He didn't fret over homework, having opted out of "obedience" school. Claude didn't whine for creative-movement lessons or copper-enamel jewelry class. He never once auditioned for a musical.

Claude was never arrested for riding his bike without a permit. He never agitated for a pet unknown to the City of Iowa City municipal code and found himself called to court to explain said goat.

Claude didn't need his space. He liked togetherness. Especially for naps.

My daughterly duties were reduced to attending events at venues that excluded dogs. Which is to say the opera and select restaurants. Claude ordered carryout in advance.

The arrangement worked nicely, though Claude, noting that I was rarely equipped with hand-crafted dog crunchies, seemed uncertain who I was and what I wanted. He found my children downright suspicious. They occasionally tried to distract his parents with skills he lacked, ones executed with opposable thumbs and crayons. Claude fended off this insult by inserting his long black snout into any snuggle, and licking. Which might explain why my children were fairly adept at same.

Best-Friend Biscuits

Makes about 3 dozen 2-inch biscuits

2½ cups whole-wheat flour

3 tablespoons vegetable shortening (such as Crisco)

3 tablespoons peanut butter

½ cup broth, any flavor

1 egg

1. Mix: Heap flour in a mixing bowl. Drop in shortening and peanut butter. With brave fingers, work in shortening and peanut butter.

2. Stir: Mix together broth and egg. Pour over dry ingredients. Stir to combine.

3. Shape: Turn out dough onto a work surface. Roll or pat ½-inch thick. Use a 2-inch cookie cutter to punch out shapes. If your friend is small, consider 1-inch cookies.

4. Bake: Set treats on a parchment-paper-lined baking sheet (not touching). Slide into a 350-degree oven and bake until good and crunchy, about 1 hour. Cool. Serve, as it were.

A PERFECT CUP

Abstinence is in. Food is out. Half of any dinner party opposes bread. The other half won't touch bacon or eggs. Vegetarians refuse the chicken. Vegans poke at the broccoli, alert to cheddar dust. The fit fear french fries. Environmentalists weep over the sea bass. Old school dieters won't eat butter. New school (which is to say old old-school) drizzle extra on their steaks. But they don't drink. Just water, thank you. Eight glasses.

Food, apparently, is evil. But hot chocolate is divine.

Not the gray drizzle leaking from the push-button box in the cafeteria. That's not hot chocolate. That's revolting.

Hot chocolate is the lava center of melted chocolate cake, minus the cake. The cheer of the chocolate chip cookie, less the cookie. It's the pliant center brownie. It's chocolate that's hot.

Hot chocolate is better than all desserts and most food, making it an ideal diet companion. Like Slim-Fast, only thick and slow and luxurious.

Molten chocolate is so compelling its promise can leaven the tedium of picking mung beans from the salad bar. Its charms can fortify the weak from the temptation of the vending machine. Its lure can draw the disciple through traffic and bath time and dirty dishes, and reward her with a single perfect cup, savored in seclusion and silence.

For those sticklers who denounce its components—chocolate and milk—there are two options. Offer the reluctant a sip. Or shrug, smugly.

Molten Chocolate

Serves 1

In a small saucepan, melt 1 ounce chopped bittersweet chocolate (70 percent) over low heat with ¼ cup skim milk. Pour in another ¼ cup skim milk and increase the heat to medium-high. Whisk constantly until the chocolate turns thick and roiling hot at the edges, about 5 minutes. Drop 1 tablespoon crème de cacao in the bottom of a small cup. Pour in chocolate. Float on a drift of unsweetened whipped cream. Sip slowly, swirling scalding chocolate and cool cream. Stop. One cup will suffice.

REMEMBRANCE *of* THINGS LOST

Mysteries abound, though none is so deeply perplexing as the location of the lost.

We are familiar with the theory positing that unchaperoned socks meet their demise in the dryer, spinning so swiftly they're drawn into a time warp. While plausible, this explanation does not account for all missing personnel, to wit: phone charger, green garlic, brown lipstick, tax refund, tulip bulb, *Swann's Way*, safe deposit box key, and the swimsuit that fits. Also the plastic figurine with hinged legs known as Monkious George.

Because we rarely launder these items (intentionally), it seems doubtful they have been sucked through the lint screen into the future. We are troubled as much by their absence as by their erratic sightings. Never when their services are required.

Likewise *peapod*, *mnemonic*, and *recidivist*. As well as a mouthful of other words, presently indisposed, that slip out at inopportune moments only to return, unbidden, at odd hours. We want to know where they have been. And with whom. Was there drinking?

And what brought them back, at this hour, sneaking in during the misty section of a dream involving madeleines? We don't need *recidivism* now! We wanted it hours ago, right in the thick of minimum sentencing, before scorching the risotto, though after, obviously, both potholders went on the lam. Who gave any of them permission? Was it collusion—or peer pressure?

We have considered a stricter curfew. Fewer privileges. Perhaps an obligatory evening drill in which everyone in the household lines up against the wall and counts off. But it's clear where that would lead. By the time the briny jar of caper swill got around to shouting out "Sir! 9,672, Sir!" the indelible pens would already have sneaked away, snickering.

Eventually, we hear, they all leave home—all but the most remote memories and recent menus. We should just be grateful for this interlude, before they, like the boy still searching for Monkious George, discover they can reach the doorknob.

Madeleines

Makes 12

1 egg plus 1 egg yolk

1 pinch fine salt

½ teaspoon finely grated
lemon zest

Seeds scraped from
½ vanilla bean

⅓ cup sugar

5 tablespoons unsalted
butter, melted and cooled

⅔ cup sifted cake flour

1. Fluff: Slide egg plus egg yolk into the bowl of a stand mixer fitted with the whisk attachment. Toss in salt, zest, and vanilla seeds. Whisk until frothy, about 30 seconds. With mixer running, cascade in sugar. Whisk until thick and pale, about 3 minutes total. Drizzle in butter; whisk until butter disappears.

2. Fold: Sift flour over batter. Fold in.

3. Fill: Scoop or pipe into the twelve shell-shaped indents of a buttered madeleine pan. No need to smooth out.

4. Bake: Slide into a 400-degree oven and bake until golden on top and springy when gently pressed in the center, about 11 minutes. Ease madeleines out of pan and onto a cooling rack. Munch; remember.

THE SECRET LIVES of GIRLS

Stricken with dread over a particularly dreadful birthday, I'd been applying the standard remedies—ointments, exercises, indexing of opportunities squandered—and had achieved the standard imperceptible results. Fortunately, I had friends enduring the same circumstance, and we believed there was solace in numbers.

Sarah, Ann, Grace, Danielle, Daryn, and I had, since junior high, relied on one another for solemn advice unfettered by fact. We agreed to meet and exchange more of same. We'd originally planned to do so under the influence of cheerful cocktails, extreme pedicures, and meals we had no hand in preparing. We understood this was called a spa.

Spas, we learned, promise to return the optimism of youth through cold mud, hot wax, and crushed pomegranate seeds. They attempt to pare guests to girlish slenderness via tai chi and carrot curls. These friendships were forged over Oreos. We did not consider carrots celebratory.

Eventually we realized we could simply stage a slumber party, like the ones at which we first discovered the intoxicating effects of little sleep, many Oreos, and boldly misguided convictions about the secret lives of boys. Back then, an evening without chaperones defined abandon. Now, an evening with no one to chaperone defined abandon.

The self-inflicted spa would spare us the embarrassment of lounging green-faced among strangers. And we could concentrate on our preferred pastimes. As Grace pointed out, "How much talking can you do during a mud/honey/cow-dung facial?"

We'd read about another group of friends who each led a retreat treatment. They went home with aromatherapy salves and improved yoga postures. That approach would have left us enlightened about drugless labor and delivery, sick infants, adolescent therapy, clean prose, and real-estate management. We agreed to cook for ourselves and send out for pedicures.

Our reunion was light on aura buffing, heavy on loafing. A spa. As in spaghetti.

Halibut Spaghetti

Serves 6

4 slices Italian bread

½ cup plus 2 tablespoons olive oil

1 bunch rapini

½ pound halibut, skin and bones removed

Kosher salt

2 tablespoons chopped garlic

1 teaspoon dried red pepper flakes

1 cup dry white wine

¾ pound spaghetti or spaghettini

3 tablespoons chopped fresh parsley

1 tablespoon fresh lemon juice

1. Toast: Settle bread on a baking sheet, drizzle with 2 tablespoons olive oil. Slide into a 300-degree oven and toast golden brown, 20 minutes. Cool. Process into crumbs.

2. Slice: Cut rapini thinly crosswise, tossing out thick stem bottoms. Cut halibut into 6 strips; season with 1 teaspoon salt.

3. Simmer: Pour 2 tablespoons olive oil into a large skillet. Stir in garlic. Set over medium-high heat and stir until garlic goes golden, 2 minutes. Add fish strips and chili flakes; stir 20 seconds. Pour in wine and bring to a boil. Turn fish over. Lower heat and simmer until just cooked through, 1 minute. Use a slotted spoon to scoop fish onto a plate. Simmer wine broth 3 more minutes.

4. Boil: Meanwhile, boil pasta until tender but firm. Dip in a measuring cup and scoop out ½ cup cooking water. Drain pasta and add it to the wine broth.

5. Toss: Turn up heat to high. When broth comes to a boil, add rapini, fish, and parsley. Toss gently, letting rapini wilt and fish flake. Drizzle with lemon juice, remaining 6 tablespoons olive oil, and ¼ cup cooking water. Toss. Pasta should be glistening, not swimming. Add a tablespoon of cooking water if need be.

6. Serve: Tumble onto a large platter. Scatter on breadcrumbs. Enjoy.

PROVENANCE: *Adapted from a recipe by Chef Carmen Quagliata of Union Square Cafe, New York.*

UPSIDE-DOWN *AND* BREATHING

Yoga, through long practice and deep concentration, achieved the status of yogurt. Ubiquitous.

Once yoga had been an exotic import, full of multisyllabic contortions. It was practiced by high-minded sorts with bare feet. Who, in all likelihood, liked yogurt.

Back then yaourt, or worse, yoghourt suffered from a surfeit of vowels and deficit of sugar. It was sour. Bulgarian. It contained bacteria, with names like *Streptococcus thermophilus* and *Lactobacillus acidophilus*. On purpose.

Over time, both yogurt and yoga acculturated. Yogurt diversified into extreme, drinkable, squeezable, frozen, whipped, cream-topped, and two-toned. It was packaged with fruit or jam or sprinkles or "interactive" mix-ins.

Yoga too stretched its market share. It flaunted hot, cold, power, therapeutic, yogaerobic, yoganetic, and yogilatic, as well as custom blends for business, depression, weight-loss, idiots, and dummies. The yoga-inclined could practice at the studio, gym, wedding, birthday party, or—with a friend—in bed.

The yoga supplicant was instructed to fold her body into shapes called asana. Loosely translated as "pose." Or "torment." A popular position, for instance, insisted the arms stretch one direction, legs another, while upside down and—significantly—breathing. Also while grasping self-respect, even though the pose was called, without irony, downward-facing dog.

The triumph of the gravity-defying headstand or pretzel-inspired lotus was merely a step toward a loftier goal: enlightenment. But in the teeth of downward-facing dog, this struck many a student as overly subtle.

Indeed, yoga, like yogurt, largely opted for the streamlined approach. Class usually closed with all hands in prayer position, and a brief chant of "namaste." Teachers translated this wisp of Sanskrit as "I salute the divinity within you." Or, for the workplace: "Have a nice day."

And yet, beneath the sugar coating lurked a complex soul. Even Rockin' Raspberry listed *S. thermophilus*. Even Rock 'n' Roll Yoga ended with meditation.

This was the part where the body, unfolded from its origami, was allowed to collapse into corpse pose. The brain unspooled onto the floor, accompanied by silence, incense, and the occasional snore. This was the big finish, the moment of release. As mysterious and transformative as live culture.

Fair Lassie

Serves 1

BLEND: 1 cup plain yogurt, 2 ripe mangoes, peeled and seeded, 1 cup ice cubes, and 2 tablespoons sugar. Pour into a tall glass. Have a nice drink.

PACKING

The toddler cowboy maintained a fierce attachment to his five-gallon hat. He could not relinquish it to the airport X-ray. He refused. He swaggered, firmly hatted, through the metal detector, which, sensing the conchos studding his hatband, alerted security personnel to danger.

There was no going back. No remedial scan. Once the bing had bonged, procedure stipulated that the suspicious passenger be searched, no matter how young, how surly, or how loudly opposed.

A wandslinger took aim. The outlaw attempted to bolt, shouting, "Don't fence me in!"

During the struggle, an armed and uniformed official formulated a plan. Commandeering a bottle of apple juice from an adjacent espresso cart, he crouched. "You can have this juice free," he said, "if you can be compliant." It was a misguided strategy. The cowboy disdained juice, expected all drinks on the house, and could not grasp "compliant."

Nevertheless he dropped his resistance. Stood transfixed. And passed his patdown. The lawman, still gripping the scorned juice, followed the cowboy's awestruck gaze to his own white button-down and its left pocket, flashing a gold star.

Every cowboy recognized the sheriff.

Cowboy Cookies

Makes about 2 dozen 4-inch cookies

4 cups water

1½ cups hazelnuts

¼ cup plus 1 teaspoon baking soda

½ pound (2 sticks) unsalted butter, softened

¾ cup brown sugar

¾ cup granulated sugar

2 eggs

1 teaspoon vanilla extract

2¼ cups flour

1¼ teaspoons salt

10 ounces thin dark (or semisweet) chocolate, broken into chunks

1. Husk: Bring water to a boil in a large saucepan, leaving room for the bubble-up to come. Add nuts and ¼ cup baking soda. Boil 5 minutes. Drain in a colander. Working under cool running water, slip the nuts out of their jackets.

2. Toast: Tumble naked hazelnuts onto a rimmed baking sheet. Slide into a 350-degree oven and toast, shaking once or twice, until golden and fragrant, about 16 minutes. Chop half the nuts coarsely (use the food processor to cut down on fugitives). Grind the other half into a powder.

3. Fluff: Using a stand mixer with the paddle attachment at high speed, cream butter and both types of sugar until light and fluffy, about 2 minutes.

4. Mix: Add eggs and vanilla extract, mixing on low speed. In a separate bowl, whisk together flour, salt, 1 teaspoon baking soda, and the ground hazelnuts. Scoop dry ingredients into the batter and mix thoroughly. Add chopped nuts and chocolate, mixing gently.

5. Scoop: Portion out batter using a ¼-cup ice cream scoop. Arrange batter blobs on parchment-paper-lined baking sheets, leaving 3 inches between neighbors. Flatten slightly with the bottom of a glass dipped in sugar.

6. Bake: Slide cookies into a 350-degree oven and bake, rotating pans once, until edges are golden and centers are just set, 13 to 15 minutes. Pack, with swagger.

CURTAINS!

Our couch coach, who saw clients on the eighth floor of Marshall Field's, sat us down at a moment of triumph. After hours of sweaty aesthetic combat, we had reached a truce: butter-colored twill, loose cushions, mahogany legs. She tucked our down payment under the cash drawer, then handed back this advice: "You two need a drink."

If, years later, our home lacked curtains, it was due to cowardice. Window treatment might have required follow up with medical treatment.

We were stumped by brocade versus floral, pleated versus flat, Roman versus French. Plain white roll downs seemed too rooming-house. Swags too house-of-ill-repute. We feared the tyranny of the decorator and the desolation of going it alone. As the home-decorating catalog warned: Measuring was a demanding art. Our spare closet, with its jumble of lonely rods and panels, concurred.

Our front rooms, done up in curtain manqué, were bright, airy, and clean. They posed no hazard of cord-entanglement. The look was inexpensive, easy to install, and maintenance-free.

Though perilous. The naked window fostered an intimacy that exceeded the bounds of standard neighborliness. We were familiar with the television preferences of the opposing household. We worried that the chef next door, having witnessed one too many family dinners served from a white carton, would tip off child and family services.

We were not entirely without protection. In summer, magnolia blossoms offered a hint of discretion. In winter, we were shielded from the curious by our own appallingly dull lives. We did little in the public rooms of our private home save lounge on the butter colored twill couch, staring at the papers. Soundtrack by Aimee Mann. We studied the fine print on the caller ID. We moved pieces of the Lego train and the Brio train and the Lionel train from box to bin, sorting, but never actually segregating, incompatible societies. Occasionally we needed a drink.

Should we have attempted the untoward, like search for clean socks dressed only in a spare swag or pull cord, we had an option handy. We used the neighbor's curtains.

Freshwater Scoundrel

Seaworthy sailors rely on the Salty Dog, a grapefruit and vodka classic, to revive them. Here's a freshwater version served by the shores of our inland ocean.

Serves 2

Mix 6 tablespoons simple syrup into 2 cups fresh grapefruit juice (with pulp). Choose red for drama in the cup. Pour into a metal baking pan and freeze until slushy, about an hour. Fluff up the ice crystals with a fork and pour into two plastic cups. Drizzle on some vodka, if you like. Gulp.

SIMPLE SYRUP: In a medium saucepan stir together 1 cup sugar and 1 cup water. Bring to a boil. Simmer 1 minute. Cool. Makes 1½ cups.

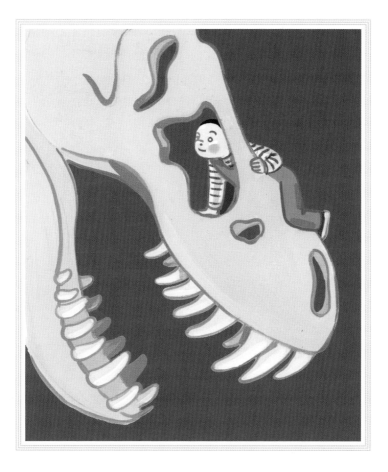

TRIAL *AND* ERROR

Paleontology suits the three-year-old career boy. It involves dirt. And digging. And dislodging a fossil, though rarely. Which inspired me to fraud.

We had a wooden puzzle that fit together into a 3-D dinosaur skeleton. I looked over the puzzle pieces. I looked at the flower patch. I meant well.

Early in the morning my paleontologist took his tin bucket and his red shovel outside and dug up bones. He didn't seem surprised. He pieced together a complete dinosaur skeleton. He said he might take his work to the Field Museum. I smiled. He said he was taking it to preschool. I panicked.

"Let's make muffins," I countered. Switching from shovel to spatula, we stirred pumpkin, sugar, and milk. We sifted cinnamon, nutmeg, and ginger. We scooped the batter into our favorite muffin pan, filling the spikes and horns of Ankylosaurus, Triceratops, Polacanthus, Stegosaurus, Protoceratops, and T. Rex. "They look fierce," I said. "But not real," he said. "Like my real one."

He had the warm Ankylosaurus. I had T. Rex. We talked about science, guesswork, trial and error. Then we set his newly discovered dinosaur skeleton on the bookshelf, where it remained on permanent display.

Dinosaur Pumpkin Muffins

Makes 6 dinosaur or 12 standard muffins

5 tablespoons unsalted butter, melted

¾ cup sugar

⅔ cup pumpkin purée (just open a can)

¼ cup milk

1 egg

1 cup flour

¾ teaspoon baking soda

½ teaspoon fine salt

¼ teaspoon ground cinnamon

¼ teaspoon freshly grated nutmeg

¼ teaspoon ground ginger

1. Whisk: Brush muffin pan with some of the melted butter. In a large mixing bowl whisk the remaining butter together with the sugar, pumpkin, milk, and egg.

2. Fold: Sift flour, soda, salt, and spices over pumpkin. Fold just until combined.

3. Bake: Scoop batter into buttered pan, filling each cup about three-fourths full. Slide into a 350-degree oven and bake until a toothpick poked in the center comes out clean, about 25 minutes for dinosaurs, 17 for standard muffins.

PROVENANCE: *I adapted this recipe from one that came with my favorite cast-iron muffin plaque. The pan came from a company called John Wright Classic Gourmet. The recipe was credited to Gerryre O'Higgins.*

CITY CHILD

Hannah hailed taxi and sushi with authority. She was swift with the speed dial, confident missing mittens would be returned by the dry cleaner. But she remained confused about the great outdoors. It demanded no batteries. Came without software. Required no waiter, tour guide, or credit card. No one rang a bell 15 minutes before closing. Nature was just there, waiting to be ignored.

She had limited exposure. She could identify the picnic-fattened squirrel, the tourist-towing horse, and the bomb-sniffing dog. She had seen wildlife, red in tooth and claw, relaxing at the Lincoln Park Zoo, where it was hand-fed sashimi by a weary keeper zipped into spatter-proof gear.

She knew the ebb and flow of the seasons, from snowplow's sludge crop to the jackhammer's rubble harvest. She observed the cycle of life: the way the butterfly struggled from its chrysalis at the Nature Museum, the way flowers blossomed year-round in the Conservatory. She knew how humans flourished, as detailed in the window display at the Pleasure Chest.

Nature seeped into her artwork. My city girl baked a city gingercake house. She spread the roof with whipped cream and jabbed in a row of Good & Plenties, like spikes. "Pointy," she explained, "to scare the pigeons away."

Gingercake Houses

Makes 12 small houses

2½ cups flour

5 teaspoons ground ginger

1 teaspoon ground cinnamon

¾ teaspoon fine salt

½ teaspoon baking powder

½ teaspoon baking soda

½ pound (2 sticks) unsalted
butter, softened

1½ cups packed dark
brown sugar

4 eggs, at room temperature

1 cup molasses

1 cup whole milk

2 cups Whipped Cream
(page 291)

Lemon Sauce (recipe follows)

1. Disperse: Whisk together flour, ginger, cinnamon, salt, baking powder, and baking soda in a mixing bowl.

2. Fluff: Using a stand mixer fitted with the paddle attachment, beat butter and brown sugar until fluffy, about 3 minutes. Crack in eggs, one at a time; beat until fluffy. Beat in molasses and milk.

3. Mix: Scatter on dry ingredients and mix just to combine.

4. Bake: Scrape into 12 buttered and floured gingerhouse molds, 12 square muffin cups, or a 9-inch square cake pan. Bake at 350 degrees until a toothpick poked in center comes out clean, 25 minutes for small cakes, 50 for large. Cool slightly. Unmold. Cool.

5. Build: Cut the 9-inch cake into cubes (house bases) and pyramids (roofs). Hold everything together with whipped cream. Decorate extravagantly with candy or simply with a shake of powdered sugar.

6. Admire: Individual gingerbread houses make a charming holiday tablescape. Before dinner they can serve as place cards. After dinner, doused with lemon sauce and accompanied by whipped cream, they can serve as dessert.

Lemon Sauce

Makes about 1½ cups

Whisk together ½ cup sugar, zest and juice of 2 lemons, zest and juice of 1 orange, and 3 egg yolks in a medium saucepan set over medium-high heat. Whisk until hot, frothy, and thickened, 10 minutes. Stir in 6 tablespoons unsalted butter, cut up. Strain. Serve warm.

POETIC JUSTICE

The family vacation is all about togetherness and you can't get more together than in a borrowed beach house, on an island, under a rain cloud, without a phone, for a week. Measured in quantity time, it was a success.

Those of us capable of reading did so, retracing Curious George's unfortunate trip to the hospital once every fifteen minutes.

In the cabin's sole cupboard, we discovered a cache of plastic parts and attempted to assemble them, eventually concluding they belonged to a battery-less remote-controlled skateboarding winged monster/princess, on the waitlist for a donor body.

We watched both videotapes. We boiled noodles. Once we suited up in Hefty bags and waded to the general store, where we stocked up on additional noodles, a plastic princess (with body), a plastic steam engine (without track), and aspirin.

The sun sparkled off the puddles as we boarded the ferryboat for home.

We were grateful to our friends for their generosity. We considered sending a case of wine, a case of noodles, or a case of full-spectrum light bulbs. Instead we left four sets of turkey-and-cheese-on-whole-wheat, no mayo, which may have lost their appeal during the interlude between our departure, sans lunch, and our hosts' return a week later.

Mercifully, no photos survive. But the memory of the beach vacation is tinged with damp noodle-scented claustrophobia and guilt pangs of kindness unrequited. It resides in the same dread closet as RSVPs ignored, condolences unsent, invitations unreciprocated, and email lost in space. Plus a few obsolete would-be gifts. Congratulatory Champagne wrapped and addressed to the couple long uncoupled. The teething toy for the tot now in braces.

I compose long letters, charming invitations, brilliant dinner parties, and thoughtful thank-yous in that parallel universe where my other self is perpetually well-dressed, poised, witty, and endowed with that home-magazine absurdity: the gift-wrapping room. Not to mention staff assigned to stand on line at the post office.

Ruth Lilly, heir to the Prozac fortune, could afford staff to stand in line at the post office. That's probably how she got her efforts mailed to *Poetry* magazine which responded with the prompt and kindly worded no-thank-you. In appreciation, Lilly sent back $100 million or so. Poetry fans are assured verse in perpetuity. The delinquent have been inspired to compose timely thank-yous. And those in the slack habit of relying on good intentions—or moldy turkey sandwiches—are forced to wonder if they're missing out on outrageous fortune—or a return invitation.

In literature, they call such torment poetic justice.

Beach-House Spaghetti

Serves 6

¼ loaf (about 4 ounces) country bread

2 cloves garlic, chopped

1 teaspoon kosher salt

2 tablespoons unsalted butter

1 pound spaghetti

½ cup olive oil

5 cups cherry tomatoes, halved (a mix of red and gold is pretty)

3 anchovies, rinsed and chopped

2 teaspoons finely grated lemon zest

1 cup slivered basil leaves

½ cup freshly grated Parmesan cheese

Freshly ground black pepper

1. Grind: Cut bread (crust and all) into chunks. Drop into the food processor or blender along with 1 clove garlic and ½ teaspoon salt. Pulse to fine crumbs. There should be about 2 cups.

2. Toast: Melt the butter in a wide skillet over medium-low heat. Add bread crumbs and toast, stirring attentively, until crisp, brown and garlic-fragrant, about 8 minutes. Set aside crumbs. Wipe out skillet.

3. Boil: Cook spaghetti in boiling salted water until tender but firm. Drain pasta and set aside.

4. Soften: Heat oil in the same skillet over medium-low. Add tomatoes, remaining clove of garlic, and ½ teaspoon salt. Cook, stirring, until tomatoes have softened (some collapsing altogether, others still in chunks), about 5 minutes.

5. Rest: Turn off heat. Stir in anchovies and lemon zest. Stir in cooked spaghetti. Cover and let rest 2 minutes. Toss in basil, cheese, and reserved breadcrumbs. Grind on some pepper. Nice, right?

RECIPE *for* DISASTER

Friday night dinner is the sort of home-bound tradition best focused on roast chicken. It's delicious. Easy. A classic. Like the little black dress, it manages to cover both extremes of the plain-to-fancy scale.

Choose a plump bird large enough to feed the family. Rinse, pat dry, and rub all over with rendered chicken fat. Don't ask. Sprinkle with kosher salt, fit into a roasting pan, and settle in the oven at 425. Expect perfection.

Should at that very moment your daughter arrive home, face crumpled in distress, realize that your recipe may have to be revised. Note that she has received a plastic kaleidoscope as a classroom party favor. That the kaleidoscope features a small view-hole. That the hole is occupied by your daughter's ring finger. That she cannot withdraw said finger.

Offer her a calm demeanor. A fresh strawberry. Give the knuckle a rinse in cold water, and rub it all over with chicken fat. Though this tactic ought to work, it doesn't. Plan to transfer the afternoon's festivities to the ER. The challah, rising in its buttered bowl, can be ignored. Bread thrives on neglect. The chicken should take a good hour. Likewise the ER. The timing might work, except for the possibility of returning to a smoldering house. Turn the oven off.

At the hospital, you will be amazed by the complexity of the kaleidescopectomy. The tools include cold water. A sterile version of chicken fat. A large sheet to wrap around the hysterical kaleidoscopically ensnared child. A large person to lie on top of the sheet to aid in the restraining effort. Anesthesia. Tugging. Consternation. And finally, gardening shears. The howling lament: "But it was the most beautiful toy I'd ever seen!" Plus Bacitracin, Band-Aids, and observation.

Back home, the abandoned chicken is neither cooked nor raw. The dough has climbed out of its bowl. Deflate, braid, and slide into the oven, at 350. While the bread bakes, bathe the fat-fingered child. Swear she will regain use of her hand. Serve bread and anything else you have handy. Say, wine. Turn up the heat to 425.

After the children are asleep, the chicken will turn a nice golden brown. Leave it cooling on the counter and a babysitter lounging on the couch. Go out. Return to find the sitter still on the couch and the chicken still on the counter. Don't ask. Refrigerate.

Saturday afternoon give the chicken a suspicious look. Carve. Serve cold on left-over challah, in the grip of bruised and swollen but otherwise functional fingers. The recipe, though tumbled and refracted, has achieved perfection.

Roast Chicken

This recipe calls for bunches of herbs—leaves, stems, and all. This is the time to clear any sad-looking herbs from the crisper drawer or trim the straggly herb garden.

Serves 4

1 (2½- to 3- pound) chicken

2 teaspoons kosher salt

1 teaspoon freshly ground
   black pepper

1 clove garlic

6 fresh sage leaves

1 tablespoon olive oil

Bunches of herbs
   such as rosemary,
   parsley, thyme, and
   sorrel, including stems

2 tablespoons
   unsalted butter

½ cup water or
   chicken broth

1. Clean: Pull the chicken out of its packaging and the innards out of the chicken. Freeze or toss innards. Plunge the chicken into a big pot of cold salted water. Let soak, 1 minute. Drain water and repeat until water is clear and chicken is clean. Pat dry with paper towels.

2. Rub: Tuck wings behind back. Sprinkle chicken, inside and out, with 1 teaspoon salt and ½ teaspoon pepper; rub lightly into skin. Cover loosely with plastic wrap or wax paper. Set on a plate. Return chicken to the bottom shelf of the fridge. Let rest, 2 to 24 hours.

3. Season: Pull chicken out of fridge and let come to room temperature, up to 1 hour. Chop together sage, garlic, 1 teaspoon salt, and ½ teaspoon pepper. Slide a finger between skin and breast, opening a pocket of space. Rub in some of the sage mix. Repeat, seasoning between the skin and meat on both sides of the breast and over the legs. Stuff herb bunches inside the chicken, filling (though not tightly packing) the cavity.

4. Roast: Meanwhile, drizzle the olive oil into a cast-iron pan that will later offer your chicken a snug fit. My go-to chicken pan is 10½ inches across the top and 3 inches deep. Slide pan into a cold oven; heat to 425 degrees. Pan and oven will heat up together. When hot, carefully lower in chicken, breast-side up. All that sizzle will ensure crisp skin. Roast 20 minutes. Turn breast down; roast 20 minutes. Flip breast up; roast 20 minutes. Chicken is

done when skin is golden and blistered, its juices run clear when inner thigh is poked, and it smells delightful, about 1 hour total.

5. Rest: Lift chicken out of pan and set on a platter. Cover loosely with foil. Tip the platter so the chicken is tipped toward the breast.

6. Deglaze: Set the roasting pan on the stovetop. Add the butter and water or chicken broth. Set over medium-high heat. Stir with a wooden spoon, scraping up any stuck bits. Let boil and thicken, about 3 minutes. Strain into a gravy boat.

7. Serve: Carve the chicken. I usually divide into 2 wings, 2 drumsticks, 2 thighs and 2 breasts, each cut crosswise into 3 chunks. Set roasted chicken chunks on a bed of spicy greens, such as arugula or watercress. Serve with gravy. What could be better?

FAR, FAR AWAY

In summer, you feel obliged to vacation. Everyone does. You consider Door County in Wisconsin. Everyone does. It's beautiful and there's a lake and it takes forever to get there. It's beautiful here and we have a lake and it takes no time to stay put. But it's summer. You go.

On vacation you attempt to vacate your mind of its usual preoccupations, like work, getting to the dentist, and the ideal kitchen floorplan. Instead you think about play and getting a nap and the ideal kitchen floorplan. You read. You eat pie. You look at the lake. You wonder why you don't spend more time in real life with book, pie, and lake.

When it's time to go, you buy a bag of dried sour cherries. You know the regulations. All personnel leaving Door County are required to show a bag of dried sour cherries at the door.

Back home you remember the lake—calm and unfettered by fretting. You remember the pie. The cherries. And—with a jolt—the dried sour cherries.

You untwist the twist tie, scoop up a handful and chew. They are sweet, tart and sticky. They might mix well in trail mix, if you tolerated trail mix. They might skulk by in granola, if you liked granola. Loose in the bag, they seem at loose ends.

You know better than to fob them off on your fellow travelers. They've got their own sacks of cherries to divest. You don't bother bothering your friends. Their upper shelves harbor upper-lake cherries too. You've been invited to dinner parties, in October, where each guest was pressed into taking home a baggie of dried cherries. You've attended Thanksgiving feasts where the hostess attempted to slip dried cherries into the stuffing. You've seen innocent Christmas cookies and beleaguered New Year's cocktails forced into cherry smuggling. The entire off-season is preoccupied with dried cherry off-load.

It occurs to you that the problem is not dried sour cherries, which, though dried and sour, don't manage to offend. The problem is dried sour cherries under false pretenses. Sneaking into stuffing. Confusing cookies. Hoodwinking cocktails. Interlopers. Poseurs.

Maybe sour cherries should accept themselves for the dried, sour fruit they are.

Or maybe these disgruntled, dehydrated souls simply need a vacation. You arrange one, in which they are encouraged to gaze at length into a lake of liqueur, enjoy some pie, and then settle down for a long, hot nap. It seems to do them good. Frankly, you know the feeling.

Casual Cherry Pie

Serves 8

½ cup dried sour cherries

2 tablespoons boiling water

2 tablespoons kirsch

1½ pounds (about 7 medium) ripe plums, skins on, thinly sliced, stones discarded

10 tablespoons sugar, plus a bit

2 tablespoons cornstarch

Crisp Pastry (recipe follows)

2 teaspoons unsalted butter, cut up

2 teaspoons half-and-half

1. Plump: Tumble cherries into a small bowl. Pour in water and kirsch. Cover and let rest 30 minutes.

2. Chop: In a large bowl stir together plums, 10 tablespoons sugar, and cornstarch. Chop cherries and add, along with their soaking liquid, to the plums.

3. Fill: Roll out pastry into a 15-inch circle about ⅛ inch thick. Roll around rolling pin and unroll onto a parchment-paper-lined baking sheet. Smooth plum mixture onto pastry, leaving a 3-inch bare border. Scatter fruit with butter bits. Fold the border up and over the fruit, shaping a 9-inch free-form pie. Brush edge with half-and-half and sprinkle with a little sugar.

4. Bake: Slide pan into a 400-degree oven and bake until crust is golden and fruit is bubbling, 35 to 40 minutes. Cool completely.

Crisp Pastry

Wraps one 9-inch free-form pie

Measure into the food processor: 1 cup flour, ¼ cup corn flour (or fine corn meal), 1 tablespoon sugar, ¼ teaspoon fine salt. Pulse to mix. Drop in ¼ pound (1 stick) cold unsalted butter, sliced. Pulse until lumps range in size from crumbs to cornflakes. Turn out into a large mixing bowl. Drizzle in about 4 tablespoons cold water, mixing gently with a soft spatula, until pastry comes together. Pat into a disk. Wrap in wax paper and chill at least 1 hour.

FRENCH DRESSING

The French eat well. The French dress well. And their style secret, reports a stylish friend, is this: one outfit. Which is good news. It demystifies the French mystique and it qualifies me for a French passport.

I've long stood steadfast by my rule: One girl, one outfit. In second grade I relied on a yellow floral maxi and copper-enamel peace pendant. I spent much of college in itchy pink capris. But basic, which is to say black, is best.

Once you've settled on a look, it will come in handy all the time. The zip-back microfiber tank dress, for instance, works with sandals in summer, a blouse in fall, sweater in winter, and T-shirt in spring. It pairs nicely with a jacket for day or pearls for night. It shrugs off playground spatter or commuter grime. It can, in a pinch, double as nightgown.

The repetitive look frees the budget for other concerns. Like double portions of shoes and handbags, which my friend assures me are the Hamburger Helper of the French fashion diet.

After a year, the French retire the old and invest in the new. I've been stretching my black-on-black best a couple of seasons now and have yet to experience the urge to shop. I'm hoping this makes me doubly chic.

Lemon Vinaigrette

I don't believe in changing salad dressing any more than clothes. I've been relying on this recipe for decades and it has yet to fail me.

Makes about ½ cup

Juice of 1 lemon

1 teaspoon Dijon mustard

1 teaspoon sugar

6 tablespoons olive oil

Fine salt

2 tablespoons snipped chives, optional

1. Mix: Pour lemon juice into a small bowl. Whisk in mustard and sugar.

2. Whisk: Drizzle in olive oil, whisking constantly, until vinaigrette is shiny and smooth.

3. Season: Stir in salt to taste and, if you're feeling fancy, chives. Stylish on any salad.

PROVENANCE: *Adapted from* The Seasonal Kitchen *by Perla Meyers.*

STRONG COFFEE

After ballet Hannah and I walked to Krispy Kreme to watch the hot glazed doughnuts roll across the conveyor belt. The sugar shower was the best part. Hannah ordered milk and I got coffee. We looked at the El trains and discussed important matters. Like barrettes. And, one week, capital punishment.

"So, you know what happens when a person does something wrong?"

"He gets a time out," she recited.

"And when a person does something really bad?"

"He goes to prison."

"And sometimes the workers at the prison, they take that criminal and, well." There was no sugar I could sprinkle on this. "They kill him."

Hannah put down her glazed cinnamon. She studied my face, trying to work out if I was recounting a fairy tale, or a Hannah-in-Charge fantasy or some morality lesson, like the puppet's nose got longer when he lied.

At our house, bad guys sometimes suffered ambush with a double-barreled Lego. They were usually treated with the doctor's kit, and released on their own recognizance. Clara used her ballet shoe to dispatch the Mouse King. But actual adults who went to jobs where they killed people? What kind of story was that?

"Now," I went on, "the Adult-in-Charge, the governor, has realized that killing prisoners is bad. The newspaper helped change his mind."

This startled Hannah, who usually spread the pages across the floor in search of zoo photos, short words, and comics. She asked: "Why the newspaper?"

"Because, that's what it's for: to help people make decisions. Today the governor is going to tell everyone: 'Don't kill prisoners.'"

Now Hannah knew where we were. The happy ending. The part where right triumphed over wrong. Familiar terrain. Familiar enough for her to finish her dough-nut, and ask for half of mine.

Coffee

No child should reach majority without knowing how to brew a decent cup of cof-fee. There's science to this process and that science is called measuring. Here's the secret: 2 tablespoons ground coffee beans to 6 ounces water. Memorize that. It's easier in larger quantities like ½ cup ground coffee beans to 3 cups water. Not any water. Cold water. Cold filtered water, ideally.

You can use an electric drip coffee maker or one of the many hand-held options, like a Melita pot. Fold a paper filter. Measure in the grounds (make sure you've got the right grind; ask a professional). If working by hand, heat the water to boiling, let it settle a few seconds. Pour the water slowly, making sure all the grounds are soaked. Stir them with a spoon or whisk (even if you're using an electric coffee-maker, stir the grounds).

That's about it. Sip. Think dark thoughts.

SELF HELP

Problems collect in hair, migrating from root to split end. Therapies include soothing comb, sunny highlight, and the scissor's radical release. All best practiced by the professional. Still, it's troubling to finish treatment disheveled.

You suspect hair failure when friends fall silent, followed by the upbeat: "You got your hair cut!" Or, when one of your younger companions says: "Your hair looks ugly and bumpy, Mom."

What this analysis lacks in tact it makes up for in truth. Your hair looks ugly and bumpy. It has been slashed, spritzed, and scrunched into bedhead. Rumple is not your do's only don't. In an attempt at the angled bob, your hair therapist has sculpted tusks.

Tusks do not become you. Curled, they impart that wild rhinoceros look. Straightened, pure Babar. Tucked into a untended tangle, the porcupine startle. Taking solace in a deep hat, you shop for bumpy, ugly kale. The checkout clerk, peering from a thicket of curls and springs, confides that his own tousle is self-inflicted.

Back home, you lock the bathroom door and find the cuticle scissors. Imitating the stylist's two-fingered grip, you clamp and sever. The results fall somewhat short of professional, somewhat short of stylish, indeed somewhat too short. But the process is liberating.

Turning to your kale crisps, you think: This must be self-help.

Chip and Dip

Serves 4

Chip

These chips are compellingly crunchy, entirely snack-worthy, and made from kale, cruciferous superhero.

1 bunch red kale

1 teaspoon olive oil

1 teaspoon red wine vinegar

½ teaspoon kosher salt

1. Chop: Fold 1 kale leaf in half the long way. Cut away the purple backbone. Slice kale crosswise into 2-inch wide strips. Repeat with remaining leaves. Soak briefly, drain and spin dry.

2. Season: In a large mixing bowl toss kale with oil, vinegar, and salt.

3. Crisp: Spread out kale on two parchment-paper-lined baking sheets. Slide into a 350-degree oven and bake until crisp to the touch, about 10 minutes. Crunch solo or with dip.

Dip

Makes ½ cup

Peel and finely chop 1 shallot and, separately, 1 clove garlic. In a small skillet heat 1 tablespoon olive oil over medium-high. Add shallot and cook, stirring, until golden brown, about 3 minutes. Add garlic and cook until brown and crispy, 1 minute more. Scrape crispy bits along with any oil into ⅓ cup plain yogurt. Add a pinch of salt and stir well with a fork.

TRIED *AND* TRUE

My criminal career began at the grocery store, trailing the shopping cart and the shopping parent. There, at young-eye height and within young-hand's grasp, rose a mountain of yellow candy. I reached, delighting in the yellow cellophane crinkle. I slipped the candy into my mouth, then out. Butterscotch, I learned, tasted corn-syrup sweet, fake-butter awful. Crime, I learned, doesn't pay.

Scared straight, I learned to bake the chocolate-studded blondie. Teenaged friends goaded: "Try butterscotch. Like chocolate, only blonde." Caving to peer pressure, I switched. One bite yielded the truth: the butterscotch chip is whey-laced, partially hydrogenated awful.

Afraid of awful, I avoided further contact with butterscotch.

One night, well into adulthood, I dined at a fresh and inventive restaurant and there poached a spoonful of butterscotch pudding. It was delicious. It tasted of butter. And—thrillingly—Scotch. The hamburger lacks ham. The doughnut lacks nut. Is true butterscotch, I wondered, the happy amalgamation of butter and Scotch?

I turned to the authorities, who claimed this "scotch" referred to scoring or "scotching" the sweet. Not one to think too literally, I cooked up a renegade pudding sweetened with caramel, thick with butter, and soothed by Scotch whisky. So good, it was practically criminal.

Caramel Butterscotch Pudding

Serves 12

1 cup granulated sugar

¼ cup water

⅓ cup heavy
   whipping cream

½ cup dark brown sugar

⅓ cup cornstarch

1 teaspoon fine salt

3 cups whole milk

4 egg yolks

6 tablespoons unsalted
   butter, cut up

1 teaspoon vanilla extract

1 teaspoon Scotch whisky

1. Caramelize: Pour granulated sugar and water in a saucepan. Stir over medium heat until sugar dissolves, 2 minutes. Turn heat to high; boil, without stirring, until mixture turns a deep golden brown, 5 minutes. Pull pan off heat; carefully pour in cream (mixture will foam up). Stir the caramel smooth.

2. Boil: Measure brown sugar, cornstarch, and salt into another saucepan. Whisk in milk. Stir over medium heat until thick and bubbling, 5 minutes. Pull off heat. Whisk in caramel.

3. Thicken: Whisk egg yolks. Temper by slowly whisking in ½ cup warm pudding mixture. Whisk yolk mixture into pudding mixture. Bring to a simmer over medium heat. Whisk in the butter, vanilla, and whisky.

4. Chill: Pour into 12 demitasses (little cups). Chill uncovered 30 minutes, then press a piece of plastic wrap directly over each pudding. Chill 3 or more hours.

PROVENANCE: *Adapted from* Salty Sweets, *by Christie Matheson.*

ALONE WITH
A FIVE-POUND BRISKET

Your education, though long and expensive, does not include brisket. You opted out of the core course, under the self-righteous teenage vegetarian exemption. Now you know regret. Because at the holidays, the hostess is expected to serve brisket. And you lack even the vague memory that enables the resourceful cook to cram, guess, or cheat.

In fact, you are ignorant of the brisket requirement until the morning of the final, when you are discovered in the produce aisle, playing hooky. Esther, a family friend, studies your cart: organic pomegranates, red-leaf lettuce, green lentils, and sullen child. She commands: "You're making brisket, aren't you?" Esther, a confidant of your own mother, holds unassailable moral authority. Your menu—soup and salad garnished with a shrug—is swiftly revised. You swear: "Of course."

You have already failed. Brisket is a two-day ordeal.

At the meat counter you are directed to a carpet of beef flung across the top shelf. You are tempted to ask, with nonchalance: "How long does that cook?" But your son, who believes you are fully credentialed, is listening. You choose your slab and lug it home. "Biscuits?" he shouts. "I love biscuits!"

You are astonished to discover that your cookbook does not list brisket. Skimming, you gather that brisket is not a dish, per se, but a chewy cut. You give it a quick pot-roast prep, set it over a low flame, and turn your attention to more pressing matters, like the child on the floorboards shouting: "What's taking so long?" You are reassured, mid afternoon, by your brother-in-law on the phone who asserts: "Brisket cannot be overcooked."

At dinner you lift the lid to discover a broad expanse of something gray and dry and crusted with burnt carrot chunks. You suspect this is not the intended effect. You carve and serve. One of your more daring guests remembers her mother relied on a similar recipe.

Your children, in fierce loyalty, declare they love it.

Later, in the quiet hours when the fine print comes into focus, you discover, under camouflage of the heading "tzimmes," detailed instructions for searing, braising, cooling, carving, resting, and serving, along with a potful of cheerful potato dumplings, brisket. You consult the footnote and learn that tzimmes translates roughly as "nuisance."

Basic Brisket

Serves 8

1 (5-pound) beef brisket

1 tablespoon kosher salt

1½ teaspoons freshly
  ground black pepper

1 handful flour

2 tablespoons vegetable oil

10 cloves garlic, smashed

4 carrots, cut into coins

2 celery ribs, chopped

1 onion, thinly sliced

1 cup dried apricots

6 sprigs fresh parsley

2 bay leaves

2 sprigs fresh thyme

¼ cup tomato paste

1 bottle red wine

2 cups beef broth

1. **Prep:** Season brisket with salt and pepper. Cover and chill 2 to 24 hours.

2. **Brown:** Sprinkle brisket with flour; shake off excess. Heat oil in a Dutch oven over medium-high heat. Brown brisket, 5 minutes per side. Lift out brisket; tumble in garlic, carrots, celery, and onion. Cook, stirring, until lightly browned, about 10 minutes. Add apricots, parsley, bay leaves, thyme, and tomato paste. Cook, stirring, 2 minutes.

3. **Braise:** Set brisket on top of vegetables. Pour in wine. Liquid should rise halfway up the side of the meat. Add broth as needed. Heat to a boil, reduce to a simmer. Cover; slide into a 350-degree oven until fork tender, 2 to 3 hours.

4. **Slice:** Let cool. Lift out meat and slice thinly against the grain. Heat liquid over medium until thick. Strain sauce; pour back into Dutch oven. Lay in sliced meat. If you have time, refrigerate overnight, lift off any fat and reheat gently. If not, simply reheat gently.

SOMETHING *to* GNAW ON

Gnocchi share much with their cousins, the pastas, yet retain a unique heritage: Rolled from potatoes. Hunched into dumplings. And led by that silent "g" cozied up to the "n."

It's a burden few words share. The gnome is used to the role of odd. He spends his days hunched underground, guarding treasure. Perhaps gnocchi.

Every now and then the gnome may emerge, gnar at some woodland creature—a grazing gnu or fluttering gnatcatcher—and settle down on a tree knot, or gnarl. The very gnarl that lends its bumpy character to gnarled and gnarly. And gnocchi. The rolled and grooved little lumps would never be named after a striated rock, like the gneiss, or the sharp shape, like the gnomon.

The gnome gnashes at a passing gnat. He gnaws on a gnocchi, thinking that gnawing is gnathic work—all jaw.

Gnome is also a phrase, tried and true. Strangely, the gnomic canon contains few aphorisms dedicated to gnocchi.

The Gnostic aspires to gnosis—capturing truth. He seeks the divine, eschews the demiurge.

But the gnome, at least the gnocchi-noshing gnome, happily submits to the demiurge, even the full urge, to heap his platter with gnocchi. Why not? The truth is that potato dumplings, boiled tender, toasted in brown butter and sizzled with sage, are divine. And valuable. Without gnocchi, what would happen to Italy, and its GNP?

Gnocchi

Serves 4 as a first course

1 large (¾ pound) russet potato, not peeled

1 egg

⅛ teaspoon freshly grated nutmeg

Kosher salt

About ½ cup flour

4 tablespoons (½ stick) unsalted butter

8 fresh sage leaves, slivered

1. Bake: Scrub potato and poke several times with a fork. Set directly on the rack of a 400-degree oven and bake until tender when poked, about 45 minutes. Alternatively, zap until tender, about 10 minutes.

2. Rice: When cool enough to handle, press through a potato ricer onto a work surface. Let cool until no longer steaming.

3. Whisk: Whisk together egg, nutmeg, and ⅛ teaspoon salt. Pour egg mixture over potato and stir very gently with a fork, just to combine. Sprinkle on about ⅓ cup flour and continue to mix very gently and sparingly with fork or fingers until a soft dough forms.

4. Test: Bring a large pot of salted water to a boil. Pinch off a bit of dough and drop it in. If it holds its shape, you're good to go. If it falls apart, add a little more flour to the dough.·

5. Roll: Divide dough in two. On a floured surface, roll each portion into a ½-inch-thick rope. Slice crosswise into ½-inch segments.

6. Groove: Flip a fork over, tines resting on table. Roll each gnocchi down the back of the fork, pressing lightly, to imprint grooves. Not absolutely necessary, but gnocchi are all about looking adorable.

7. Boil: Drop gnocchi into boiling water in two batches. Gnocchi will sink. Then, in about 1 minute, float. Wait 10 seconds. Scoop them out with a slotted spoon and drain on a clean kitchen towel.

8. Sizzle: Heat butter over medium-high heat in a medium skillet. It will melt, then brown. Add sage, sizzle 1 minute. Add cooked gnocchi and toast, tossing gently until lightly browned, about 1 minute. Nice as an appetizer or scattered on an arugula salad, crouton-style.

FOSTERING CONFIDENCE

The child is supposed to prepare her own breakfast. It says so in *Scholastic Parent & Child*. It says pouring milk inspires independence and confidence. It shows, in full-color cheerfulness, a child feeling confident.

You want your own child to pour milk and feel confident. You have been depriving her of this benefit. You are a bad parent. Soon you will be profiled in *Bad Parent & Child*.

Fortunately the magazine explains how to make amends. First, transfer the oat-bran flakes from their cardboard box to a plastic jar with flip-top, so that your child can serve cereal with confidence. Transfer the milk to a bulbous syrup pitcher with spring-loaded lid, so that your child can pour milk with confidence. Transfer the yogurt to the bottom shelf of the refrigerator so that your child can browse with confidence. Cut your sponge into a star shape so that your child can bus and clear with confidence.

You recognize that rules change. You remember the friend who, a generation ago, stocked the foot of the crib with snack packs of Lucky Charms, in the interest of an additional six minutes of sleep. And while you understand—indeed share—her goal, you know her technique would now inspire glossy coverage in *Feloniously Negligent Parent & Child*.

Still, you resist the kitchen reorganization. Until, contemplating an unruly stack of bills, you are overwhelmed by the desire to boost your child's confidence. You shift the carrots up and the strawberry jam down and relocate the organic Cocoa Oatios.

Then you download a map to Ikea. Because there's no way to bolster a child's early-morning confidence without a set of those flower-shaped melamine dishes. It gives a girl confidence to know that no matter how perplexed she may be by the physics of uniting toast square with jam lump, her microwave-compatible, dishwasher-safe, impact-resistant plate won't shatter.

At Ikea, beside the dice slipcovers and the bumble-bee umbrellas, sits a crate overflowing with flower-shaped plates, six for $1.99. Talk about confidence. Also matching cups and forks and knives and spoons. No bowls. Discontinued.

At home you move the pie tins to a high shelf and the new plasticware to a low shelf and tell your child she can get her own breakfast. She looks confused.

There's something about a child hovering over a small orange daisy plate—jug of Crunch Berries in one hand, pitcher of milk in the other—that makes you suspect you will soon need a star-shaped sponge, as well as a mop. It's a prediction you make with complete confidence.

Strawberry-Rhubarb Jam
Makes about 1½ cups

1 pint perfectly ripe strawberries, hulled and halved

1 cup rhubarb, trimmed and sliced into 1-inch lengths

¾ cup sugar

1. Thicken: Heap berries, rhubarb, and sugar into a medium saucepan. Set over medium heat and cook, stirring occasionally, until thick and beginning to set, about 15 minutes.

2. Cool: Pull pan off heat; let cool. Scrape into a glass jar. Seal. Chill.

3. Serve: For the simplest of breakfasts spread on toast, waffle, or English muffin or stir into yogurt.

'COCCO'

GOOD THINGS

Procrastination is a waste of time. Especially if you've been meaning to make hamantaschen and then, out of the blue, your grandmother, who has been folding the triangular cookies for most of her ninety-eight years, expires. What now? How will you re-create the cookies that arrived twice a year, packed into a foil-lined shoe box, size 6½ wide, beige?

Certainly not from the recipe she sent you. Your grandmother never lost the smooth skin and lilting delivery she imported from Hungary. She spoke English mixed with Hungarian and wrote—copiously—in flowing transliteration. Her instructions call for mixing doe from flower and a pond of butter.

You have tried this recipe. It yields a pond of melted butter. You've edited, seeking assistance of cream cheese and some nicely reduced preserves. But you know deep in your second-generation heart that your Cuisinart-churned hamantaschen are not the lowly, lumpy, lovable hamantaschen you grew up on. The ones you believed only came stuffed with "woolnuts" until you discovered, years later, that your mother had been looting the apricot layers.

Haman, Biblical namesake of hamantaschen, was famous for treachery.

You've studied other recipes. Notably the one practiced by your husband's family, also Hungarian immigrants, one still enamored of the prepackaged pleasures of the New World. It calls for mashing vanilla ice cream into flour, rolling and filling with jelly. Obviously a crime.

You could have joined your grandmother on a trip to Hungary. She drove, cursing at inept "old people," until ninety. She traveled until ninety-seven. You could have gone to Florida, and stood in her humid kitchen, idled except for the percolator, and insisted she show you, step by step, with her bent but smoothly manicured fingers. You thought: later.

You tried to get her advice long distance. It was knaidlach, those little potato footballs your older brother called Istenem!, in honor of your grandmother's frequent and feisty use of the Hungarian oath. She was distracted by other concerns. Like pain. "Focus," she said, "on good things."

Now you look over your collection of her letters—ballpoint scrawls stuffed into the back of a cookbook. Chees Blintz. Woodka Punch. Each ends with a pat on the back: "I have no doubt. You will make a good job of it." Followed by a sharp elbow: "Eny question? Use the fone!"

You go to Florida to say good-bye. Stealthy as Haman, you snag a slim blue cookbook from her vacant apartment. Checkmarks in the index note her accomplishments: Baba Rum Cake. Bridge Cocktails. Dry Martini. No hamantaschen. You close the book and sigh. It's titled, of course, *Your Just Desserts*.

Vinaigrette

Makes about ½ cup

2 tablespoons cider vinegar

1 teaspoon Dijon mustard

½ teaspoon kosher salt

1 clove garlic, mashed

2 teaspoons finely chopped
fresh chives

2 teaspoons finely chopped
fresh parsley

2 teaspoons finely chopped
fresh tarragon

6 tablespoons olive oil

Whisk together all ingredients except the oil. Slowly drizzle in oil, whisking constantly, until thick.

MAKING IT LOOK EASY

Talking and eating go together. Unlike talking and cooking. Such an unsavory mix has yielded many a dehydrated roast and many a dispirited hostess. Then there's talking and grilling, a pairing that approaches fatal.

The worst dinner party I ever managed was preceded by a heated dispute. At the time I lived in a small apartment with a small balcony that held a small grill. I believed I could pull full meals from this picnic tag-a-long while maintaining a cool demeanor and hot debate.

Phone pinched between shoulder and ear, I sliced the onions into lopsided circles and neglected the timer and oversalted the fish, while upbraiding my friend Rose for failing to deliver chicken soup to our friend Brigid.

Rose countered that she could make her own decisions. And while my view (empathy! responsibility! matzoh balls!) had merit, Rose won. Because at the end the of the phone call she had a glass of wine and went to bed exhausted while I had a dinner party and went to bed ruined.

One of my guests actually stacked up the charred salmon and the blackened potatoes and the tortured pepper-onion marmalade in a tower, restaurant style, in an attempt to hide one gruesome corpse from another. Though still years from the enlightenment that parenting can bring, I had the compassion to offer him a PB&J.

Since then, I've learned a thing or two about casual entertaining. Beginning with the insight that nothing is actually casual. Making it look easy calls for an ancient cooking technique: cheating.

Which is to say, cook ahead. Salads and casseroles have earned their reputations as dependable backyard basics. But even the hot-tempered grill can benefit from cool foresight.

Choose a spring menu of tender, savory lamb. Enjoy the ingenious time-management technique of the marinade, which allows you to prep while you sleep. You can even grill in advance—the finished dish is enchanting hot or warm.

Once you've dispatched the spatula to the dishwasher and changed into a fresh dress you can simply point to the platter, fully composed. You'll look, to the casual eye, like a casual genius. And if anyone disagrees, you can give that point of view your full attention.

Grilled Lamb
Serves 6

1 (4-pound) boneless leg of lamb, butterflied to an even 1½ inch thickness

1 tablespoon kosher salt

1½ teaspoons freshly ground black pepper

2 tablespoons olive oil

3 tablespoons chopped garlic

3 tablespoons chopped fresh rosemary

3 tablespoons chopped fresh thyme

1. Season: Rub lamb with salt and pepper. Cover and chill overnight.

2. Smear: Measure olive oil, garlic, rosemary, and thyme into the food processor and pulse to a fragrant paste. Smear all over both sides of the lamb. Settle the meat in a glass dish, cover tightly with plastic wrap and chill, 1 hour.

3. Sizzle: Let meat come to room temperature, up to 1 hour. Grill directly over a medium-hot fire, until nicely browned, about 5 minutes per side. Move to indirect heat and cook until done (130 degrees for medium rare), about 5 more minutes.

4. Serve: Let the meat rest, loosely covered with foil, 10 minutes. Slice into thin strips. Douse with any accumulated juices.

EARLY MORNING
SURRENDER

Nature provisions each child with a parent, as a way of ensuring her survival. And each parent with a child, as a way of ensuring her demise. Call it natural population control. Part of ensuring your child grows up is to feed her and this will inevitably be your undoing.

It doesn't look like a difficult task. Just pour the cornflakes into the bowl and let nature take its course. Which means the cornflakes will settle into a sullen hush and so will the child. And while you might leave matters at that, dispatching cereal to the disposal and child to school, you suspect that such haste would render you derelict in your duty: sustaining life.

You try the usual lame antics: threats, rewards. You feel foolish pointing to the uncooperative chair or the jelly bean jar at 7 a.m. In a moment of calm you consider that mealtime is the soul of family life and that young palates are tender and that convenience almost always ends up inconvenient.

So you attempt to appease your girl gourmet. You shirr eggs and toast up ginger waffles and draw tiny renditions of Matisse's Jazz in melted Nutella on crushed pecan griddlecakes. And while all this activity amuses Hannah, none of it reaches the stage of digestion when actual nutrition is achieved.

Then, from some deep recess of your sleep-deprived brain, comes a vision. It's a prosaic vision, being brown, and rectangular, and raisin-spotted, but it is a vision no less. A vision from a time when, pre-parenthood, you lingered over brunch at Ina's and indulged in scrapple and vegetable hash and poached eggs and coffee with real cream. And sometimes, while waiting, in one of those heavenly oatmeal squares—or rather rectangles—dotted with raisins. You don't even like raisins. But these blocks were so chewy and homey and delicious they always struck you as the perfect square (or rectangular) breakfast. Breakfast in a bar. A concept long since ruined by the granola lobby, the Power Bar elite.

You call Ina Pinkney. Gracious as ever, she copies down the recipe. It's full of raisins and walnuts and oatmeal—wholesome breakfast elements all—suspended in a cloud of butter and molasses enticements. You stay up late beating and spreading and in the morning have a breakfast strategy at the ready: One plate stacked with four oatmeal bars.

Hannah, sensing brownie, bites. You smile a sly mother smile. By the time you dose your coffee with cream, you find a mound of walnuts and oatmeal and raisins heaped on the plate, the bar's sticky connective tissue having been skillfully gnawed away.

Youth and ingenuity triumph, again.

Sly Oatmeal Bars

Makes 16 bars

¼ pound (1 stick) unsalted butter

¾ cup sugar

2 eggs

6 tablespoons molasses

1 teaspoon vanilla extract

1½ cups all-purpose flour

¼ cup whole-wheat flour

1 teaspoon baking soda

¾ teaspoon fine salt

1½ teaspoons ground cinnamon

2 cups rolled oats

1 cup raisins

½ cup chopped walnuts, toasted

1. Fluff: Using a stand mixer fitted with the paddle attachment, cream butter and sugar until light and fluffy, about 3 minutes. Add eggs, molasses, and vanilla and beat until the batter looks fluffy again.

2. Mix: In a separate bowl whisk together both types of flour, baking soda, salt, and cinnamon. Add flour mixture to butter mixture and blend. Stir in oats, raisins, and walnuts by hand.

3. Bake: Heap batter into a 13 x 9 x 2-inch baking pan (you know, the lasagna pan) lined with parchment paper. Pat down with a damp hand. Slide into a 350-degree oven and bake until rich brown and slightly puffed, about 25 minutes. Cool completely, cut, and serve. Or store in the freezer for those mornings when breakfast prep seems daunting.

TRAINING *for* THE MARATHON

Greece was an exotic destination, one I knew by way of sunny postcard, flaming cheese, and mental file labeled "Legends of the Fifth Grade." I imagined it dominated by superhero Odysseus, supermodel Helen, and superpatient Penelope, who waited twenty years for her husband to return from work.

I was particularly entranced by the way the average Greek god, storming a foreign palace, was welcomed with hot bath, hot-oil massage, and hot meal. I considered this custom as I trained for an Olympian feat: taking in 1,210 hours of Olympic programming, including kayak slalom, men's epee, and dressage. Greek to me.

It would take mental focus to achieve even a qualifying Nielsen rating. I remembered the story of the original marathon, in which a messenger dashed from Marathon to Athens to announce: "Rejoice. We Conquer." Then expired.

I prepared by anointing chunks of filet mignon with oil and herbs. I roasted the meat, chilled tzatziki, and warmed up the television.

Lacking the patience to wait for Bob to return from work, I settled into an appreciation for athletes who test the limits of mortals. I wondered if there was something untoward about lounging on pillows, tzatziki-suffused, while my compatriots sweated it out on-screen. I considered the wisdom of the Greek chorus, stationed a safe distance from the action.

"Rejoice," I thought, raising a goblet. "We conquer."

Filet Mignon Kebob

Serves 4

½ cup dry white wine

½ cup olive oil

1 teaspoon kosher salt

2 cloves garlic, chopped

1 tablespoon mixed pickling spices, optional

1 tablespoon fresh oregano, chopped, optional

1 pound beef filet mignon, cut into 1-inch cubes

Tzatziki (recipe follows)

Pita bread

1. Marinate: Mix wine, oil, salt, and garlic in a gallon-size zip-top bag. If the sultry mystery of cardamom, cinnamon, and cloves appeals, add the pickling spice. If not, substitute the oregano. Tumble in the meat, seal, and chill at least 1 hour. Meanwhile, soak wooden skewers in cold water.

2. Skewer: Thread the meat onto the skewers.

3. Sizzle: Slide kebobs under the broiler or over a hot grill. Cook, turning once, about 5 minutes. Serve with tzatziki and pita.

Tzatziki

Makes about 1½ cups

1 cup plain nonfat yogurt

1 medium cucumber

1 teaspoon fine salt

1½ teaspoons red wine vinegar

2 teaspoons olive oil

1½ teaspoons finely chopped fresh dill

1½ teaspoons finely chopped fresh mint

1½ teaspoons finely chopped garlic

¼ teaspoon ground white pepper

1. Drain: Line a strainer with two lengths of cheesecloth, crisscrossed. Set the strainer over a bowl. Pour in the yogurt, tie loosely at the top, and let drain, 2 hours at room temperature or in the refrigerator overnight.

2. Salt: Peel the cucumber. Split it in half lengthwise; scrape out the seeds with a small spoon. Slice, as finely as possible crosswise. Dump the crescents into a colander and season with salt. Let drain over a bowl, 30 minutes. Rinse, gently press, then roll up cucumber crescents in a kitchen towel to dry.

3. Season: Combine yogurt and cucumbers in a bowl. Add the remaining ingredients and mix gently with a soft spatula. Chill.

GOAL-ORIENTED

The scholar/athlete must choose her sport. And should she be ignorant of all sports, soccer will choose her. For the girl who is seven and has feet, soccer is hard to avoid.

Hannah found she liked soccer. Especially the green striped jersey and the Velcro-tight shin guards and the camaraderie of slapping palms after someone—else—scored a goal.

The nuances of the game remained a mystery. She was aware that there was a ball and that the ball was to be kicked, one direction and then the other. She was willing to lope behind the pack of green-striped girls, first one direction and then the other, without ever achieving contact—even eye contact—with the ball.

This workout pleased her. She belonged to a team. She wore a green-striped jersey. She loped. Then she noticed that certain girls were capable of controlling the ball, even willing it into that net thingy. She realized, with an upwelling of bitter tears, that her soccer skills were deficient.

Leaving her oatmeal warm in its bowl Hannah descended to the driveway to dribble. She skipped rope. She repeated: "I think I can."

Then one sleet-soaked Saturday Hannah—or her coach—was determined she would score. She stood, as ordered, near the opposing goal. As the nimble green girls skittered the ball down the field, the coach screamed, "Pass!" The ball rolled directly to Hannah's muddy cleats. She lurched, and scored. There was much high-fiving.

Back home I peeled off Hannah's dripping striped jersey and soggy green socks, right down to her clenched blue toes. I settled her into fleece warm-ups and pink knee-highs and offered her a bowl of black-bean soup thick with masa balls, each of which rolled directly from spoon to goal, and scored.

Greens and Beans

Serves 6

1 pound dry black beans

4 chipotle peppers in adobo*
(fished from the can)

3 cloves garlic, chopped

½ small white onion, sliced

¼ cup olive oil

1 cup fresh masa for
tortillas* (or ¾ cup dried
masa harina* mixed with
⅔ cup hot water)

About 2½ teaspoons
kosher salt

¾ cup chopped
fresh cilantro

6 ounces (1½ cups)
crumbled queso fresco*

6 cups stemmed,
sliced chard

Corn tortillas**

1. Boil: Rinse the beans, scoop them into a large pot, and add 2 quarts cold water (skim off any beans that float). Simmer, partially covered, stirring now and then, until creamy and tender, about 2 hours.

2. Thicken: In the food processor or blender, purée peppers with garlic, onion, and ½ cup cold water. Press through a medium-mesh strainer into a bowl. In a large saucepan, heat 2 tablespoons oil over medium-high. Pour in the purée and stir until thick, about 5 minutes. Add to cooked beans and simmer another 30 minutes.

3. Knead: In a large bowl, knead together the masa (fresh or reconstituted) with the remaining 2 tablespoons oil, ½ teaspoon salt, ¼ cup of the chopped cilantro, and the cheese. Roll into 48 small balls. Cover with plastic wrap.

4. Simmer: Season the stew with about 2 teaspoons salt. Add dumplings one at a time. Simmer over medium heat, 5 minutes. Add greens, stirring gently, and simmer until tender, about 7 minutes.

5. Serve: Ladle stew into bowls, sprinkle with remaining chopped cilantro, and serve with hot tortillas.

PROVENANCE: *Streamlined from the indispensible* Rick Bayless's Mexican Kitchen.

*Chipotle peppers in adobo, masa (corn tortilla dough), masa harina (corn tortilla flour), and queso fresco (fresh crumbly cheese) are available in the Mexican aisle of many grocery stores and at Mexican markets.

**To steam-heat corn tortillas: Dampen a clean kitchen towel. Wrap around a stack of tortillas. Zap 2 minutes in microwave.

BACK IN COLLEGE DAYS

Our first college apartment indulged in all the clichés of its genre. Cindy and I decorated one room in spare futon chic, one in "unfinished" style, and one in thrift-shop shabby. Terribly grown-up.

We practiced many a new ritual, like sliding the rent check under our landlord's door. And keeping the electricity flowing, most of the time. New Year's Eve, mid-toast, we realized that the first of the month arrives whether you are in town or not.

We learned that when you go on vacation, it's okay to leave your spare/unfinished/shabby apartment empty. And that it's not okay to leave your spare/unfinished/shabby apartment refrigerator full.

We were also schooled in the habits of neighborliness. We were amazed that our sole neighbor—a grownup with an actual job—did not share our taste for late hours and loud music.

In the spring our neighbor, the one with the job, invited us in for lobster. Being students without jobs, we had never steamed a lobster. Perhaps we'd never seen a lobster.

Our neighbor set her dining-room table with huge platters of craggy red creatures, and tiny bowls of butter for dipping. That first crack, dip, and bite was a revelation. One of many that year, and one of the best.

Lobster Rolls

Serves 4

1 pound cooked lobster
meat, chopped*

½ cup mayonnaise

1 tablespoon freshly
squeezed lemon juice

1 tablespoon snipped fresh
chives

1 teaspoon finely grated
lemon zest

Kosher salt

4 tablespoons (½ stick)
unsalted butter

1 clove garlic, smashed

4 top-loading buns**

Butter lettuce

1. Mix: Settle lobster, mayonnaise, lemon juice, chives, and lemon zest in a bowl. Mix gently with a fork. Season with salt. Cover and chill, 1 hour to 1 day.

2. Toast: Melt butter in a skillet over medium heat. Add garlic; sizzle 1 minute to scent the butter. Add buns and toast the outsides until golden, 1 to 2 minutes per side. Discard garlic.

3. Fill: Line each toasted bun with lettuce. Fill each with a quarter of the chilled lobster mixture. Enjoy.

*Choose a live lobster and ask the fishmonger to steam and shell it. One 1½ pound lobster yields about ½ pound meat, so you'll need two for this recipe.

**Aka split-top buns or New England buns. Like hot-dog rolls, but split top down. If your grocery store doesn't carry them, substitute standard hot-dog rolls.

THE GENIUS *of* BARBEQUE

Barbecue is not positioning steak over flame. That, your huffy cookbook enunciates, is grilling. Barbecue, in the noble southern tradition, is subjecting a tough chunk of beast to smoke until it collapses. The ancient art, known to many men as a form of meditation, draws on the natural elements—earth, wind, fire, and beer.

Prep for you, a novice, involves buying a grill and following the 12-step assembly pictogram, dragging home sacks of charcoal and chunks of wood and hunks of meat. Meditation can be exhausting.

The cut in question, though taken from the upper front leg of a pig, is termed, indelicately, pork butt. And must be patted with a mix of salt, sugar, and spices, providing ample opportunity to juxtapose "rub" and "butt."

And afterward, smoke. Pork butt only transforms into barbecue in narrow confines: 180 to 250 degrees Fahrenheit. Steadying a hardwood-charcoal fire takes attention. Constant, obsessive attention.

Chuck, of Chuck's Barbecue, offers concise instructions: If the fire is too hot, stop down the vent. If it's too cool, add charcoal. Check, following the wisdom of grill gurus Chris Schlessinger and John Willoughby, every 30 to 40 minutes or after each beer, whichever comes first. Repeat for 8 to 12 hours. You understand why this holiday is named Labor Day.

Forgoing beer for clipboard and thermometer, you toss hickory chips, twist vent. Then you are met with an interval during which the job is, essentially, nothing. That's when you are visited by a profound insight. These foamy interludes of nothingness are why guys like this job.

You fixate on these empty expanses, some of which stretch to several minutes. Soon you are sprinting inside, loading the dishwasher, sorting lights from darks, spreading peanut butter on toast, and trimming crusts. Soon your thermometer reads zero.

Now you know the ignominy of refiring the rapid-fire chimney starter, long after having started. Hot-cheeked, you hew closer to code; you open an actual beer. You twist and toss for a total of 16 hours and 22 minutes, and at midnight shred an impressive pile of pork. The crispy outside shards and tender inner strands are scented earth, wind, fire, and beer. As are you.

Your friends, heaping tender meat onto soft buns, declare you a barbecue genius. "Eat up," you smile. You're never going near that grill again.

Pulled Pork Sandwich

Serves 12

5 pounds Pulled Pork
(recipe follows)

2 cups North Carolina BBQ
Sauce (recipe follows) or
other barbecue sauce

6 cups Mustard Slaw
(recipe follows)

12 soft fluffy white buns

Gently heat sauce and mix with the meat. Heap onto a bun. Top with a scoop of slaw. Roll up your sleeves. Eat, heartily.

Pulled Pork

Makes about 5 pounds

2 tablespoons
granulated sugar

2 tablespoons brown sugar

2 tablespoons kosher salt

6 cloves finely
chopped garlic

4 teaspoons ground paprika

1 tablespoon chili powder

2¼ teaspoons black pepper

2¼ teaspoons
mustard powder

1½ teaspoons
cayenne pepper

¾ teaspoon
ground cinnamon

1 (8-pound) pork butt,
bone-in, untrimmed
(all that fat, melted for
hours, is what makes
the meat so tender)

1. Toss: Mix all ingredients except meat in a small bowl.

2. Rub: A day before you're in the mood for a pulled pork sandwich, cover the meat with half the rub, wrap in plastic, and refrigerate overnight. Also soak a bucket of hickory chips or chunks in water. Early the next morning, use remaining rub to rerub the butt.

3. Smoke: Wake up early. Don't shower. Position a disposable aluminum pan on one side of the charcoal grate in the bottom of a kettle-style grill, to catch drips. Light a small heap of natural wood charcoal using a chimney starter. Pour the hot coals (carefully!) next to the aluminum pan. When the coals are nice and hot, scatter a handful of wood chips on top. Position the pork butt, fat-side up, on the top rack above the aluminum pan, not above the coals. Cover the grill. Situate the lid vent directly above the meat and close any other vents. This will force the smoke to travel past the meat.

4. Check: If your grill does not have a temperature gauge, slip a thermometer in the vent hole. Keep the grill temperature between 180 and 250 degrees. If it gets too hot, close the vent a little; if it gets too cool, add more charcoal. Cook pork butt 8 to 12 hours, adding wood chips every 45 minutes for the first 4 hours and then every hour or so. Meat is done when it reads 180 degrees on an instant-read thermometer and is very tender when prodded with fork or finger.

5. Pull: Pull the meat apart with tongs or two forks or (if cool) fingers and remove all visible fat.

Mustard Slaw

Makes 6 cups

6 cups cabbage, shredded

1 small onion, finely chopped

½ cup half-and-half

¼ cup sugar

3 tablespoons
    yellow mustard

3 tablespoons cider vinegar

2 tablespoons mayonnaise

1 clove garlic

1 teaspoon kosher salt

Mix cabbage and onions in a large bowl. Blend everything else in the blender. Pour over cabbage and toss.

Simple North Carolina BBQ Sauce

Makes 2 cups

1½ cups cider vinegar

½ cup ketchup

¼ cup dark brown sugar

2 teaspoons kosher salt

1½ teaspoons freshly
ground black pepper

1 teaspoon chili powder

½ teaspoon cayenne pepper

Swirl in the blender. In the North Carolina tradition, this is a thin sauce.

Cheater's Sandwich

If you'd rather not spend the day squinting at your grill, trim the pork butt before rubbing. Brown on all sides in 2 tablespoons canola oil in a large ovenproof pot. Cover and bake at 325 degrees until it shreds easily, about 3 hours. The meat will not be smoked, but it will be tender and tasty. Don't tell Chuck.

THE PLEASURES *of* URBAN LIFE

The urban bee contends that the city is a fine place to raise a family. Indeed superior to the arid conditions and floracultural poverty found in many a rural setting. The bee, like the rest of us, thrives here.

The local wildlife tends to construct shade-casting towers and concrete-covered streets. But they are also given to planting things. Things that bloom. In park, median, or window box. And because humans water their décor, the hardworking honeybee enjoys snack-shop convenience all over town.

In North Lawndale, west of downtown, a bee can find an attractive home and prosperous living. Behind a chain-link fence marked Sweet Beginnings stand thirty-five beehives. Not the old-fashioned curvilinear sort, but modern condominium-style hives: bright white, squared off, five stories high and neatly spaced, like a surrealist vision of dresser drawers on a field trip. In high season each houses fifty thousand bees. Within an easy commute the forager can find aster, golden rod, and, happily, sweet clover in abundance.

The beehive development has amenities including two huge watering tubs with wine-cork floats to accommodate the thirsty worker or drone. Bees raise brood in frames, conveniently prestamped with the hexagonal pattern favored by bees of all social classes.

The queens are pleased. Each has commanded her hive to produce surplus honey, which human workers harvest spring and fall. Many are learning beekeeping under an employment program for the formerly incarcerated. The city is all about opportunity.

The worker people spin out the honey, bottle it, and sell it under the label Bee-love. The bees don't seem to mind. The honey tax is one of the costs of city living.

Honey Apple Tart
Serves 8

5 tablespoons unsalted butter

½ cup sugar

¾ cup ground almonds (aka almond meal or almond flour)

1 egg

⅛ teaspoon almond extract

1 package (about 1 pound) all-butter puff pastry, defrosted

2 apples, peeled, cored, and thinly sliced

3 tablespoons honey

1. Fluff: Beat 4 tablespoons butter and the sugar until light and fluffy. Beat in, in order: almonds, egg, and almond extract.

2. Cut: Unfold puff pastry onto a lightly floured surface. Cut into 8 sections (squares are efficient, but circles suggest apple). Set pastry on a parchment-paper-lined baking sheet.

3. Fill: Spread a generous spoonful of almond cream onto each tart, leaving a ½-inch border bare. Arrange apples over the cream in a pleasing pattern. Melt together the remaining 1 tablespoon of butter and the honey; drizzle over apples.

4. Bake: Slide into a 400-degree oven and bake until golden and thoroughly puffed, about 20 minutes. Serve warm.

A HEX ON SHELF HOGS

The dedicated cooking utensil annoys me. Who needs a springerle mold, asparagus steamer, or tortilla crisper? They work minimal hours, take up maximum storage space, and spend most of their time loafing.

So when a bitter night called for chicken paprikash, I found my kitchen batterie deficient. The recipe demanded the ordinary tool, like large pot, and the extraordinary one, like spaetzle maker. As if.

The technique is to stew chicken until it collapses into a rich red bath of paprika. Spaetzle, chewy lumpy dumplings, intercept the sour cream swirl. The idea is to leave the meal so heavily anchored as to be impervious to chill.

The challenge is to produce a dumpling up to the task. Standard instructions suggested beating together eggs and flour, then forcing the dough through the holes of a gadget into long lumpy strands. Lacking gadget, I tried alternatives. Like a spoon. And, in a fit of inventiveness, the drowsy potato ricer. The separate streams of dough managed to reunite before plummeting into the pot, yielding a single spaetzle scramble.

Neither cold weather nor chicken paprikash relents in a single day. By my second go-round I had purchased a certified spaetzle maker. It's something like the pasta machine that hibernates on my top shelf, with a German accent.

"With the Spaetzle-Hex you have now a 'good witch' in your household," read the insert. It could conjure three sizes: "soup spaetzle," "side-plate spaetzle" and "like homemade spaetzle." I braved all three, following the instructions to "let the extruded dough swim to the surface of slightly bubbling water" and to drain the dumplings "in a riddle." Actually I improvised the riddle.

Just as I was scooping out the squiggles, my mother dropped by. She cast a skeptical eye at my kitchen witch, scooped up a handful of dough and squeezed. The dough streamed from fist to pot. Her dumplings promptly swam to the top: authentically large, lumpy, and chewy. Excellent sauce catchers all.

Which solved the riddle: Stick to simple tools, like hands.

Chicken Paprikash

Serves 6

3 tablespoons
  unsalted butter

3 onions, thinly sliced

6 tablespoons sweet paprika

¼ teaspoon hot paprika
  (or cayenne pepper)

3 tablespoons flour

2 cups chicken broth

4 cloves garlic, chopped

1 teaspoon kosher salt

1 teaspoon freshly ground
  black pepper

2 (3½-pound) chickens,
  quartered, rinsed and
  patted dry

1 cup sour cream

1. Soften: Melt butter over medium heat in a large, heavy pot. Add onions. Cook until golden, about 10 minutes. Sprinkle with both paprikas and the flour. Cook, stirring, 1 minute. Stir in broth, garlic, salt, and pepper.

2. Simmer: Bring to a boil. Add chicken. Cover and simmer tender, turning chicken once, about 45 minutes. Pull chicken from pot and set aside.

3. Thicken: Let the sauce settle. Skim off fat. Squeeze sauce through a strainer lined with cheesecloth. Discard solids. Return sauce to pot, increase heat to medium and simmer thick, about 20 minutes. Reduce heat to low and stir in sour cream.

4. Heat: When chicken is cool enough to handle, remove and discard skin and bones. Return meat to pot, heat and serve with spaetzle.

Spaetzle

Serves 6

Whisk together 2 eggs and ½ cup water. Stir in 1½ cups flour, ½ teaspoon baking powder, and ¾ teaspoon salt. Beat well with a wooden spoon. Heat a large pot of salted water to a boil. Scoop up a handful of dough and squeeze, dropping small bits of dough into the water. Each dumpling should be about 1 inch long, ¼-inch wide and lumpy. When spaetzle float to the surface, in about 1 minute, scoop them out with a slotted spoon. Spread spaetzle out to dry on a clean kitchen towel. Heat 2 tablespoons unsalted butter in a medium skillet over medium heat. Toast spaetzle, tossing occasionally, until edges are lightly browned, about 3 minutes.

GERM WARFARE

Germ theory has its proponents, like germs. And its opponents, like the rest of us. Their team, obviously, is winning.

The germ is stupid, the young and afflicted complain. And yet, it shows intelligence. The germ never works alone; it leads a complex social life. Confining our own to bathrobe, bunny slippers, and a daily call to the school nurse.

Just when pharmacists hit on a recipe both tasty and lethal to the ordinary microbe, it turns up its tiny nose. Resistant. Cunning. Even, we hear, opportunistic.

And so we are left with our standard remedies: vile cough drop, sticky syrup, whining. And soup. Which offers the only effective over-the-counter relief.

Red-Hot Pepper Cure
Serves 8

1 head garlic, unpeeled

1 teaspoon vegetable oil

Kosher salt

2 tablespoons olive oil

1 onion, chopped

4 bell peppers, any color, seeded and chopped

2 jalapeño peppers, seeded and finely chopped

3 tablespoons grated ginger

8 cups chicken broth

2 cups cooked shredded chicken, optional

1 bunch cilantro, chopped

Freshly ground black pepper

Juice of 1 lemon

1. Roast: Separate garlic cloves and drizzle with vegetable oil. Wrap in foil and toss in a 400-degree oven until soft and fragrant, about 30 minutes. Let cool. Squeeze roasted garlic cloves from their skins. Use a fork to mash with a pinch of salt.

2. Soften: Heat the olive oil in a large soup pot over low heat. Add the onion and cook, stirring occasionally, until tender, about 10 minutes. Add the peppers, roasted garlic, and ginger and cook, stirring, for 1 minute.

3. Simmer: Pour in the chicken broth, increase heat to medium-high, and simmer for 3 minutes. Add chicken, if using, and cilantro and cook 1 minute more. Season with salt and pepper.

4. Serve: Stir in lemon juice and serve hot.

PROVENANCE: *A version of this easy cure ran in the* New York Times *about twenty years ago. I keep the tattered clipping in my go-to file and dig it out whenever I've got the sniffles. Works like a charm.*

ADVENTURES ON ICE

N oah envisioned his fifth birthday as an Arctic adventure, and I was willing to comply. Why not visit the Arctic, at least by way of the freezer?

First, there was provisioning. This polar expedition would require polar bear, easily acquired at the zoo gift shop. And igloo, not so easily acquired.

I considered the options. Building one—hindered by lack of skill. Subcontracting—hindered by lack of igloo professional. Faking it—hindered by fear. My Arctic scout might take offense to teepee, pup tent, or yurt.

I prowled toy store and outfitter, comparing blow-up, pop-up, and hard-bodied igloos. None would do. The igloo I imagined knew authentic curviness, easy-to-assemble tolerance, and a slim storage profile. I gave this project a sautéed snowball's chance of success.

Then I came across the ideal igloo: lightweight, roomy enough for boy and bear, but one that melted down to puddle dimensions. Available via online auction.

I admired the original igloo—the way its sturdy confines were fashioned from Arctic detritus: snow. Much the way the sturdy online auction house was fashioned from urban detritus: clutter.

Securing the igloo called for clicking and fretting and relinquishing information I considered personal. As did my scandalized work-station computer.

Followed by hourly phone calls to the postal distribution center and a brief interlude during which I slid down the sidewalk, waving USPS Delivery Notice/Reminder/Receipt Form 3849 and shouting at a frightened postal employee. The wrong frightened postal employee. Noah, watching from the frost-glazed window, wore a puzzled expression.

The igloo arrived. Seven minutes before the guests. I was otherwise prepared in the tradition of Admiral Byrd, with bear, cake, Klondike Bars, lettuce icebergs, and a platter heaped with fried fish and french fries, preferred meal of my Arctic explorer.

I once actually traveled to the actual Arctic, and there enjoyed precisely this menu, minus the Klondike Bar. The potatoes had likely been dragged in by a fur-fringed postal employee, but the Arctic char was local, having been fished out from under five feet of solid ice.

Which is nothing compared to shopping on eBay.

Small Fry

Serves 4 small fry

1 egg white

1 teaspoon kosher salt

1 tablespoon dry sherry

1 tablespoon cornstarch

1 pound Arctic char or other firm fish, filleted, boned, and skinned

1½ cups pecans

2 tablespoons sugar

Peanut oil

1. Whisk: Blend egg white, salt, sherry, and cornstarch in a shallow bowl, whisking smooth any lumps.

2. Coat: Cut fish into sticks, about 3 inches long and one inch wide, and toss with the egg-white mixture.

3. Grind: Measure pecans and sugar into the food processor or blender. Grind fine. Transfer to a plate.

4. Roll: Fish fish out of the eggs and drop into the nuts, rolling to coat.

5. Pan-fry: Heat a shallow slick of peanut oil in a cast-iron pan over medium. Crisp fish in batches until crust is deeply colored and fish is cooked, about 2 minutes per side. Drain on paper towels. These freeze perfectly and reheat nicely in the toaster oven. The recipe works well with boneless skinless chicken breast as well.

Fresh Fries

Start with one big Russet potato per person. Scrub but don't peel. Balance it on one of those old-fashioned wall-mounted potato-slicers and in one clean sweep, shred into slender sticks. (Lacking slicer, a mandoline or knife will do.) Soak slices in water for at least half an hour. Rub with a kitchen towel to dry thoroughly. Bring at least 2 inches of peanut oil to 325 degrees and fry in small batches until just beginning to color, about 3 minutes. Drain on paper towels. Cool. Fry again at 375 degrees until crisp and golden, about 2 minutes. Drain on paper towels. Salt. For extra-deliciousness, use truffle salt. For extra-cute, wrap in a waxed-paper cone.

THE RETURN *of* SPRING

Bleak times call for intervention. Which is why International Women's Day was invented. Yet both strife and March persist.

Sarah spent years in a Soviet outpost where the holiday was observed, under orders. Now, out of nostalgia or habit she continues to live on a wind-bitten prairie, in Iowa. Her winters are leavened by elaborate parties, including International Women's Day.

"We all need two hours free from responsibility," she instructs. Setting aside her study of ancient Greece, where Lysistrata, cleverly, led a bedroom strike against war, Sarah turns her piercing concentration to recipes. She stays up for a week, cooking as for the return of the czar. Or spring.

I participate long distance by looking up the recipe for lemon tart. But one year I thought: "Why not?"

Sarah put me to work arranging roasted vegetables and slicing mocha roulade. When the table seemed in peril of collapse there was a moment of awed silence. And then the pursuit of bread and peace, via cake and chatter.

Over pissaladière, a boutique owner and I discovered that each of our sons curates a stick collection. During the cheese course, a pastry chef confessed her addiction to Doritos. Across the terrine a lawyer and I commiserated about the lot of all wives: alone in their appreciation of eggplant. Mid-chocolate cake, an elderly scholar recounted the day she left her four boys unsupervised so she could attend a lecture by Dr. Spock.

Soon it was time to recoup my own children. But not before slicing a square of lemon tart. Its gritty pat-in-the-pan crust captured the pleasures of the windswept beach. Its pale yellow custard quivered somewhere between snowdrift and sunshine. It glistened with sharp lemons poached sweet. Each bite captured all the aching bittersweet anticipation of spring. And all the solace of friendship.

Almost-Spring Tart

Serves 8

8 lemons

2 cups sugar

½ cup water

2 eggs

½ cup heavy
  whipping cream

1 pinch salt

Tart Shell, partially baked
  (recipe follows)

¼ cup apricot jam

1. Zest: Grate the zest from 2 lemons and juice them. Measure ⅓ cup juice. Peel the remaining 6 lemons with a sharp knife, cutting deeply enough to remove all the white pith and expose the flesh. Slice crosswise into ¼-inch-thick disks. Lift out any seeds.

2. Poach: Combine 1½ cups sugar and the water in a saucepan. Bring to the soft-ball stage, 238 degrees. Add the lemon slices and return to a simmer. Pull off heat. Set aside at least 1 hour.

3. Bake: Beat together reserved lemon juice, zest, remaining ½ cup sugar, and eggs. Stir in cream and salt. Pour into the cooled, partially baked tart shell (still in its pan, pan still on a baking sheet) and slide into a 350-degree oven until just set, about 20 minutes. Cool to room temperature.

4. Decorate: Carefully lift the lemon slices from the syrup and lay them on the tart. Two forks might be helpful. In a small saucepan combine 2 tablespoons of the cooking syrup with the apricot jam and boil thick, about 5 minutes. Strain. Brush this glaze over the lemon slices. Serve as soon as possible.

PROVENANCE: *Adapted from* Pies & Tarts, *Williams-Sonoma Kitchen Library (out of print).*

Tart Shell

Makes 1 (9-inch) tart shell

Toss together 1¼ cups flour, 3 tablespoons sugar and ¼ teaspoon fine salt. Drop in 10 tablespoons unsalted butter, cut into chunks. Cut butter into flour using a pastry blender until the mixture resembles rolled oats. Stir together 1 egg yolk and 1 tablespoon cold water in a small bowl. Pour the egg mixture over the flour mixture and stir gently with a fork. The dough should be damp enough to clump. If not, add a few drops of water. Gather dough into a ball. Drop pastry into a 9-inch tart pan and pat, with lightly floured fingers, across the bottom and sides. Poke all over with a fork. Freeze firm.

To partially bake: Line tart shell with two layers of foil. Set on a baking sheet and slide into a 425-degree oven for 8 minutes. Lift out the foil and continue baking until golden and crisp, about 4 minutes. Cool on a rack.

To fully bake: Set on a baking sheet and slide into a 375-degree oven until crisp and golden, about 35 minutes.

THE "SAVE" FILE

The recipe is a neglected form, scrutinized, stained, folded, and saved, and yet rarely exalted. The university confers its diploma on the student intimate with poem, essay, novel, or play. Not recipe. While the sonnet reclines on the divan, pale and breathless, the recipe hustles around the kitchen, scrubbing potatoes. The recipe is working-class prose.

And yet, the recipe has plenty to offer by way of plot, thickened, perhaps, with roux. It's full of intrigue, suspense, and delicious dénouement. The scholar is always left with something to chew on.

Consider that classic text, Maida Heatter's French Chocolate Loaf Cake, which contains this line: "For the first dozen or so years that I tried to make this, I concentrated on recipes with only 1 or 2 spoonfuls of flour and only about 15 minutes of baking." Here is a masterwork that in eight ingredients and three bossy pages cuts cleanly through years of floury failure. Can haiku be more rigorous, or more enlightening?

Which is why the lone recipe, torn from newspaper, clipped from package back, or scrawled onto the odd envelope, commands a place of honor in the kitchen. Shoebox, say. Unruly heap. Or, among the intently tidy, the binder, file box, or zip drive.

None of which assists the cook in the most laborious of prep jobs: recipe location. She scans and stacks, forming cookbook stalagmites along the linoleum. She wonders if that stew, that one with the carrots (or was it spinach?) is listed under Carrot or Spinach or Stew or worse, Hearty. She curses the inept reference professional, one who likely survives on improvisational grilled cheese.

She turns to her last resort: the cookbook pressed into service as stray-recipe catch basin, its pages salted with interlopers. Employing a technique natural to the disorderly, the cook hugs the bulging book, reaches in and pulls out the right crumple. Carrots. And spinach.

Someone should figure out how to organize these things, she thinks, scraping happily. And be granted an honorary PhD.

Found Stew

Serves 8

3½ pounds boneless lamb
  shoulder, trimmed and
  cut into 2-inch pieces

1½ teaspoons salt

½ teaspoon freshly ground
  black pepper

1 to 3 tablespoons olive oil

1 large onion, chopped

1 celery stalk, chopped

3 cloves garlic,
  finely chopped

4 teaspoons ground cumin

2 teaspoons
  ground coriander

2 cups water

1 (14- to 16-ounce) can
  whole tomatoes in juice

6 medium carrots,
  cut crosswise into
  2½-inch pieces

1 bunch spinach, coarse
  stems discarded

1. **Brown:** Pat lamb dry. Sprinkle with 1 teaspoon salt and the pepper. Heat 1 tablespoon oil in a medium cast-iron skillet over medium-high heat. Brown lamb in batches, turning occasionally, about 4 minutes per batch, adding more oil as needed. Transfer to Dutch oven.

2. **Soften:** Pour off all but 1 tablespoon fat from skillet. Add onion and celery and cook over medium heat, stirring occasionally, until golden, about 3 minutes. Add garlic, cumin, and coriander and cook, stirring, 1 minute. Deglaze with 1 cup water then pour mixture over lamb.

3. **Boil:** Pour juice from the can of tomatoes into stew, then coarsely chop tomatoes and add them along with the remaining cup water and remaining ½ teaspoon salt (liquid should almost cover meat). Bring to a boil.

4. **Braise:** Cover pot and slide into a 350-degree oven for 1½ hours. Stir in carrots and continue to braise until carrots and lamb are tender, 20 to 30 minutes.

5. **Chill:** Cool, uncovered, then chill, covered, overnight. You can skip this step, but it does deepen the flavors.

6. **Finish:** Lift off any fat. Reheat stew over medium heat on the stovetop. Stir in spinach by handfuls. Cook, uncovered, stirring occasionally, until spinach is tender, 5 to 8 minutes.

PROVENANCE: *Ripped from the pages of* Gourmet, *and adapted.*

COMPANY IN THE KITCHEN

S hould you like to cook you will find yourself, frequently, in the kitchen. And should the person you cook for not like to cook, you will find him, frequently, not in the kitchen.

Generally you don't mind pounding and shredding and prodding solo. The more demanding recipe demands it. But once you get down to a sensitive dish, béarnaise say, you don't want it picking up off-flavor bitterness. Better to infuse the atmosphere with camaraderie.

There are ways to lure the reluctant to the kitchen. The most obvious—and perilous—being crumbs. Should you expend considerable effort brushing clean and slicing thin and sautéing fragrant a pan full of mushrooms and garlic and butter, and then scrape the mix onto a saucer to cool while you turn your attention to clean-up detail, you will be disappointed to find the saucer empty and the late-arrival full. You will sharpen your knife with renewed determination.

You have something better: a chair. Not a standard kitchen chair, all sit-up-straight-and-eat-your-broccolini righteousness. No. A chair whose ample girth, high-density foam core and alluringly soft upholstery are embroidered: Sit down, have a drink, stay a while.

You know this chair is counterindicated by the decorating professional. Its soft expanses attract aioli, yet resist the advances of the scrubby sponge. Its sprawl oversteps the approved armchair footprint. But this is not a chair. It's a cooking tool.

The operating instructions for the easy chair are familiar to the noncook, unlike those governing, say, the zester. It requires the end user to sit, drink, digress. And stay away from the cooking surfaces. Keeping the designated cook on task.

For best results, use in conjunction with a round of dumplings, installed chair-side. The dumpling's plump and pleated generosity suggests the throw pillow. Its chive-brightened filling is filling enough to stave off ravenous impatience. Its compact packaging, from crispy bottom to tender top, offers single-serve convenience. And multiple-choice charm.

Should the cook settle down to join the dumpling dipping, the recipe can be doubled to double for dinner. Easily.

Dumpling Pillows

Makes about 35

1 pound ground pork

3 tablespoons hoisin sauce*

2 tablespoons finely
chopped fresh cilantro

2 tablespoons finely
chopped scallion

1 tablespoon finely
chopped garlic

1 tablespoon Sriracha*
(Thai hot sauce)

2 teaspoons finely grated
fresh ginger

2 teaspoons Asian
fish sauce*

1 tablespoon finely
chopped fresh basil
(Thai, if possible)

1 (12-ounce) package round
dumpling wrappers*

Peanut oil

Simple Dipping Sauce
(recipe follows)

1. Mix: In a large bowl, gently combine all ingredients except wrappers, oil, and dipping sauce.

2. Fill: Set a dumpling wrapper on a flat surface. Run a wet finger around the edge. Spoon 2 teaspoons filling into the center. Fold to close (pleat if you're feeling fancy). Press edges to seal. Set filled dumpling aside, covered by a clean kitchen towel, while shaping remaining dumplings.

3. Crisp/steam: Measure 2 teaspoons oil into a large, heavy nonstick (or cast-iron) skillet. Heat over medium. Fit in a crowd of dumplings. Crisp bottoms 1 minute. Hold the pan lid like a shield and carefully pour in 1/3 cup water. Cover and let steam until pork is cooked through and tops gleam translucent, about 6 minutes. Use a spatula to lift dumplings to a serving platter. Repeat with remaining dumplings.

4. Serve: Enjoy warm with dipping sauce.

Simple Dipping Sauce

Stir together 2 tablespoons soy sauce, 1 tablespoon sesame oil, 1 tablespoon rice vinegar, and 1 pinch sugar.

PROVENANCE: *Adapted from a recipe by chef Bill Kim of Urban Belly, Chicago.*

*Available in the Asian foods aisle of many grocery stores and at specialty markets. I'm particularly fond of Golden Boy fish sauce for the eerie glowing baby on the label.

UNCHARTED WATERS

Noah didn't seem surprised that his dad had switched desks, to one in another state. A state, he knew from his junior-kindergarten studies, meant far away. A state, he knew from his sibling studies, also meant that giddy inclination that lead sister and brother to transgress the house rules and jump on the bed. Perhaps this new desk was a good thing.

On weekends, when his dad was back on duty, he resembled the original, misplaced, Chicago-based dad. Except he brought home snow globes and sweatshirts and tiny drinking glasses decorated with plastic crabs, and chocolates wrapped up in pictures of his new town's baseball team, the Oreos. Noah approved of this new habit. He offered positive feedback.

Eventually Noah was invited to visit this other state, the one with the desk. He packed his red pajamas, portable snowdog, and tin of crayons. He had to take a plane there. Or perhaps—given what he discovered—a rocket ship.

Turns out that while Noah was soldiering through the school week back home, his dad had been secretly lounging in luxury. He lived in a palace called Corporate Condominium. It had an elevator! It had a TV that worked! It had a kitchen stocked with nothing but Froot Loops! It had two king-size beds so unfettered with fussy linens that here children were allowed to jump with abandon.

For five days he did nothing but ride the elevator, watch cartoons, and jump on the bed. Froot Loop-fatigued, he relished restaurant meals, each of which featured a massive heap of french fries garnished with crab cake: a sweet, lemony, butter-fried puck cavorting on a saltine mattress. Capable, mysteriously, of easing parental crabbiness. He came to appreciate why his dad had switched jobs. And why they called this place Merry Land.

Crab Cakes

Serves 4 to 6

½ pound scallops

1 pound crabmeat

¼ cup mayonnaise

½ cup scallions, white and
tender green, thinly sliced

1 tablespoon freshly
squeezed lemon juice

Finely grated zest of 1 lemon

1½ teaspoons Old Bay
seasoning

1 cup fresh white bread
crumbs

2 tablespoons
unsalted butter

2 tablespoons canola oil

12 saltine crackers

1. Chop: Pile scallops, one-quarter of the crabmeat, the mayo, scallions, lemon juice, lemon zest, and Old Bay into the food processor. Using the pulse function and a light touch, chop just until the mixture holds together, with some large chunks remaining. Use a fork to mix in remaining crab.

2. Pat: Shape 12 cakes, each about 2½ inches in diameter and ¾-inch thick. Spread the breadcrumbs on a plate. Pat each cake in the crumbs to coat.

3. Fry: Heat butter and oil in a large cast-iron skillet set over medium. Pan-fry 6 cakes, cooking until well browned, about 2½ minutes per side. Drain on paper towels. Keep warm in a low oven while frying the second batch.

4. Serve: For authentic Maryland style, set each crabcake on a cracker.

FIRST RECITAL

Music is not my forte. I know this because I've tried. First recorder, an instrument so rudimentary as to rank a single evolutionary notch above kazoo. Then piano. My teachers always praised my command of music theory. If not music practice.

And yet I find myself attracted to the mandoline. The classical mandoline slicer demands a firm hand, steady beat, and appreciation of the thin-cut vegetable. Perhaps this is an instrument I can master.

The beginning student learns on a rental. But I'm convinced I'm ready for retail. I know from the late-night advertorial that the mandoline can shred, slice, or shave the unsuspecting potato. I know from the emergency-room professional that it can shred, slice, or shave the unsuspecting finger. I choose a mid-range model with a sturdy look.

Unpacked from its case, the acoustic mandoline features a long grooved fingerboard broken by a sharp cutting blade. Frets switch from straight to crinkle. A single peg tunes thickness. The bow, or "food holder," glides back and forth, forcing lumpy cucumber or cabbage into smooth, undulating, or shredded melodies.

I read through the sheet music and follow along as best I can. The first exercise, the "Twinkle," as it were, is bell pepper, crosscut. I strive for the suggested "quick and smooth" motion and even tempo. Next, julienne. The carrot refuses to let go, producing orange mop. But with added pressure, I achieve strips.

I attempt the last variation. Pinning a radish in the prongs of the food holder, I slide it across the ripple blade. Then, with a pause for a quarter radish twist, I slide again. The cellist calls this move a hook. My wrist calls it ow.

I stop, shove aside the mandoline and discover a single waffle-cut radish slice. Thin-sided, perfectly even, and riddled with ripples.

In the silence of my kitchen, I earn my first "bravo."

Radish Salad

Red radishes

Sour cream

Heavy whipping cream

Fresh chives

Kosher salt

1. **Slice:** Cut the radishes into slim red-rimmed waffles with a mandoline.

2. **Dress:** Thin a spoonful of sour cream with a drizzle of heavy cream in a bowl. Gently mix in sliced radishes. Snip on chives and season with salt. Admire.

MISERY'S CURE

Parenting calls for mistakes and you submit yours at the standard clip of about one per diem. Some—like tickling the strawberry-filled child—merely require clean up. Others demand self-medication. Like subjecting the minor to *Les Miserables*.

It started innocently enough—with desperation. During carpool your daughter and her companion take to listening to the soundtrack of *The Lion King*. Twice a day. For a year. Driving the other driving parent to suggest an alternative: *Les Miserables*. Then those bus ads started rolling around town, the ones with the waif and the tattered flag and the phone number. Resistance was a lost cause.

So you find yourself installed in row F, seat 106, in such proximity to the action that you, your terrified children, and your outraged credit card are equally stunned.

In the privacy afforded by dark theater and thundering score you take stock of your folly. This musical is three hours long, six times that of carpool, in traffic. It is performed without pause for dialogue, explanation, or (given the wait) bathroom break. As the playbill synopsis attempts to clarify, it distills Victor Hugo's 1,400 page novel into two convoluted acts and thirty-four ballads. Your youngest viewer is moved to ask, repeatedly, "Is that guy bad?"

Mostly: yes. You take in theft, profanity, child abuse, and an upbeat number about the pleasures of prostitution. There's a dead mom, a dead child, and the barricade, which rotates to reveal piles more dead. Plus gunfire, corpse robbing, and suicide. You wonder if pediatric psychiatrists offer family discounts.

Finally there's a finale. The house lights come up to reveal your children, pink-cheeked and awestruck. "That," your daughter shouts, "was definitely worth T-shirts!"

Too shaky to cook, you take your children out to eat. Or in your case, drink. You search the menu for something corrosive and French: absinthe. Real absinthe, lurid green abstract of the wormwood shrub, is outlawed—merely for inducing the sort of hallucination that inspired Hugo. Leaving direct descendant Pernod to add bitter anise charm to drink or dish.

"So," the youngest wrinkles his damp forehead, "the stealing man was good, and the policeman was bad. How can that be?" "Theater is illusion," you explain, feeling somewhat less miserable. "The stagehands are now regluing the broken chairs for the evening performance." Your children plead for tickets.

Aperitif

Pernod, Ricard, Pastis, or
other anise liqueur

Cold water

1. **Dose:** Pour about ½ inch liqueur into the bottom of a small, straight-sided glass. One filched from a sidewalk café and embossed "Pernod" would be ideal.

2. **Dilute:** Add cold water. Five parts water to 1 part Pernod is considered prudent.

3. **Drink:** Sip. Brood.

'OO(OO'

FOR THE BIRDS

Entertaining should be entertaining, and yet it is not. Being entertained is entertaining. Entertaining is torture. At least as practiced in my household, by me.

I've long entertained the conviction that entertaining involves cooking, which, I gather from the carryout convivia I've attended, it need not. Still, I opt for cooking. The sort that involves a grocery list and an afternoon darting from farmers' market to supermarket to World Market.

The entertaining magazine suggests that entertaining also involves redecorating. The sparrow, expecting company, tucks strands of tinsel between the twigs. I plump pillows, then give in to the more fanciful nesting instinct.

For one particularly breezy evening, I am inspired to lay the table with sod. Technical difficulties reroute me to sowing seed, which sprouts, takes one horrified look at the cotton placemat to which it has been spray-glued, and dies.

I turn my attention to wheatgrass. Live wheatgrass, being live, lives somewhere and that somewhere is dirt. It occurs to me that dirt on plate is a counterintuitive choice.

Eventually I solve the dirt problem with a white-on-white tabletop tower at each place: a shallow white pizza box packed with a flat of wheatgrass nestling a tiny

white bowl coddling two speckled quail eggs. The table, a smooth expanse of linen cutwork, punctuated by ten trim patches of green, looks fresh and inviting, poised to host a family of cows.

I accomplish dinner by banishing the children and hiring a housecleaning service and corralling my mother into mothering the roast while I weave watercress into arugula.

My guests arrive. I retreat to the bedroom and lie face down on the clean sheets, wondering what what normally comes in a pizza box.

Quail-Egg Nest Salad

Serves 6

12 quail eggs*

3 ounces arugula

1 bunch watercress

2 tablespoons olive oil

1 tablespoon walnut oil

1 clove garlic, slivered

¼ cup walnuts,
  coarsely chopped

1 tablespoon
  balsamic vinegar

Kosher salt and freshly
  ground black pepper

1. Boil: Settle eggs in the bottom of a medium saucepan. Cover with cold water. Bring to a boil. Cover, turn off heat, and let stand 4 minutes. Rinse under cold water.

2. Arrange: Discard the thick stems from the arugula and watercress. Feather 6 nests with the greens, working with small bowls and a bird's sense of style. Nestle 2 unpeeled eggs in the center of each and set out for your guests to admire.

3. Crisp: Heat olive oil, walnut oil, garlic, and walnuts in a small saucepan over medium heat. Stir until garlic is crisp, about 2 minutes. Remove from heat. Let cool a moment. Stir in vinegar, cautiously; it will sputter. Season with salt and pepper.

4. Serve: Let your guests crack off the speckled shells (have a receptacle handy). Drizzle warm vinaigrette over salad.

*Quail eggs are available at many grocery stores and Asian markets. Or substitute 6 standard eggs. Increase standing time to 16 minutes.

THE PICNIC

The watermelon is a friendly fruit, all broad pink smile and abundant generosity. And yet, its rotund condition attracts snide remarks.

True, it takes determination and core strength to befriend the forty-pound watermelon. It calls for teamwork to heave one through the checkout, or worse, up the stairs. In the close confines of the fridge, the watermelon may inadvertently flatten the foil-wrapped lasagna or squeeze dry the squeeze yogurt. Watermelon is a shelf hog.

Sweating on the countertop, the watermelon exudes an inert hippopotamus charm—cold, copious, and thick-skinned. It's not much for table manners—all drippy seed-disposal quandaries. In the restaurant setting the watermelon may suffer refinement into spiced sorbet or minced yuzu salad, but in its natural state, it's a slob.

And so, we understand, even if we don't embrace, the advent of the personal watermelon.

The personal watermelon has been raised by strict agribusiness executives in California to stay small and sweet and well-behaved. The little round cutie doesn't spill juice. It can snuggle into the crisper drawer.

The novelty is not entirely novel. Half a century ago housewives appreciated the space-saving benefits of the so-called icebox melon, also known as the New Hampshire midget.

And while we admire the goals of tidy or thrifty or practical, we find the means somewhat antisocial.

Where, precisely, is the application for the personal melon? Perhaps the remote family reunion. At the scheduled hour, far-flung relatives, each seated on a personal picnic blanket, aligned on a personal lawn square, log on via a handheld personal computing device. Simultaneously, each cues the iPod, cracks open a minimelon, and begins.

Raising some questions about the traditional mid-melon spitting contest.

Watermelon

Serve small watermelons very cold, cut in quarters. Complete the picnic with fried chicken and corn salad.

Tumbled Corn Salad

Serves 10

10 ears corn, husked

1 cup sugar snap peas

2 cups grape tomatoes, halved on the diagonal

¼ cup olive oil

¼ cup rice vinegar

Kosher salt and freshly ground black pepper

12 fresh basil leaves, snipped

1. Boil: Bring a large pot of water to a boil. Drop in corn and cook until shocking yellow, about 7 minutes. Drain.

2. Blanch: Bring a small pot of water to a boil, add peas, and cook until bright green, about 1 minute.

3. Toss: Cut the corn kernels from the cob and tumble into a large bowl. Cut the sugar snap peas in half (on the diagonal is nice) and add to the corn. Add the tomatoes, olive oil, and vinegar. Toss gently. Season with salt, pepper, and basil.

PROVENANCE: *Adapted from the now defunct Trotter's To Go, Chicago.*

Picnic Chicken

Serves 8

2 cups buttermilk

3 tablespoons kosher salt

4 pounds bone-in chicken breasts, cut in quarters

2 pounds bone-in chicken legs, cut into drumsticks and thighs

2 cups flour

2 teaspoons ground cayenne pepper

1 quart vegetable oil

1. Marinate: Pour 1 cup buttermilk and 1½ teaspoons salt into each of two 1-gallon zip-top bags. Add half the chicken pieces to each, seal, and shake to coat. Refrigerate 2 hours to 2 days.

2. Dredge: Whisk flour with remaining 2 tablespoons salt and the cayenne in a pie plate. Dredge chicken.

3. Fry: Heat oil to 350 degrees in a cast-iron skillet. Add half the chicken, avoiding spatter, and fry until golden on one side, 10 minutes. Turn and fry until golden, juices run clear, and chicken reaches 165 degrees inside, about 10 mintues more. Drain on a rack. Return oil to 350 degrees. Repeat with remaining chicken.

SUMMER MEMORY

We stayed in a cabin. One room where the grownups and us kids slept, plus a tiny kitchen. When it rained we worked macramé, pinning strands of sisal to a spongy board, tying the lumpy cord into the lumpy potted-plant holder. It was, after all, northern California. Compliant children, we sat cross-legged on the floor, patiently securing the square knots.

Otherwise, we were rarely indoors. We spent our days roaming the rocky coast, which was windy and wild and would have laughed at bikini or beach novel. We untangled ropes of seaweed caught in the crags. Damp salt-scented kelp, with its bulbous float and trailing stem, makes a fine microphone, handy for broadcasting the vacation morning news. The five-day forecast: buoyant.

We collected rippled shells and smooth stones and brought them back to the cabin. Some were speckled with tiny holes; these we saved to tie up in the macramé.

Evenings we walked into town to watch *The Perils of Pauline*, silent but for the organ. Invariably the villain tied Pauline to the tracks. Probably with square knots. One night on the way home we bought a pie at the Sea Gull Inn. It was low-slung, dense, and golden. In the tiny kitchen we passed out the tin plates and sliced a tumble of sticky, sweet apricots, brilliant as the seaside sunset. The next night we walked back for another.

Eventually, we had to return the keys. We packed the car with our half-finished macramé, our rocks, our heaps of damp sweaters. And one apricot pie.

It was vacation; the sort where children get to act like adults and stay up late watching old movies. The sort where adults get to act like children and, while driving, stick a tin fork in the pie. Miles down Shoreline Highway we all missed Mendocino. We doubled back for one more sunset pie.

Apricot Pie

Serves 8

2 tablespoons cornstarch

1 cup sugar, plus a bit

1½ pounds ripe apricots, pitted and sliced into 1-inch wedges

Flakey Pastry (recipe follows)

1 tablespoon unsalted butter

Half-and-half

1. **Toss:** Whisk together cornstarch and 1 cup sugar in a large bowl. Add apricots and toss to coat.

2. **Fit:** Roll out the larger round of pastry on a lightly floured surface and fit into a 9-inch pie plate. Refrigerate while you roll out the smaller round of pastry.

3. **Fill:** Scrape apricots and any accumulated syrup into the pastry-lined pie plate. Dot with butter. Cover with top pastry and crimp the edges. Brush with half-and-half and sprinkle with a little sugar. Use kitchen scissors to snip a starburst vent in the center.

4. **Bake:** Set pie on a rimmed baking sheet and slide into a 450-degree oven for 15 minutes. Lower heat to 375 and bake until golden and bubbly, about 40 minutes. Cool.

Flakey Pastry

Lines and covers one 9-inch pie plate

2½ cups flour

1 tablespoon sugar

½ teaspoon fine salt

12 tablespoons (1½ sticks) cold unsalted butter, cut into chunks

4 tablespoons cold vegetable shortening (such as Crisco), cut into chunks

6 tablespoons ice water

1 tablespoon cider vinegar

1. **Mix:** Whisk together flour, sugar, and salt in a large bowl. Cut in butter and shortening with a pastry blender until lumps range in size from crumbs to corn flakes.

2. **Clump:** Stir together water and vinegar; drizzle into dough, folding with a soft spatula, until damp enough to clump.

3. **Chill:** Gather pastry and pat into two disks, one slightly larger than the other. Wrap in plastic and chill at least 1 hour.

PROVENANCE: *Reconstructed from memories of Helen Kiefer's famous apricot pie.*

A TOAST *to* BUTTER

Buttering toast is a demanding art form, practiced in our household by the fatherly half of the parenting team. The remainder of the culinary chores are handled by the motherly half. Our children smile toast-flecked smiles at their accomplished dad.

After all, butter is practically a miracle. Who is not awed by butter's smooth feel and creamy taste, its sauce-soothing serenity, its crust-crisping character? To the tender palate, butter renders loathsome broccoli lovely. To the sophisticate, it turns the standard baguette sublime. Butter makes fine food and fine art.

We smile toast-flecked smiles knowing that every summer cold and talented hands shape the butter cow, pride of the Illinois State Fair. We are amazed by the butter cow's six hundred pounds of bovine contentment. We are moved by her perishable poise. We relish her all-butter bounty. And appreciate her cow-made-from-butter-made-from-cow perplexity. We savor her surrealist scale.

And yet the deep thoughts inspired by the butter cow seem plodding compared to the aims of the yak-butter artist. In Tibet, or the many Tibetan outposts, monks carve butter into the meandering bas-relief of the deity, flower, or yak. The finished tableaux, celebrating victory in an ancient miracle match, are admired briefly before meltdown. Not that anyone minds. The monks carve butter to enhance world peace, end hunger, and achieve enlightenment. A state to which the hefty butter cow cannot aspire.

After the fair, leftover butter is packed into buckets and stored in an ice-cream plant. Should you find yourself with leftovers from your personal toast-enhancing sculpture, make flavored butter. Sliced and stored on the ice-cream shelf, sweet or savory butter can enhance whirled peas, curb hunger, and enlighten any number of dishes, steak to scone. Consider it as essential and capricious as the butter cow—or yak—herself.

Herb Butter
Makes ½ cup

½ clove garlic

¼ teaspoon kosher salt

2 tablespoons finely chopped fresh chives

1 teaspoon each finely chopped fresh thyme, rosemary, and parsley

½ teaspoon finely grated lemon zest

¼ pound (1 stick) unsalted butter, softened

1. Smash: Chop garlic and salt together to form a thick paste.

2. Mix: Mash garlic mix, herbs, and zest into butter with a small spatula.

3. Roll: Gather up butter and heap onto a length of parchment paper. Roll into paper, shaping a log about 4 inches long. Twist shut ends. Refrigerate.

4. Store: Unwrap chilled butter, slice into ¼-inch thick rounds, rewrap, and freeze up to 1 month. A pat of herb butter offers a fresh finish to risotto, pasta, steamed vegetables, or soup.

Anchovy Butter

Makes ½ cup

8 anchovies

½ clove garlic

½ teaspoon freshly ground black pepper

¼ teaspoon finely grated lemon zest

¼ pound (1 stick) unsalted butter, softened

1. Smash: Chop anchovies and garlic into a thick paste. (Don't be tempted by that tube of anchovy paste; this is better.)

2. Mix: Mash anchovy mix, pepper, and zest into butter with a small spatula.

3. Store: Press into a small dish and cover with plastic wrap. Refrigerate up to 3 days. A spoonful adds delicious depth to grilled fish, steak, chop, or burger.

Citrus Butter

Makes ½ cup

Finely grated zest of 1 orange

Finely grated zest of 1 lemon

1 teaspoon sugar

1 teaspoon orange liqueur

½ teaspoon vanilla extract

¼ pound (1 stick) unsalted butter, softened

1. Mix: Mash zests, sugar, liqueur, and vanilla into butter using a small spatula.

2. Store: Press into a pretty mold, small or large. Refrigerate up to 3 days or freeze up to 1 month. Hold a warm kitchen towel against the bottom of the mold briefly to release. Turn out and serve with hot muffins, pancakes, scones, or toast.

TRY SOMETHING NEW

Happy camper is a demanding job, calling for dexterity with the lanyard, style on the Slip'N Slide, and patience gluing googly eyes to the Bug of the Week. To sustain him in these efforts, the camper relies on bug juice, a drink so sweet it attracts flies and so bright it glows. High praise from the under-six set.

I suffer typecasting as the sort of pro-fruit parent who frowns on bug juice and its sole ingredient: powder. And yet, I learn, camp is all about trying new things.

One sweaty afternoon my camper announces he intends to dye his hair. Having already endured Pajama Day and Costume Day, I accept news of Wacky Hair Day. In my enthusiast's limited life experience, wacky can only mean this: red.

I am hardly in a position to frown on hair enhancement. My computer secures instructions for coloring young hair with a benign agent: bug juice.

Borrowing rubber gloves from the kitchen sink, I mix red powder with conditioner and apply it to my son's innocent curls. I manage this maneuver with embarrassingly professional swagger.

Fifteen minutes later, I panic. I rush Noah's plastic-wrapped hair to the bath and know a kind of ER revulsion as the water turns blood red. To my relief some of the color washes out. To his relief, much of it stays in.

Wacky Hair Day proceeds at a wacky clip, ruled by the girl who tethered her pigtails to helium balloons.

Later I scrub my son's hair. Repeatedly. But the bug juice refuses to shoo. Given an average curl length of two inches, I calculate four months of red bath water to go.

Leaving certain concerns about actually drinking this drink.

I blend instead a round of bubble tea—bug juice, of sorts, for the post-camp crowd. Once confined to the Asian strip mall, the cool drink has bubbled over everywhere. It comes laced with balls of chewy tapioca meant to slip and slide through a fat straw. And though it once featured tea and milk, it has evolved to smoothie-style freshness. No powder necessary. Bubble tea might also come in handy, just in case camp decides to stage Wacky Drink Day.

Mango Bubble Tea

Bubble tea ranges in complexity from tea to milkshake. This fruity version strikes a nice balance.

Serves 4

1 teabag orange, peach, or other fruity tea

½ cup black tapioca pearls*

4 mangoes, peeled, fruit sliced away from seed

3 cups orange juice

3 cups ice

1 cup Sugar Syrup (recipe follows)

½ cup coconut milk

1 fresh lime

1. Steep: Bring ½ cup of water to a boil, pour over teabag, and steep until flavorful, about 3 minutes. Let cool.

2. Boil: Prepare tapioca pearls according to package directions. Note that overcooking yields gummy balls. Drain and rinse under cold water. Heap into a bowl. Cover with cooled tea and ½ cup Sugar Syrup. Chill.

3. Blend: For each drink, measure ¾ cup fruit into the blender. Add ¾ cup orange juice, ¾ cup ice, 2 tablespoons sugar syrup, 2 tablespoons coconut milk, and a squeeze of lime juice. Blend smooth.

4. Serve: Scoop ¼ cup pearls and tea bath and settle into the bottom of a large glass (or clear plastic cup, as would be traditional). Fill with mango mixture. Add a very fat straw. Slurp, chew, smile.

*Tapioca pearls are available in black or white at Asian markets and some supermarkets. Don't be put off by the description "starch balls." They're pure cassava, an actual plant. Cooked, they look like enormous caviar and taste like not much. Should the idea of slurping starch balls from the bottom of your smoothie strike you as revolting, omit this ingredient, or consider fresh currants as a cheerful and decidedly nontraditional substitution.

Sugar Syrup

Makes about 1 cup

⅓ cup dark brown sugar

⅓ cup granulated sugar

⅔ cup water

Bring both kinds of sugar and water to a boil in a small saucepan. Simmer 5 minutes. Remove from heat. Cool.

Chapter 3: Whisk

When I was single and living in New York, I spent a weekend with my parents in Chicago. They took me out for a taco. It was extraordinary: tender hand-made tortillas, crisp catfish, charred scallions. If this was a taco in Chicago, I thought, I should live in Chicago.

Later I learned that not every Chicago taco matched the work of Rick Bayless. But I'd already moved.

Chicago is an exceptionally delicious town. I wrote the column for its home cooks, but I was inspired by its restaurant chefs. Sarah Stegner taught me never to refrigerate a tomato. Bruce Sherman showed me how to meld upscale and down home. Paul Kahan's crisp sardines shook up my idea of a snack.

Every chef I spoke with—Grant Achatz, Michael Kornick, Rick Tramanto, Gale Gand, and many others—proved generous and gracious. Each readily shared a recipe. Few of which worked. I was shocked. "A world-famous chef gave me this?" I fumed, stomping around my kitchen. It took me a while to grasp that restaurant cooking and home cooking shared next to nothing. Chefs had access to different ingredients; they butchered their meat. They worked with high-heat, large quantities, and precision plating. I picked up a new skill: translating Chef.

Chicago was tasty in other ways. I loved biking the lakefront to work. I loved riding the El, hand-in-hand with Hannah in tutu. I loved bird-watching at the lily pool with Noah. I loved our friends. Even after Bob started working in Baltimore I didn't want to leave.

One night when I tucked Noah in, he said he'd had a good day: He'd hardly missed his dad at all.

"You miss him?" I asked.

"Just every minute of every day."

We put our condo up for sale. My editors at the *Tribune* agreed to let me continue writing from afar.

Bob swears we looked at fifty houses before, in a musical-chairs moment of panic, we grabbed one. It had a wide, rotting front porch and a spacious, weed-infested backyard. It had wood floors and high ceilings and a kitchen that longed for a sledgehammer. We agreed: "It's got potential."

I knew the working-class Jewish Baltimore glimpsed in *Diner* and the drug-war Baltimore that sizzled across *The Wire*. The Baltimore we found was also the wide streets of our new neighborhood and the cheerful classrooms of our new school. Baltimore was many things, almost none of them, in those days, restaurants.

At first I flew back to Chicago frequently, stuffing five meals into a single day. Then I started looking around my new town—seafood glistened, Southern cocktails winked. I had a lot to learn.

Our life was more compact: Hannah and Noah at the same school, me and Bob in the same city—he downtown in the *Sun* newsroom, me at home, balancing my laptop on a stack of moving boxes. We tended the creaky house, the ornery garden, and the feisty puppy. We faced each domestic drama over a good meal. Most, like it or not, made at home.

MOVING

The realtor is, by trade, a realist. In a single sweeping glare he takes in your home—its tightly-wedged bookcases, its fully stocked kitchen, its 165 million dinosaurs—and sees this: clutter.

Clutter, he insists, doesn't sell. And his business is sell.

Gamely, you straighten up. You square heaps of mail into stacks. You crack apart the forty-eight pieces of Our Solar System and cram the universe into the black hole of the puzzle cupboard. You pace the kitchen, snapping at blender and mixer and microwave: backs against the wall. These efforts earn you that tight-lipped smirk perfected at the leading schools of realty.

Not what he had in mind. What he had in mind was this: storage. You gasp, then reach to cover the ears of the smaller pieces of furniture.

One moving truck, four men, four hours, and fifty-four boxes later, your home seems relieved. You encounter walls you had forgotten. You discover a room previously dedicated to closet duty. You find patches of the sparse desolation featured in the Hold Everything catalog. You don't need to hold everything. Your storage corral already does.

Some time after the truck has pulled away and the dust pterodactyls have landed, you wonder about the contents of those fifty-four boxes. Presumably nothing important.

Storage, you concede, isn't all bad. You have long admired the storage potato, harvested at first frost, cured and held cool through the winter. The storage potato has thick skin, dense flesh and a perseverance that keeps us all in hash browns and pierogis through the off-season.

But spring offers an alternative: the new potato, that darling Ping-Pong ball turned up early. The new potato flaunts delicate skin, creamy texture and, when gently boiled and tossed with butter, innocent charm.

Suddenly, it seems like the right moment for the new potato. And, given that you can't find a thing in the kitchen, a new potato pot.

New Potatoes

Serves 4

2 pounds tiny new potatoes

2 tablespoons
unsalted butter

⅓ cup snipped fresh chives

¼ teaspoon kosher salt

¼ teaspoon freshly ground
black pepper

1. Wash: Gently rinse potatoes but don't peel. New potatoes are best "jacketed" as the English say; or, as the French would have it, "en chemise."

2. Melt: Melt butter, stir in chives, salt, and pepper.

3. Boil: Settle potatoes in a large pot. Cover with cold salted water by 1 inch. Simmer tender, about 12 minutes. Check by piercing a potato with a fork—it should be easy work.

4. Toss: Drain potatoes in a colander. Return them to the pot, set over low heat, and shake gently until dry, about 1 minute. Pour in butter and toss gently to coat. Serve warm.

UPWARD MOBILITY

purchased a new brain. You'd think it would have required deep thought or comparison shopping, but I just walked into the Apple store and pointed to the one with the aluminum-alloy good looks.

After plugging in my new brain, importing my old memories, and upgrading my powers of concentration, I found myself oddly efficient. Once I wired for wireless I found I could roam from room to room, carrying my brain. This was an improvement over my old life, when I could only think in the corner outfitted with power strip and dial-up.

Like many thinking people, I liked to bring my brain when I went out. But it didn't work everywhere. Turned out my brain, like me, would only get with the program after a $5 cup of coffee and an aluminum-hard scone. I don't remember asking for the external scone drive. It must come standard.

What if I needed to complete a thought in a scone-free zone? I posed this problem to my brain, and in .13 seconds it came up with 1.88 million scone thoughts, most of which were recipes that called, bitterly, for currants. I thought up my own recipe, baked a batch, and uploaded. Each scone offered about an hour of cinnamon-flecked thought. And, true to the promise of wireless, didn't require currants.

Coffeehouse Scones

Makes 12

1 ounce milk chocolate

1 teaspoon ground cinnamon

1¾ cups flour

2¼ teaspoons
    baking powder

¼ cup sugar, plus a little

¼ teaspoon salt

1¼ cups heavy
    whipping cream

2 tablespoons unsalted
    butter, melted

1. **Pipe:** Zap chocolate just to melt, about 1 minute. Stir in cinnamon. Scrape into a zip-top bag. Snip off one corner and pipe mini cinnamon chips onto a parchment-paper-lined baking sheet. Let set, 10 minutes (or slide into the freezer for 5 minutes).

2. **Mix:** Whisk together flour, baking power, ¼ cup sugar, and salt. Pour in cream, stirring with a fork, once or twice. Slide in cinnamon chips. Mix a few more turns of the fork, just until dough comes together. Turn out onto a parchment-paper-lined baking sheet. Pat into a disk, about 8 inches in diameter and ¾-inch high.

3. **Brush:** Use a long, heavy knife dipped in flour to slice disk into 12 wedges. Separate wedges about ½ inch from each other. Brush tops with melted butter. Sprinkle with a little sugar.

4. **Bake:** Slide into a 400-degree oven and bake until tops turn golden and scones are set, about 16 minutes. Good warm or cooled.

THE PLEASURE PRINCIPLE

"Be the best you can be" has a rousing ring to it. Unless your best happens to be somewhat slimmer and swifter and smarter than you currently find yourself. Then "be the best you can be" carries a distinctly bossy tone. It suggests sweaty sweats, plateside math, and miniature meals that promise a better tomorrow at the price of a blander today.

You don't mind the idea of eating healthfully. As they say, you just don't want to be there when it happens.

Then one morning, while working out with your credit card, you come across a delicious-looking book whose cover promises "A New Way to Cook." Back home, you indulge in an old way to not cook: lounging in a comfy chair, imagining your better self actually shopping for, prepping, and serving these sumptuous dishes. Indeed you come so close to such model behavior that you consult the fine print and are shocked to discover that this weighty cookbook is designed to produce slim meals. You are horrified. And fascinated.

You turn to the introduction. There, under a glamour shot of ragout, you find a manifesto titled "Moderation and the Pleasure Principle." Skimming the moderation part, you delve straight into the principle. Pleasure, it says, and cheer and conviviality are as nutritionally beneficial as counting . . . whatever it is we're supposed to count this time. Yes, you murmur, yes.

Comfort me with Cumin-Crusted Quail with Cilantro Gemolata. Tart, Ethereal Lemon Curd. Boneless Leg of Lamb Stuffed with Crushed Olives. And though this book has a tiresome tendency to tick off the various measures of good this and bad that, you forgive it. You even overlook the unduly explicit recipe titles, such as Saucing Pasta with Flavorful Fats. You prefer to file your flavorful fats discreetly under "butter."

You try saucing pasta with flavorful fats and discover that author Sally Schneider has a good thing going. She is particularly fond of boiling broth with a bit of butter or bacon into a thin sheen thick with flavor. Soon, so are you.

It's a technique that strikes you as swift and slim and smart. Just the way you like to imagine yourself, should you ever manage to be your best.

Revised Ravioli

Serves 4

2 tablespoons olive oil

10 cloves garlic, thinly sliced

1 pinch red pepper flakes

10 large fresh sage leaves, cut into ¼-inch strips

Kosher salt

1 pound cheese ravioli

Freshly ground black pepper

¼ cup grated Parmigiano-Reggiano cheese

1. Crisp: Combine oil, garlic, and pepper flakes in a small heavy saucepan. Cover and cook over low heat until garlic begins to frizzle and turn golden, 5 minutes. Scoop the garlic onto a plate, using a slotted spoon. Add the sage leaves to the pan and cook until fragrant, dark, and crisp, 3 minutes. Turn off the heat; scoop sage leaves onto the plate with the garlic.

2. Boil: Cook pasta until tender but firm. Measure out ½ cup cooking water and set aside. Drain pasta.

3. Meld: Add ¼ cup pasta water to the saucepan with the garlic-scented oil. Boil vigorously for 30 seconds, or until emulsified.

4. Sauce: Return pasta to the pot and toss to coat with the sauce, adding 1 or 2 tablespoons cooking water if the pasta seems dry. Season with salt and pepper. Serve in shallow bowls, sprinkled with reserved garlic and sage and lightly dusted with cheese.

PROVENANCE: *Adapted from* A New Way to Cook *by Sally Schneider.*

A BRIGHT IDEA

Cooks have long suspected that sunshine could star in the kitchen. It is, after all, hot. Now, after five billion years of preheating, the solar oven is sizzling. With spectacular results.

And stunningly simple design. The solar oven is a box. The schoolchild can construct one from a pizza carton and plastic wrap. But why bother? For the price of a large deep dish with anchovies, the backyard barbecuer can buy a solar oven, plunk in a slab of ribs, and let daylight handle the details.

Freeing him to focus on other demands, such as the nap. The upside is obvious—like not having to burn gas or fell trees or, in certain hostile climates, spend half the day picking up sticks. This box is hot. And yet, underutilized. Especially in its natural habitat: the tailgate.

Consider the plight of the tailgate host. He has steered his beer-cooling and rib-marinating vehicle through bumper-to-bumper aggravation. Paid supersized stadium-lot rates. Flipped open, popped up, and spread out. And now, at prime time for asphalt socializing, must attend to the rigors of igniting and basting and turning and checking.

He needs the solar oven. Park the ribs in a dark pot and the pot in the oven. Drink beer, eat nachos, and be merry. Sunlight, focused through the oven's clear plastic face and trapped in its black interior, maintains a meltingly sweet slow cook, just as it does for the spare crayon on the backseat upholstery. Allowing the tailgater to concentrate on the pre-game. And on working up an appetite for ribs so tender lawnchair quarterbacks swear they outscore charcoal-grilled.

Should the festivities extend until kickoff, the ticket holder can toss the oven in the trunk. No need to cool down, lock up, or dispose of burning briquettes. After all, it's a plastic box. Which should provide the fan of the underperforming team something to cheer about.

Fair-Weather Ribs

Serves 4 fans

2 cloves garlic

2 teaspoons kosher salt

¼ cup dark brown sugar

2 teaspoons Dijon mustard

1 tablespoon ground
chipotle pepper

1 teaspoon ground cumin

2 racks (about 4 pounds)
baby-back pork ribs,
divided in two,
membrane removed

2 cups prepared
barbecue sauce

1. Rub: Chop garlic and salt together into a grainy heap. Mash in sugar, mustard, pepper, and cumin to form a thick paste. Rub into ribs.

2. Prep: Settle ribs into 2 black metal pots (speckle-ware is ideal), meat-side down. Pour ½ cup barbeque sauce into each. Cover. Set pots in solar oven and turn so that the shadow falls directly behind oven. Twist 15 degrees clockwise.

3. Wait: Your chores are done. No turning, basting, adjusting, watching, or tending. Enjoy the novelty of cooking while consuming beer, not fuel. After about three hours of unencumbered parking-lot leisure, peek. Ribs should be tender and delicious. Serve with remaining sauce.

4. Cheat: If game day is cloudy or you can't find your solar cooker, prepare at home. Cook in a large oven-safe pan, securely covered with a lid of foil, at 225 degrees for 3 hours. Baste with additional sauce 10 minutes before the clock runs down. Wrap in foil and go.

NOTE: For more information on building or buying a solar oven, contact the Solar Oven Society.

RISING *to* THE OCCASION

Organized religion calls for a skill set I lack, being inherently disorganized. I'm always misplacing the spare tradition or reading from the wrong page. I can't lift, much less carry, a tune.

Still, the average holiday calls for family squeezed around a table and a table crowded with food; these are customs I understand.

At the Jewish New Year I'm willing to simmer carrots into bounty and coax apple and honey into togetherness. If the year's sweetness is determined by what's on the plate—as this holiday's superstitions hold—I'm not one to risk serving wasabi.

I am happy to bake challah. It's a pleasure I indulge, religiously, on the last day of the year and occasionally on the last day of the week. The warm milk and honey bath comforts. The industrious determination of yeast inspires. The measured pace of knead and wait and knead soothes. Uncovering the puff of doubled dough, I fold a fist, sink it in, and—at the end of the day—exhale.

Now comes the pleasing symmetry of long division: two loaves, three segments each. The rhythmic progress of rolling each into a thick stretch of rope. The orderly charm of braiding. New Year's challah calls for an extra twist: coiling the braid into a circle, predictable and convoluted as the seasons. I brush the top shiny, heat the oven, and wait for the house to smell like home.

Outside, challah is all golden glow. Inside, all that rolling and twisting and curling yields strands that are sinuous and intertwined and eagerly followed from one bumpy knob to the next. Slice not.

Folklore has it that leftover challah, should such exist, can be fried into fluffy French toast. I prefer to adapt another ritual: casting crumbs (recast as transgressions) into the lake. It's one of those rare traditions that I can figure out how to operate. And, as far as I know, requires neither precision timing nor singing.

Challah

Makes 2 big loaves

1½ tablespoons active
    dry yeast

⅓ cup sugar

½ cup warm water

¼ pound (1 stick)
    unsalted butter, cut
    into small cubes*

2½ teaspoons fine salt

1 tablespoon honey

1 cup whole milk*

5 eggs

6½ cups flour

1 tablespoon unsalted
    butter, softened*

1. Proof: Whisk yeast and a pinch of the sugar into the warm water. Let stand until creamy, about 10 minutes.

2. Scald: Pour remaining sugar into a large bowl. Toss with cubed butter and salt. Drizzle with honey. Bring milk to a boil (watch closely; it will bubble up). Pour scalded milk over butter. Stir until butter has melted and mixture is no longer hot.

3. Enrich: Briefly whisk together 4 of the eggs. Stir into milk mixture. Test temperature by dropping a spot on your wrist; it should feel neither hot nor cold. Stir in yeast mixture.

4. Knead: Stir in about 5 cups of the flour, 1 cup at a time, until dough is exasperatingly sticky. Turn out onto a floured work surface and knead, adding more flour as needed (you may not use it all), until you achieve a smooth elastic dough, about 10 minutes.

5. Raise: Smear softened butter around a large bowl. Settle in dough, turning to coat with butter. Cover bowl with a stretch of plastic wrap, then a kitchen towel, and let rise until doubled, about 1 hour. Sink in a fist, deflating dough. Pat into a ball, cover, and let double again, about 1 hour.

6. Braid: Punch down dough. Turn out and cut in half. Cover one half. Divide the other in three. Roll each third into a rope about 16 inches long and 1 inch thick. Lay the three ropes side-by-side and braid. I find it easiest to braid from the center, turn the bread and braid from the center again (this time tucking strands under, rather than over). Turn end strands under and pinch securely. Divide, roll, and braid the other half.

7. Rest: Line two baking sheets with parchment paper. Settle one loaf on each sheet. Cover with plastic and let rise, until puffy, 45 minutes.

8. Glaze: Beat remaining egg with a 1 teaspoon water. Brush over loaves. If you like, sprinkle the top with a little flaky salt or a few sesame seeds. (Feel free to wrap and freeze now. When ready to bake, transfer frozen loaf to hot oven and add 10 minutes to baking time.)

9. Bake: Slide into a 350-degree oven and bake until challah is golden brown on top and sounds hollow when rapped on the bottom, about 30 to 35 minutes. Cool on a rack.

10. Serve: Gently tear off a knob and enjoy.

*This challah calls for milk and butter. Bakers who eschew dairy products can substitute mild oil (such as canola) for the butter and water for the milk.

PROVENANCE: *I learned these proportions from* Baking With Julia *by Dorie Greenspan and the technique from many, many loaves.*

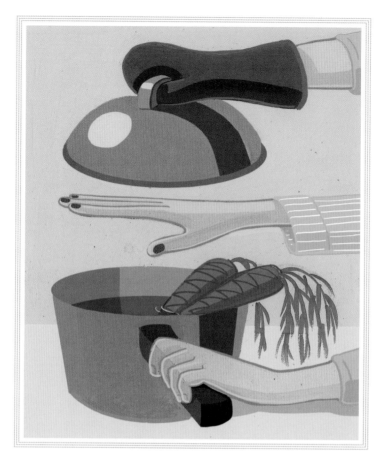

TOO MANY COOKS

Should your mother teach you to cook, as a child, you will be grateful. And should she continue to teach you to cook, as an adult, you will be grouchy. You believe this condition afflicts only you. You learn, knife in hand, it cuts both ways.

Out of town on house-hunting duty, you press your mother into Moma duty. She spends two days following your schedule, an eight-page grid detailing how much toothpaste to apply and the number of minutes each child is permitted to stall before lights out. You leave nothing to her innate creativity, not even the number of millimeters of milk in each bunny cup.

And yet, this experiment goes well. Everyone survives. No one says what transpired between good-bye kiss and what-did-you-bring-me hug. It is only later, in a quiet moment stringing beans, that Hannah mentions how much she enjoyed Moma's salmon. And how much Moma enjoyed preparing it. "She said it was fun," the junior reporter reports. "She said it was fun cooking in your kitchen. She said it was fun cooking in your kitchen, especially without you."

This revelation comes back while you are sizzling carrots for Thanksgiving carrot purée. You make this dish every year. And every year, your mother slides a lid over the bubbling carrots. You flick it off. You turn up the heat, she turns it down. You shout, "Don't touch my carrots." You consider running the Sharpie down the middle of the island so neither of you will be voted off.

At dinner, everything is delicious. Especially the turkey, which your mother has prepared in absolute privacy on the east end of the kitchen. And the tarte Tatin, which you constructed on the west. The carrot purée reigns superior. Probably because you managed to sizzle the carrots without interference. Or maybe because your mom secretly dropped a shallot into your food processor. Collaboration, you discover, can sometimes be smooth.

Carrot Purée

Serves 8

1 small butternut squash, about 2 pounds

1 orange, zested, peeled, and broken into segments

1 shallot, halved

4 teaspoons unsalted butter

1 pound carrots, peeled and cut into 1-inch lengths

2 cups chicken broth

1 tablespoon sugar

¼ cup sour cream

Kosher salt

1. Bake: Scrub the outside of the squash, because your mother says so. Split the squash in half the long way. This will take a heavy knife and some muscle. Use an ice-cream spoon to scrape out seeds and strings. Lay the two halves, cut-side down, on a rimmed baking sheet. Bake at 400 degrees for 30 minutes. Flip over. Fill each cavity with, in order: half the orange zest, half the shallot, half the orange segments and 1 teaspoon butter. Continue to bake until very soft, another 30 minutes.

2. Boil: Settle carrots in a medium pot. Cover with chicken broth. Add remaining 2 teaspoons butter and the sugar. Bring to a boil, reduce heat to a lively simmer, and continue to cook. Don't let some

kitchen busybody fiddle with the heat or slide on a lid or call it quits. The pleasure of this technique comes from sticking it out until the broth has evaporated, the carrots are sizzling sweet and nearly stuck to the bottom of the pan, 1 long hour.

3. Purée: Tumble the cooked carrots into the food processor. Scoop the orange zest and pulp, shallot, and soft flesh out of the squash shell and into the food processor bowl. Add sour cream and purée until smooth. Salt lightly. Transfer to a serving dish. Serve right away or keep warm in a low oven, covered with foil. Or reheat in the microwave, covered in wax paper.

HEIDI MAKES USE *of* WHAT
SHE HAS LEARNED

When I was young and impressionable and spoke abysmal high-school French, I spent a summer in Switzerland with a family that was old and impervious and spoke impeccable—and nothing but—French. I was bewildered.

One evening we suited up in foul-weather gear for dessert. It started mildly enough, with a sail on a placid lake. After a supper of cold ham and boiled eggs, the captain squinted through binoculars and announced we'd soon have éclairs. I welcome the éclair on land or sea, but the crew turned frantic. Sometime later, perhaps during the downpour or between thunderbolts, I was struck by a new understanding of "éclair." Fishing out my soggy vocabulary list, I penciled in "lightning."

The foreign-exchange student is supposed to exchange ignorance for experience and I, being ignorant, arrived prepared. Switzerland, as I understood from *Heidi*, featured the intrepid family hiking the Alps armed with pocket knife and chocolate bar. Yodeling.

My second day on the job, I found myself trailing the intrepid family through the Alps, armed with pocket knife and chocolate bar. Yodeling.

We came across an ancient ring of rocks where we (ok, they) built a bonfire. Mr. Intrepid shrugged down his rucksack and muscled out a wheel of cheese about the size of a spare tire. He sawed the wheel in two and set each half on a stone to warm. Using his pocket knife, he scraped off one melting slab, letting it tumble onto a tin plate where Mrs. Intrepid had arranged a huddle of pickles and boiled potatoes. I uncrumpled my vocabulary list and added "Raclette."

Creamy, nutty, hole-speckled Raclette cheese makes a mild snack cold and a national obsession when melted. It offers a simple and hearty meal, especially welcome after a day hiking the Alps or the avenue, shouldering a massive cheese or an armload of shopping bags. You can prepare it at home with the assistance of an electric melting contraption, but why bother? Like the fondue pot, the dedicated cheese grill will dedicate its post-cheese hours to shelf sprawl.

Try something more resourceful. Build a fire (outdoors or in) and melt the cheese. It'll make you feel intrepid. Even if, after a summer of yodeling, you're not.

Raclette

Serves 4

2 pounds small potatoes, in their jackets

Kosher salt

1 jar cornichons

1 jar tiny boiled white onions

½ pound thinly sliced prosciutto or Serrano ham or 2 links flavorful sausage, grilled and sliced into coins or, nontraditionally, a few crisps of bacon

1 pound Raclette

Freshly ground black pepper

1. Boil: Scrub potatoes and settle in a large pot. Cover with cold salted water by 1 inch. Simmer until just tender when poked with a fork, about 12 minutes. Drain, sprinkle with salt, and keep warm.

2. Arrange: Tumble potatoes onto a platter. Pile pickles, onions, and meat in appealing heaps.

3. Serve: Let each guest choose a few potatoes, breaking open the larger ones with a fork. Accompany with a handful of pickles and onions and a fold of ham or stack of sausage.

4. Melt: Build a fire, set half a wheel of the cheese on a nearby rock. As the cut face of the cheese softens, scrape it onto a potato-prepared plate.

5. Improvise: Lacking urban campfire, heat the oven to 450 degrees. Trim the rind off the cheese. Slice four slabs of cheese (each about ½ inch thick) and lay them on a parchment-paper-lined baking sheet. Slide sheet into the oven. Watch. After 1 or 2 minutes, when the cheese goes soft and shiny, pull out the baking sheet and scrape one melty fold of cheese over each guest's potato composition. Grind on lots of pepper. Enjoy hot, while melting the next cheese set.

TIME BENDS

Time is one of those sturdy products, like spare change and parking tickets, that's easy to pile up and count.

And yet, time strikes us as sneaky, stretchy, and sly. How can the six hours between the child's departure for school and his return last 15 minutes? And yet the half-hour between Scooby-Doo toothbrushing and goodnight kiss takes four hours and 45 minutes? It's a mystery no Minnie Mouse wristwatch can resolve.

Kitchen time is no more reliable. We know plodding recipes for quick bread. And slow-roasts prepped in minutes. None of which inspire the sticky kitchen timer to budge.

Consider that classic time-bending recipe, cassoulet. A proper cassoulet, French authorities maintain, can be achieved in three long days, most of it spent bickering over whether to add goose fat or cracked mutton bones.

Which seems like a worthy cause, especially in February. We consult the six-page summary in *Mastering the Art of French Cooking*, heartened by Julia Child's candor. All the simmering and sniping, she confides, produces not "a kind of rare ambrosia" but baked beans. Tasty baked beans.

And yet, three days is a lot to ask for beans. We take interest in the streamlined two-day update listed under "Cassoulet de Canard" in *The Gourmet Cookbook*. But chickening out, consider instead: "Easy Cassoulet" (4 hours), "Simple Cassoulet" (3 hours), "Cassoulet-Style Beans" (2½ hours), and a pile of time-saving improvisations, most of which result in full thermoses and empty stomachs. We stop short of the canned-bean-and-cubed-ham approach (30 minutes).

At the end of an endless week, we settle on a two-hour compromise that focuses on the good parts (duck) while forgoing the frustration (pork rind).

We feel no compunction about calling it a shortcut. After all, even the sober scientists in Greenwich sometimes mess with the mechanism. One New Year's they slipped in an extra second, padding the clock for a planet that's been rotating more slowly. Probably due to a surfeit of cassoulet.

Two-Hour Cassoulet

Serves 8

1 pound dry navy beans (or other small white beans such as great Northern)

4 prepared duck legs, confit*

2 onions, chopped 8 cloves garlic, chopped

⅓ cup red wine

4 cups cold water

2 cups beef broth

1 (14-ounce) can whole tomatoes, puréed with their juice

1 small chunk celery

3 sprigs fresh thyme

1 bay leaf

2 sprigs fresh parsley

¼ teaspoon black peppercorns

1 teaspoon olive oil

1 pound smoked kielbasa, sliced

1 teaspoon kosher salt

¼ teaspoon freshly ground black pepper

½ baguette, ground into 2 cups fluffy breadcrumbs

*Purchase duck legs confit (duck legs preserved in fat and spices) at the meat counter (just ask) or from one of the fancy food stores. D'Artagnan is a good producer.

1. Plump: Rinse and sort beans, discarding any suspicious specks. Scrape into a large pot and fill with enough cold water to submerge beans by 2 inches. Bring to a boil, simmer 2 minutes, remove from heat and let stand 50 minutes. Drain.

2. Prep: While the beans are soaking, pull the skin off the duck legs and discard. Pull off the meat and set aside. Scrape the soft white fat from the confit into a large soup pot. Save the bones.

3. Brown: Melt the duck fat over medium heat. Add the onion and garlic and cook over medium heat until golden brown, 15 to 20 minutes. Turn up the heat and deglaze the pot with the wine. Pour in the water, broth, and tomato purée.

4. Simmer: Tie up the duck bones, celery, thyme, parsley, bay leaf, and peppercorns in a square of cheesecloth. Add this packet to the pot. Add the beans. Bring to a boil, lower to a simmer, and cook until beans are tender and sauce is flavorful, about 50 minutes.

5. Crisp: Meanwhile, heat the olive oil over medium-high heat in a medium skillet and cook the sausage until nicely browned, 3 minutes per side.

6. Bake: Remove and discard cheesecloth packet. Season beans with salt and pepper. Stir in the sausage and duck meat. Aim for a harmonious mix of elements, neither brothy nor dry (reference cassoulet's American cousin, franks and beans). Pack into a casserole with a cozy fit. Sprinkle with breadcrumbs and bake at 350 degrees until sides are bubbly and top is golden, about 20 minutes.

ANTI-FREEZE

Skiing is a great sport. Except for being out in the cold. And going downhill. And dressing like a stuffed potato. The scenery is terrific, especially when compared with wincing through the Pilates DVD on the laundry-room floor.

After skiing comes après ski. This is when the skier congratulates herself for having spent the whole day in the cold, going downhill, while dressed like a stuffed potato. In celebration of these accomplishments, and of not having broken anything critical, she is rewarded with hot drink, hot snack, and hot tub. Après Pilates, she is grateful simply to stop.

The child benefits from early exposure to this sport. If he gets used to skiing while short, he doesn't mind staying outside and facing downhill and dressing like a potato.

But the ski professional frowns on simply stuffing the tot into tater suit and giving him a push. The small skier must attend ski school. Which has certain advantages. According to the report card folded into his pocket, he learns to operate a pair of skis safely, including how to turn and how to stop. And he takes all day doing it. Freeing the parent to, well, ski.

For two whole days, I dress like a potato, brave cold, careen downhill. I even join my children on the slope for one brief run, after which the larger of the two small potatoes fixes her goggles on mine and asks: "Can't you at least try to keep up?"

The next morning I reevaluate. Is it possible, I wonder, to omit certain parts of the skiing routine, like the suit and the cold and the hill? And yet retain other elements, like the drink and the snack and the tub? It might, I reason, be efficient. And so, after dropping Hannah and Noah at the foot of the mountain, I stop by the après-ski outfitter and stock up on equipment, including beef and Burgundy and actual potatoes. I spend the day working on parallel slicing and smooth turns with the wooden spoon. I remain warm, level, and dressed in an apron.

When the skiers come back, cold and tired, moods heading perilously downhill, I show them the results of my workout: steaming bowls of beef bourguignon, heaped over potato pancakes. They take this in, enthusiastically. Après après ski, I review my report card. No one suggests I can't keep up.

Après-Ski Stew
Serves 6

4 pounds beef chuck

4 carrots, chopped

2 onions, chopped

3 cloves garlic, chopped

2 tablespoons olive oil

1 teaspoon dried thyme

1 bay leaf

Ingredients cont'd

1. Marinate: Trim fat from chuck. Cut into 1½-inch cubes. Heap into a large bowl along with carrots, onions, garlic, oil, thyme, bay leaf, 1 teaspoon salt, and the pepper. Pour in wine. Cover and refrigerate an hour or a day. Drain, reserving marinade and vegetables separately. Pat meat dry.

2. Crisp: Heat a large oven-safe Dutch oven over medium. When hot, scatter in bacon and cook, stirring, until crisp and brown, about 4 minutes. Scoop

2 teaspoons kosher salt

1 teaspoon freshly ground
black pepper

1 bottle red wine

⅓ pound bacon, frozen
and diced

10 shallots, whole, peeled

1 tablespoon sugar

¼ cup flour

½ cup chopped
fresh parsley

out and drain on paper towels, leaving rendered fat in the pot.

3. Brown: Sear meat in batches until darkly colored on all sides. Set aside. Caramelize shallots in the remaining fat. Set shallots aside. Add vegetables to the pot and caramelize, about 7 minutes, adding sugar during the last minute of cooking.

4. Thicken: Add flour to the pot with the vegetables, cook one minute. Add reserved marinade, boil 2 minutes. Sauce should be thick. Season with remaining 1 teaspoon salt. Add meat, cook one minute.

5. Meld: Cover, slide into a 325-degree oven, and cook for 2 hours, stirring once or twice. Add reserved shallots and cook another hour. Let rest.

6. Serve: Spoon off any accumulated fat. Add parsley. Heat on stovetop. Spoon into bowls, over potato pancakes if you like. Sprinkle each serving with reserved bacon crisps. Feel hearty.

Potato Pancakes

Makes 12

Grate 1 russet potato on the big shredding holes of a box grater. Grate 1 russet potato on the small shredding holes. Scoop up potatoes by the handful and squeeze dry. Stir in 1 beaten egg, 2 tablespoons flour, 1 teaspoon baking powder, ½ teaspoon kosher salt, and a good grind of black pepper. Heat ½-inch peanut oil in a heavy skillet set over medium-high heat. Scoop 1 tablespoon potatoes into the pan and nudge with a spoon into a circle. Add as many pancakes as fit happily, no crowding. Fry golden brown, 2 minutes per side. Drain on paper towels. Repeat, frying all cakes.

NOSTALGIA TRIP

The film fan passing through Baltimore dines at the diner. Not any diner; the diner in *Diner*.

He comes to find Barry Levinson's Baltimore, an anxious, post-adolescent, 1959 (as remembered in 1982) Baltimore. He may also know John Waters's flamingo-pink vision and David Simon's dark-blue versions. The city's tidier districts often double for D.C., but its leading screen credit remains *Diner*. That's the one where young Steve Guttenberg and Paul Reiser prep the prenuptial football exam, put money on Mickey Rourke's chances with the girls, and help an edgy Kevin Bacon maintain his grip on reality.

The actual diner launched its career in 1954 on Long Island, working the roadside restaurant scene. It switched to acting in the 1980s, relocating to Baltimore and striking a desolate waterfront pose. It landed roles in *Tin Men*, *Liberty Heights*, and *Sleepless in Seattle*. In the 1990s it took a new name, the Hollywood Diner, and moved downtown to a spot underlooking the highway.

The film student eager to re-create the all-night camaraderie celebrated in *Diner* will have to manage it over breakfast between 7 and 9 or lunch between 11 and 2. The location doubles as a job-training program for troubled teens. The program's funding troubles limit its hours.

Should the visitor be tempted to order the left side of the menu, as a minor character with a major appetite does in the movie, it's eggs first shift and sandwiches second. He's advised to get the open-faced hot turkey on white, with the native side: fries and gravy. The dish rightfully belongs to those late-night hours when the plates hustled out of any diner's stainless-steel kitchen seek not to dazzle but to soothe. That, and to soak up the last round.

Here the waitstaff maintains a no-wait policy—pick up your own tuna on styrofoam at the cash register. But the enthusiast who orders the hot turkey gets an upgrade to a real plate, real fork, and real knife.

So abundant and abundantly soggy a sandwich demands a firm grip on reality—even if it was made famous on film. It's served in a Baltimore still anxious, still certain that growing pains are best eased by friendship. And by french fries, doused with gravy.

Hot Turkey, Side of Fries

Serves 4

1 (2-pound) boneless turkey breast, rolled*

1 tablespoon unsalted butter, softened

Kosher salt

4 russet potatoes

2 tablespoons oil

2 tablespoons unsalted butter, cubed

2 tablespoons flour

1½ cups chicken broth

Freshly ground black pepper

8 slices white bread

1. Roast: Rub the turkey breast with 1 tablespoon softened butter. Season with salt. Settle in a heavy oven-safe skillet and slide into a 450-degree oven. Roast until golden outside and 160 degrees inside, about 45 minutes.

2. Crisp: Given that the oven is hot, may as well go with oven fries and roast them along with the turkey. What they lack in greasy authenticity, they make up for in convenience. Peel potatoes and cut into french fry shapes. Dry thoroughly. Toss with oil. Spread out on a rimmed baking sheet and slide into the 450-degree oven along with the turkey. Roast, shaking now and then, until crisp, about 45 minutes. Salt liberally.

3. Thicken: Move turkey from the skillet to the cutting board and let rest. Hold onto your potholders—that skillet is oven-hot. Set skillet—empty, save the tasty bits stuck to the bottom—directly over a burner on medium heat. Melt in the cubed butter, scraping the pan with a wooden spoon. Whisk in flour; cook 1 minute. Add broth and any accumulated turkey juices. Reduce over high heat, stirring, until thickened, about 3 minutes. Season with salt and pepper.

4. Assemble: Slice turkey thinly. Overlap two pieces of white bread on each of four heavy white plates. Top each bread pair with a heap of sliced turkey. Pile up fries in any remaining plate space. Douse everything with gravy. Tackle with a knife and fork, distractedly, while discussing football, marriage, LP filing, or other matters of consequence.

*Some meat counters carry turkey breast already boned and rolled. If not, ask the butcher. If you plan to do the prep work yourself, start with a 3-pound breast.

SWEET SORROW

Dicing can bring the competent cook to tears. Especially if the dicee happens to be an onion. But who would forego onion?

The cook is not unduly sentimental. She is inured to the drama of the innocent bulb lolling on the chopping block. Calmly, she sharpens her chef's knife. She slices off the stem end, generously, then the root end, stingily. Lifting away the crisp curve of brown skin, she admires its translucent beauty. She pulls off the stretchy layer that separates outer from inner. She takes professional pride in the peeled onion, shiny and smooth.

Then she falls to pieces. She follows the rules: Cut cleanly through the meridian. Lay the two halves flat. Make several slices stem-end to root-end, stopping shy of the root, which holds the layers together. Holding one hand flat on top to steady everything, slice horizontally, twice or thrice. Crosscut (starting from the stem end) releasing a snowy heap of onion cubes. Her knife skills are strong. But her life skills are weak. She cries.

Is it gratitude to the onion that sacrificed its life to the cause of soup? Is it regret for reducing the whole to bits? Existential angst? Or mere melancholy?

The moment is profound, and predictable. Yet the kitchen scientist swears these bitter tears can be dried. He flaunts facts, like sulfuric acid and eye irritant. He's got methods. For instance, snap on a scuba mask. The theory being that annoying vapor, wafting eyeward, will take one look at the goggle-eyed cook and laugh. This approach does provoke ridicule. But does not defang vapor.

Dicing underwater—eyes open or closed—may work. But the sage cook declines, being fond of all ten fingers. Chopping with the window wide merely affords the curious robin a good look at the cook, sobbing. Relying solely on the sweet onion strikes the cook as confining. Clenching a mouthful of water (or bread, or lemon, or matchsticks) strikes her as ridiculous.

Then one afternoon the plumber stomps through. She offers the weepy cook a handkerchief and a fix: candlelight. The flame draws in air, she says, along with airborne menace.

The cook lights a stubby candle and sets it on the counter. The flame casts a golden glow over cutting board, onion, knife, and cook, in tears. She decides to adopt this method as a standard part of her technique. It doesn't staunch the tears, but it does set the proper mood for onion chopping, with all its attendant sorrows.

Onion Tart

Serves 8

2 tablespoons olive oil

4 medium onions, chopped

¼ cup sherry

3 egg yolks

½ cup heavy
 whipping cream

3 ounces blue cheese,
 crumbled

2 tablespoons fresh thyme,
 finely chopped

½ teaspoon freshly ground
 black pepper

1 package (about 1 pound)
 all-butter puff pastry,
 defrosted

1. Caramelize: Heat oil in a large heavy skillet over low heat. Add onions and cook slowly, stirring occasionally, until deep brown and sticky sweet, about 1 hour. Turn up the heat, add sherry, and deglaze the pan, scraping any browned bits off the bottom. Cool.

2. Mix: Beat 2 of the yolks briefly in a small bowl, then stir in cream, cheese, thyme, and pepper. Stir in onions. (If you're working ahead, transfer to an airtight container and refrigerate until you're ready to bake the tart.)

3. Bake: Unfold the puff pastry onto a baking sheet. Score with a pastry wheel into 3-inch squares. Separate slightly. Paint the pastry with the remaining egg yolk, lightly beaten. Slide into a 375-degree oven for 10 minutes until pastry begins to puff. Remove from oven. Spoon the onion filling onto each square, leaving a ½-inch bare border. Return to oven and bake until fully puffed, about 30 minutes. Serve warm.

PROVENANCE: *Adapted from the Chopping Block Cooking School, Chicago.*

FAST FRIENDS

The new girl blew in on a gust of wind, a hurricane that swept her out of New Orleans, across the country, and landed her on a heavy wooden chair in third grade, right next to Hannah.

The new girl was like a sparkly rock or a symmetrical pine cone: an unexpected find. Her name was Daniela.

Hannah showed Daniela the girls' room. How to borrow a book from the library. Where to eat lunch. Before Daniela arrived, Hannah had been the new girl and Sophie had been her guide.

Side by side they worked the assignment from the blackboard. "Needs," they wrote in wobbly cursive. Hannah started her list: "Oxygen. Food. Water. Shelter. Medasen." Then she tallied "Wants:" "Laptop. Candy. Cell phon. Confort. Love."

Hannah showed Daniela the playground. And how, if you swing at exactly the same pace as the next girl, it's called getting married. Soon Hannah and Daniela and Sophie were married.

In the clear blue arc above the wood chips, swinging in perfect time, they told their secrets.

Before her year in New Orleans, Daniela came from Nicaragua. In Spanish class, she knew the answers. At lunch, she sneaked the girls slices of fried plantain.

They had a sleepover, except they didn't sleep. They wrote a list of all the boys they hated. And a list of all the boys they loved, including Elvis and Beethoven.

When she turned nine, Daniela brought a cake to school. It was low and white and sticky sweet. "Tres Leches," she said. "Three milks." The three girls scraped their paper plates clean.

And then, before spring, Daniela said she had to go. All the way back to Nicaragua, to her old life. One without the swinging friends, the sleepless sleepover, and the secret crush.

Sophie bought a necklace inscribed "best friends forever." It was shaped like a heart. A heart snapped in three, threaded onto three separate strands. Each girl strung one purple sling around her neck and vowed never to take it off, unless her mom insisted or it was bedtime. They pressed the three shards together, tightly.

And then Daniela was gone. She left a letter. "You might be a bad speller," Daniela confided in Hannah, "but that's not what counts." She left a photo of three girls gathered around a low sweet cake. They smile milk-white smiles. They know, deep in their broken hearts, that love is both want and need.

Tres Leches Cake

This recipe isn't particularly hard, but it calls for a sturdy mixer and close attention. Start by gathering the ingredients, a reliable timer, and patience.

Serves 3, twice

1 orange

1 lemon

1 lime

6 eggs, at room
   temperature*

1 cup sugar

1 cup sifted cake flour

⅔ cup evaporated milk

⅔ cup sweetened
   condensed milk

¾ cup heavy
   whipping cream

1 teaspoon vanilla extract

1. Prep: Finely grate the zest of the orange, lemon, and lime. Squeeze the juice of all three fruits. Strain. Measure ⅓ cup mixed juice.

2. Beat: Separate one egg. Set aside the white. Slide the yolk and remaining five whole eggs into the bowl of a stand mixer. Pour in ½ cup sugar. Using the whisk attachment, beat at high speed until pale, thick, and tripled in volume, about three minutes. Reduce speed to medium and mix in the flour and zest.

3. Bake: Scrape batter into an 8 x 8-inch oven-safe glass baking dish. Slide into a 350-degree oven and bake until the center springs back when gently pressed, about 30 minutes. Set pan on a rack to cool.

4. Shake: Meanwhile, whisk together the three milks (evaporated, condensed, and cream) along with the vanilla. Chill.

5. Fortify: When cake has cooled somewhat (about 15 minutes), use a fork or the blunt edge of kitchen knife to lift the brown skin off the cake and discard. Slowly pour the three-milk blend over the cake. It will take a minute or two to soak in. Chill.

6. Whisk: Using a stand mixer fitted with the whisk attachment set on high, beat the remaining egg white until foamy and white, 1 minute.

7. Boil: Combine ⅓ cup reserved fruit juice with the remaining ½ cup sugar in a small saucepan. Bring to a boil and cook, stirring, until the syrup reaches the soft-ball stage. This will take about 6 minutes. Test by dripping a bit of syrup into a saucer of cool water. It should form a blob.

8. Fluff: Pour the hot syrup onto the egg white, turn the mixer to high and beat to a glossy, thick icing, about 6 minutes.

9. Frost: Cover the cooled cake with the icing. Chill until ready to serve.

*Eggs must be at room temperature to achieve full fluff. Count out eggs into a bowl and leave it on the countertop overnight. Or, fill the bowl with warm water and let the eggs warm, about an hour.

THINKING BIG

It took me a while to get with the big shop. And to get to the big shop. So long I had to stop for gas. And a snack. And directions.

Even when I finally found it, and found a vacant spot in the parking sprawl and walked in, even then, I wasn't there yet. In order to shop for really big things, you first have to present credentials, like a driver's license and phone number and membership fee.

There were TVs there, and jeans jackets, and generators, and "fully functional garden art." And, at the far end of what seemed like a very spacious and very neat garage, food. Enormous food. Massive muffins plastic-packed by the dozen. Slabs of spare ribs. Buckets of yogurt. Cinder blocks of cheese. Backbreaking sacks of rice.

At first I felt like I'd shrunk. Become a dollhouse person sneaking around the big people's pantry. I kept worrying one of those Gorgonzola blocks was going to topple over and flatten me. But once I steered my doublewide grocery trailer down the cereal aisle, I got with the program. Maybe I did need a nine-pound tower of oatmeal. Maybe I needed nine more children to fill with oatmeal. Maybe I needed to open a restaurant. Then I'd have a good use for those barrels of mayonnaise, those jugs of chocolate syrup.

And the packaging! Pick up a twenty-pound box of Tide, if you can, and you've got yourself a readymade Warhol.

Eventually I reached the far reaches, where caves of canned soda stood in chilly silence. There was a room that looked like a carwash, squiggly plastic curtain and all, marked "Fresh Produce." Lots of fresh produce. Suddenly I needed crates of mangoes, quarts of blueberries, a five-pound clamshell, as the sign said, of straw-berries. Flouting the "eat seasonal, shop local" directive, I loaded my cart with fruit that traveled on passport. I peered over one shoulder, then the other. No sign of Alice Waters.

It wasn't until I idled at the checkout, searching for my new big-shopper ID card, that I started to wonder what I was going to do with a clamful of strawberries. Then I remembered that the warehouse sells freezer bags. As well as freezers.

Classic Smoothie

Serves 2

Pour 1 cup fresh orange juice into the blender. Drop in 1 frozen banana, broken into chunks, and 1 cup frozen strawberries. Blend smooth.

Berry Smoothie

Serves 2

Scrape 1 cup strawberry yogurt into the blender. Add 1½ cups frozen strawberries and 1 cup frozen raspberries. Thin with tart cherry juice, as needed. Blend smooth.

WELL SEASONED

My kitchen has good points, like lots of floor space. And bad points, like little storage space. Mitigated by its nicest point—location. It's just a brief dash from one of those sumptuous cooking-supply stores that stock everything.

Whenever I find myself stumped by the thought of dinner—again—I drop by and browse. Who knew there was a tool designed solely to decapitate the boiled egg? But when I actually cook, I rely on my cast-iron skillet.

I used to use all sorts of fancy cookware. The wide stockpot and the tall pasta boiler and the mini saucier. Coated with dark this and shiny that and slippery the other. Each guaranteed to deliver cook and kitchen high-style joy.

Then one day at the hardware store, while stocking up on cupboard-organizing equipment, I noticed the cast-iron skillet. I couldn't resist its heavy-duty fortitude and lightweight price tag. Not to mention its low-style charm.

At first I was stumped by seasoning—sealing out malicious rust agents. It's a process that involves vegetable shortening and low heat and patience, three of my weak areas. Then I remembered the clerk at the hardware store practiced an alternative approach: Fry up a pound of bacon. That worked.

I put my seasoned skillet to work crisping chicken and sizzling steak. Eventually, out of pure laziness, I let it swirl a sauce. Scramble an egg. Bake cornbread. Soon it was my go-to pan. It cooks most everything, without a fuss. And as long as it never gets curious about the blessings of the dishwasher, my well-seasoned pan just keeps getting darker, slicker and better at spreading low heat low and throwing high heat high.

The cast-iron pan is heavy, but there's no point in putting it away—should you have somewhere to put it. In fact, it can expand kitchen storage space. Once committed to cast iron, you can toss the rest of your cookware.

Works for me. Then again, I live awfully close to egg-topper resupply.

Saucy Chops

Serves 2

For vinaigrette:

2 teaspoons finely minced shallot

2 cloves garlic, degermed and smashed to bits

1 tablespoon fresh thyme leaves, whole

2 teaspoons finely chopped fresh rosemary

2 tablespoons capers, drained and rinsed

¼ cup fresh lemon juice

2 tablespoons olive oil

For lamb:

1 pound (8) single-cut lamb rib chops

Kosher salt and freshly ground black pepper

½ teaspoon butter

½ teaspoon olive oil

Butter lettuce

Fresh parsley

1. **Whisk:** Mound shallots, garlic, herbs, and capers into a small bowl. Whisk in lemon juice, then oil.

2. **Sear:** Season lamb chops lightly with salt and pepper. Heat butter and oil in a large cast-iron skillet over medium. When hot, add chops and cook until just done, 2 minutes per side. (Thicker cuts may need an extra half-minute per side.) Arrange chops on two plates.

3. **Serve:** Scatter a few lettuce fronds and parsley sprigs alongside the lamb. Douse greens and meat with vinaigrette. Serve with crusty bread for mopping up sauce.

UNDER THE INFLUENCE

Good food is a good idea. Not good like chocolate Vesuvius good. But good like brown rice with kale good, the good we are supposed to both practice and preach.

Good, however, is good and shifty. There's high-protein good and high-carb good and low-fat good and French good, which presumably shares much with actually good.

I tend to go with tastes good, even if it means choosing contraband. Now that I'm a parent, however, I'm supposed to stick with good-for-you good.

I know this because Noah, my youngest scientist, brings home the good news.

He classifies the early-morning toast as grain. And the lunchbox mango as fruit. At dinner he eyes the macaroni and cheese suspiciously. "Mom," he asks, "is pepper a vegetable?"

He knows about the food pyramid, that monolith erected in "George Washington, D.C." Being grown up, I remember the old pyramid, which made sense. Things you were supposed to eat a lot of lounged at the fat bottom and things you were supposed to eat little of squeezed into the point. The new pyramid seems sideways; its stripes run top to bottom.

The junior nutritionist applies himself to his kindergarten homework. Which is to say, waking at a criminal hour and ripping pages from the glossy food magazine. He points; I cut. He plans to glue these stylish meals to the classroom food chart via "paper crochet." He packs his backpack. I fill my coffee cup.

After school, the kindergarten teacher tracks me down by the swingset, brow furrowed. She holds out a glossy page. "In which section of the pyramid," she asks pointedly, "does this belong?" I look. The photo shows, with frosty clarity, two martinis.

Later, when both Hannah and Noah are wedged into bed and the cocktail glasses are wedged into the freezer, I reflect on this question. I come to the conclusion that it belongs to that portion of the pyramid reserved for dark chocolate and habanero pepper and stiff drink. That underrated yet very good section marked "adult."

Martini

Serves 2

The original martini is made with gin and as little vermouth as possible. Winston Churchill kept his straight by simply glaring at the vermouth bottle while pouring the gin.

Chill two martini glasses in the freezer for ½ hour. Fill a shaker with ice. Pour in ¾ cup (6 ounces) gin and dash of dry vermouth. Shake or stir, following your personal convictions. Add a splash of olive brine, if you like your drink cloudy. Strain into frosted glasses. Garnish each with a green olive or two (plain or fancy), skewered on a toothpick.

GO, DOG! GO.

A dog takes training and, given that we wanted a dog, we were training, hard. Every dog we met we asked to pose for petting practice. We debated dog names. We were thinking of a chocolate Lab, named Chip.

On a trip to Chicago, we learned that the city was spotted with dog bakeries, so we decided to practice treat selection. We engaged Vishnu and Nelson for an afternoon excursion. They, in turn, invited their people.

Nelson was one of those thin, energetic sorts with wide-angle ears commonly known as "brown." Vishnu had a pink freckled face dominated by a big black nose and a searching expression. Searching, we soon learned, for a snack.

We started at Galloping Gourmutts, where we planned to conduct a rigorous taste test, to compare, say, the mailman-shaped crisp to the human-grade pizza puff. But ranking proved impossible. According to our focus group, every sample rated "excellent."

Perhaps there was some fine gradation in gratitude. Vishnu awarded the beef biscuit the four-paw sprawl his people referred to as "down." While Nelson greeted the carob-covered cookie with an exuberant two-legged stretch presumably termed "up." Followed by frantic sniffing easily translated as: "More. Now."

We attempted further study at Famous Fido Dog Deli, where customers strained for real-cheese cheesecake and vivid orange cookies. Many in the dog-treat business rely on the industrial dehydrator to give their product sturdy bite and year-long shelf life. But this sweet spot specialized in chewy. "Dogs don't like dog food," confided chef Gloria Lissner. "Dogs like people food."

It was a moment the social scientist would term "ah-ha." It had the perfect pitch of truth. The honest dog would admit, 100 percent of the time, that he would just as soon snub the kibble bowl and have at the dinner plate.

This got us wondering why the human dog companion bothers with the "human-grade" dog treat. The dog-grade dog wants more, now. He wants his human to exhibit good behavior: to grill a steak, set it on the table, then turn to answer the phone. This inadvertent treat would surely be met with a swift "up." Followed by the prolonged, and enthusiastic, "down."

Good-Dog Cheesecake

Serves 12

1 cup rolled oats

½ cup wheat germ

5 tablespoons vegetable oil

1 pound cream cheese

¼ cup whole-wheat flour

3 eggs

6 ounces (1½ cups) grated
   mild Cheddar cheese

1 tablespoon milk

½ cup sour cream

1. Crumble: Pulse oats and wheat germ in the food processor until crumbly. Pulse in oil.

2. Crisp: Pat crumble into the bottom of an 8-inch spring-form cake pan. Bake the crust at 350 degrees until crisp, about 15 minutes. Cool. Reduce heat to 300 degrees.

3. Beat: Using a stand mixer, beat the cream cheese soft and fluffy, 1 minute. Add flour. Beat in eggs.

4. Swirl: Melt Cheddar and milk in a medium saucepan over medium-low heat. Pour into the cream-cheese mixture and swirl briefly for a marbled effect.

5. Bake: Scrape batter onto the crust in the spring-form pan. Smooth the top. Bake at 300 degrees until just set, if a tad wiggly in the center, about 50 minutes. Cool completely in the pan, at least 1 hour, out of paw's reach.

6. Frost: Release sides of the spring-form pan. Smooth sour cream over the top. Refrigerate until playgroup. Reward your good dog with a small slice; this is a rich treat.

HOME REMEDY

Health makes us queasy. Who wants to ruin a perfectly good kale sauté wondering if germ warfare is being fought in the foliage? Who wants to dampen a walk in the woods by counting footsteps, dividing by body mass, and discounting for doughnut? Who wants to pass the physical, only to fail the challenge of filing the forms?

We concede the standard appalling condition is best met with the standard appalling treatment. But we submit that stress—that bulging hamper of damp and dirty discouragement—is best undone with alternative medicine.

Massage, for instance. Beach idyll. Room service. Any mood-enhancement device, including morange lipstick, curvy slides, and bunny-eared phone case. Yoga, of course. Cushy yoga mat. Consultation with buff yoga instructor. Stress-reducers all.

We're certain an actual scientific study would find that these measures improve life and longevity. And that the tab compares favorably to that of traditional treatment. Perhaps muckrakers will discover collusion between the pharmaceutical industry and the anti-yoga lobby.

The health-conscious can also turn to the home remedy. For instance, the truffle. This collusion between bittersweet chocolate and heavy cream is strong medicine. It comes packed with mood-boosters best abbreviated as caffeine, calories, and chocolate. It's indicated for the mild depression experienced by the overworked and underappreciated. It's also a tonic for afternoon slump, laundry, or exasperation.

The standard dose of two truffles should be administered at the first sign of surliness. The only known side effect is addiction. Small price to pay for mental health.

Extra-Strength Truffles

Makes 36 truffles

8 ounces high-quality bittersweet chocolate (70 percent), finely chopped

2 tablespoons unsalted butter, cut up

1 cup heavy whipping cream

1 tablespoon whole espresso beans

2 tablespoons unsweetened cocoa powder

1. Toss: Line a (9 x 5 x 3) loaf pan with one long stretch of plastic wrap. Toss chocolate and butter together in a mixing bowl.

2. Scald: Heat cream and espresso beans in a small heavy pan. Just as cream comes to a boil, strain over chocolate and butter. Discard beans. Let rest, 5 minutes. Whisk chocolate smooth and shiny.

3. Chill: Scrape chocolate into loaf pan. Fold over plastic wrap to cover. Refrigerate until firm, 3 hours.

4. Dust: Sift half the cocoa powder onto a clean, dry cutting board. Unwrap truffle block onto cocoa. Sift remaining cocoa powder over the top. With a large heavy knife, cut into 36 1-inch cubes. Trust us: the truffle cube is even easier to dispense than the truffle sphere, and quite a bit tidier to produce. Toss to dust all sides with cocoa powder.

5. Store: Pile truffles into a glass or plastic container. Seal securely. Refrigerate or freeze.

6. Dose: During the moment of stress, say, an unruly child's bedtime, unreasonable deadline, or unbelievable heap of dishes, take two. Keep out of reach of children.

NATURAL SELECTION

The garden is filled, right to the top, with dirt. Yet the gardener never drags out vacuum or mop. Apparently dirt helps the plant do whatever it is the plant does. Like grow or turn green or make a strawberry.

Dirt comes in flavors. Bad, for instance, which is full of sticks and rocks and broken glass and evil clumps, inspiring the tender strawberry sprout to hitch up its roots and flee. Or good, which has been sifted by a gardener with a sore back and pointy tools. Giving the plant the feeling it can stay awhile, settle down, make a berry. And gourmet, which is to say compost.

Compost I lack. Or lacked, until my parents came to town. When they discovered my garden bereft of compost heap they nearly hitched up their wheelies and fled. Then they spent a week constructing one.

Compost occurs naturally when the carrot peel or eggshell loiters so long that the local worm gets annoyed and bites it. But even nature needs prodding and that prodding required five forays to Home Depot and a truckload of two-by-fours and a bale of wire and a power saw and half the garage and several sweaty afternoons, which my father handled.

My mother commanded supplementary Home Depot runs, stockpiled pointy tools and applied them to the clumps. She patrolled the kitchen sink, on alert for any miscreant edging carrot peel or eggshell toward the disposal.

It took all three of us to heave the compost superstructure out of the garage and onto the finely-combed dirt. My mother released the liberated carrot peel and eggshell. My father twisted on a big orange lock, presumably to keep the worm task force on task. Then my parents grabbed their wheelies and fled.

Apparently if I keep up the eggshell routine and don't get voted off my block and think good thoughts about worms, I'll achieve gourmet dirt. Next year. Then I can pluck fresh strawberry or chive or lettuce leaf, confident that each knew a happy, well-nourished sprouthood.

In the meantime, just in case my mother springs a surprise inspection, I'm securing the garbage disposal with a big orange lock.

Savory Strawberry Smash

Makes 5 cups

2 pints strawberries

2 cups sugar

¼ cup balsamic vinegar

½ teaspoon freshly ground
   black pepper

1 box powdered pectin

½ cup water

1. Mash: Wash and hull berries. Cut them in half and tumble into a large heatproof glass measuring cup or other flat-bottomed container. Crush with a potato masher (or the bottom of the balsamic bottle); leave some chunks. Stir in sugar, vinegar, and pepper.

2. Thicken: In a small saucepan, combine pectin and water. Bring to a boil over high heat. Boil 1 minute, stirring smooth. Pour hot pectin over berries; stir until sugar has dissolved, 3 minutes.

3. Set: Pour strawberry mixture into 5 clean 1-cup jars, leaving ½-inch space at the top. Cover with lids. Let rest at room temperature until set (though not as thick as jam), 24 hours.

4. Store: Refrigerate up to 1 month or freeze up to 1 year. Strawberry smash works nicely against soft cheese, alongside yogurt, or over vanilla ice cream.

PROVENANCE: *Inspired by* The San Francisco Ferry Plaza Farmers' Market Cookbook.

ON THE GO

Rice is nice. Not the first thing I'd grab from the sinking stateroom, but nice heaped in a warm bowl, keeping company with gingered green beans. Nice backstroking through chicken soup or showing solidarity with peas and Parmesan. Rice does a nice job backing up sushi, soaking in curry, or padding paella. Rice isn't nice as pudding; it's lumpy.

Nice as rice might be, it never occurred to me to invite it on vacation. Once I'm packed I just flick off the kitchen light. No hugs, no tears. The dishwasher can use the downtime, and the knives and spoons seem comfy enough, lolling in their drawers. No one shouts, "Take me! Take me!" Not that I offer.

So when I ran into my friend John off-duty in the Rockies, I was fascinated he had brought along his rice cooker. I have my standard traveling companions. The laptop constantly thirsty for juice. The phone that never, ever seeks solitude. Not once a rice cooker.

John got me thinking I should expand my social circle. I dropped by rice resupply and chatted up a few steamers—the heavy commercial model, the plastic three-cup cutie. It was hard to resist the charm of anyone named Neuro Fuzzy. But its barrel chest was pocked with enigmatic options like "porridge" and "semi-brown." I picked a medium capacity model, big handle, one switch.

Also a bag of rice. Over the last 8,000 years, some 8,000 varieties have proved popular. These days there's red and white and black and semi-brown. There's long, short, jasmine, basmati, and forbidden. Best of all is the best of all, sold only in Japan. I stuck with sticky.

Back home I filled the cooker and pushed the button. After a while it let out a growl of steam and clicked from "cooking rice" to "keeping warm." I snapped open the top and scooped out fat fluffy grains. This rice was better than nice. It didn't seem like sidekick or backup. It seemed like it could sustain life on earth. It was the sort of dish I'd want anywhere. Even on a rice-shopping vacation in Japan. Besides, with that good grip and roomy interior, my new rice cooker might make an attractive carry-on.

Nice Rice

Serves half of humanity

Water

Rice

1. Measure: Pour cold water into the bowl of the rice-cooker, following the guidemarks. These ensure compliance with the ancient water-to-rice ratio of 2:1.

2. Rinse: Measure rice, using the cup that may have come with your cooker. Rinse rice thoroughly in a colander and add to the bowl.

3. Activate: Flick switch. Wait.

4. Enjoy.

Salmon Escort

Salmon fillet, skin-on, about ½ pound per person

Orange marmalade

Soy sauce

Ginger

Garlic

Red pepper flakes

1. Prep: Rinse and pat dry salmon. Tease out any pin bones that seem annoying. Tweezers or pliers are helpful here.

2. Glaze: Stretch out salmon on a lightly oiled broiler pan. Melt a few spoonfuls of marmalade (the micro-wave might actually come in handy); brush it across salmon. Shake on soy sauce, generously. Finely chop a little fresh ginger and garlic and scatter across the salmon. Shake on a bit of red pepper.

3. Broil: Slide glistening fish into the oven, about 5 inches from the flame. Broil until just done; flesh will be flaky at the surface and bright pink inside, about 8 minutes. Serve with rice.

PREP SCHOOL

Preparation is in, prebooked at the premeeting, previewed in the prequel, predicted in the primary. Even the dinner party is preceded by predinner: appetizer, hors d'oeuvre, light bite. The waiter, solemnly centering tuna wisp on tomato jus, announces the amuse-bouche. My mouth is not easily amused.

Nor does the rest of me take readily to forefare. I'm happy to prepare the standard succession, consommé to crème brulée. But pondering the precourse, I'm stumped. Appetizer impaired, the ADA terms it.

Leading to the predictable: cheese on plate, say. Though the heavyweight appetizer is prone to fell, then flatten the ordinary appetite. Olive in bowl speaks simplicity. Yet seems insufficient. Likewise nut on napkin.

I've experimented. Strawberries dipped in whipped cream once struck me as clever. Until my guests, thinking dessert, left. I've also served nothing, under the motherly not-to-spoil-your-appetite prerogative. No one requested the recipe.

I once lived down the block from a market that specialized in fresh pasta and handmade hors d'oeuvres. Lobster this and truffled that, boxed and ready to go. That winter I knew cocktail confidence, backed by lobster puff and truffled pouf, freshly removed from box. When I moved away, I turned in my swizzle stick.

"Hors d'oeuvre" might be fairly translated as "outside the work." A time when I feel entitled to overtime. Or time off. I'm not amused by hours of puffing and poufing.

The light bite should weigh lightly on the workload. Yet meet the demands of its job: Serve with one-handed, one-bite dispatch. Function independent of fork or plate. Prove easy to operate while holding drink and holding forth. It should report for duty neatly dressed. Tease, not trample, the tastebud.

This is why filo dough endures. The Greek (or Turkish) pastry staple must, by tradition, be stretched transparent under secretive conditions, far away. Perhaps in Greece (or Turkey). The cool smooth sheets, stacked and rolled like parchment, are sequestered in the freezer section, boxed and ready to go. No one, not even the tyrannical telechef, suggests DIY. Brushed with butter and wrapped around a spoonful of fresh this or spicy that, filo makes a minuscule meal. Thoroughly amusing. Even to the preoccupied prehostess.

Crisp Asparagus Rolls

Makes about 2 dozen spears

1 pound mid-sized asparagus

1 teaspoon olive oil

¼ teaspoon kosher salt

¼ teaspoon mustard seed

3 tablespoons freshly grated
   Parmesan cheese

¼ pound prosciutto,
   very thinly sliced

½ pound filo dough,
   defrosted

4 tablespoons butter, melted

1. Roast: Snap off the tough root ends of the asparagus and discard. Settle on a rimmed baking sheet. Drizzle with oil, sprinkle with salt and mustard seed. Slide into a 425-degree oven and roast bright green (but not thoroughly cooked), 10 minutes. Cool. May as well leave the oven on.

2. Wrap: Sprinkle asparagus with cheese. Shred proscuitto into long strips. Wrap one strip around each asparagus spear. No need for full coverage—aim for the demented candy-cane look.

3. Cut: Unroll filo dough. Cut a stack of 6 x 6-inch squares. Cover with a clean kitchen towel. Save any remaining filo for another project.

4. Fill: Brush one filo square with butter. Settle on 1 wrapped asparagus spear, running diagonally from corner to corner. Fold over filo, forming a triangle. Brush triangle with butter and roll up tightly. Brush again. Repeat with remaining spears.

5. Bake: Set finished spears on a rimmed baking sheet (feel free to reuse the asparagus sheet, no need to wash), no touching. Slide into a 425-degree oven and bake crispy, about 10 minutes. Arrange like sharpened pencils in a tall jar. Crunch.

TABLE SURFING

Do you like food? Do you dream of a place where everyone else likes food? Have you heard of California? Perhaps you never noticed it, far-left. Perhaps you— too sober for stargazing or sunshine—ignored it. Seriously, California is serious about food.

Book a flight to San Francisco. Refuse vile airplane snack. Take a cab directly to Chez Panisse in Berkeley. So what if it's postlunch and predinner? You need to wedge in as many meals as possible.

Order the seafood cakes and the chanterelle toast and the halibut with wispy green beans and fat yellow potatoes. Wonder how the plain potato can taste of earth, wind, and fire without anything so obvious as, say, sauce. Offer your underaged traveling companion the wide plate of pluot sherbet with gingersnaps. Twice.

Look up old friends. Let them lead you, gleefully, perhaps gloatingly, through their Oakland neighborhood, stocked with espresso bar and tapas bar and bar bar. Wander from bracingly minty drink to pickled sardine, garlic sausage, roasted pepper, and sumptuous crème caramel.

Sleep, happy as a fat potato. In the morning, aim for the Berkeley armory-turned-chocolate-factory. Order layer cake. For breakfast. Buy an enormous dark chocolate acorn filled with dark chocolate squirrels. Squirrel it away.

Walk, slack-jawed, the halls of the San Francisco Ferry Building, where the adorable meringue-topped cake flirts with stacks of creamy cheeses. Rush your sack of treasures back to Aunt Ruth's tiny, perfect garden, your home-away-from-home. Crack open the pungent cheese and chewy bread and brilliant apricot preserves and preserve, for one afternoon, perfection.

Even if you are suffused with satisfaction, press on. Steal out late for pork-stuffed dumplings and tender eggplant and ripe figs. It's not easy, cramming California into a single weekend.

Attend a long, sunny celebration in Daryn's long, sunny garden, that culminates in handmade bread and home-smoked salmon. Wonder why so few of your hometown habitués smoke their own.

Drop in on friends. Sit outside. Stare as they pluck tender lettuce leaf and red-gold tomato and toss together a sublime salad. Served, along with artichoke pizza, under the stars. Compose your expression into something resembling interest, if not tight-lipped envy, as they describe repeating this scene, all winter. Attempt nostalgia for the wind-bitten walk to Treasure Island.

Get up early. Take a cab to the airport. Don't even glance at the Peet's Coffee kiosk. Why stay alert for the long flight home?

California Ravioli

Serves 8

For filling:

1 medium butternut squash (about 2 pounds)

1 tablespoon plus 1 teaspoon olive oil

2 cloves garlic

¼ cup water

2 medium shallots, finely chopped

¼ cup grated Parmesan cheese

¼ teaspoon finely chopped fresh sage

¼ teaspoon kosher salt

⅛ teaspoon ground white pepper

⅛ teaspoon freshly grated nutmeg

⅛ teaspoon ground sage

For ravioli:

48 square wonton wrappers

Ingredients cont'd

1. **Roast:** Cut the squash in half lengthwise and rub each side with ½ teaspoon oil. Slip 1 clove garlic in among the seeds of each half. Settle the squash halves, cut-side down, in a roasting pan, pour in the water and slide into a 350-degree oven until tender, about 1 hour. When cool enough to handle, discard seeds. Scrape flesh and garlic into the food processor. Whirl smooth. Scrape into a medium mixing bowl.

2. **Soften:** Heat remaining 1 tablespoon oil in a small skillet set over medium heat. Add shallots and cook soft, 3 to 5 minutes. Stir shallots into the squash along with remaining filling ingredients. Taste for seasoning.

3. **Fill:** Heap 1 teaspoon filling in the center of a wonton wrapper. Brush wonton edges with water and fold into a triangle or rectangle, pressing firmly to prevent squash leakage. Set finished ravioli on a floured baking sheet and cover with a damp kitchen towel. Repeat, filling all wrappers.

4. **Whirl:** To make pesto: With clean food processor running, drop garlic down the chute, buzzing it to bits. Add spinach and basil; pulse a few times. With the machine running, slowly pour in the oil in a fine stream. Add black pepper and cheese.

For spinach pesto:

2 cloves garlic

2 cups spinach (or a mix
of arugula and parsley)

1 cup fresh basil leaves

½ cup olive oil

¼ teaspoon freshly ground
black pepper

⅔ cup grated Parmesan
cheese, plus more
for garnish

5. Boil: Bring a large, deep skillet of water to a simmer. Cook half the ravioli until they are hot in the center and float to the top, about 3 minutes. Scoop out with a slotted spoon. Repeat with remaining ravioli.

6. Serve: Spoon on just enough pesto to coat ravioli, mixing very gently. Sprinkle with Parmesan. Serve immediately.

PROVENANCE: *Adapted from* The New California Cook *by Diane Rossen Worthington.*

COME, SIT, STAY, EAT

Theo joined our family the indifferent sort. His interests centered on his bowl, which was often empty. And his stick, which was often lost.

The rest of the family—it seemed to us it seemed to him—served as waitstaff. Handy when the bowl was empty. Irrelevant when it was full.

Then the dog savant came to visit. She explained that we could develop a deeper relationship with our dog. We could bribe him.

Turns out that Theo is capable of learning language. "Theo," for instance, means: "I am about to offer you something delicious." From there we worked up to "Theo, come." And "Theo, sit." Shorthand for "a superb if regrettably small sliver of lamb."

This rudimentary vocabulary allowed us to establish an intimate connection with Theo. While he previously trained his attention on bowl and stick, now he focuses on us. He tries a variety of poses—sit, stare, imploring head tilt—hoping one will break the lamb lock.

Not that we always have a lamb handy. We don't need to. The dog savant says the dog can learn delayed gratification via a technique perfected in the secluded sections of Las Vegas. In this system the dog occasionally wins big—say, the whole leg of lamb. And, replaying this happy memory, is willing to bet that one of these "come" or "sit" expeditions will score big, again. Apparently this hope will keep the dog focused for years.

We know the feeling. The happy memory of certain meals—years past—keeps us doggedly repeating the same recipe. Plum ice cream churned thick and pink always conjures a scene of sticky sidewalk hopscotch. That fragrant couscous, the one with the tomatoes and the fresh herbs, always scents the kitchen sunny. Once its bright cilantro and warm cumin tasted of sophistication and independence. Now, even with a mint update, it's soothingly familiar.

At dinnertime, we come. We sit. We stay for something delicious, something that fetches memories of meals past. Happily gnawing on a stick of grilled lamb, hunched over a jackpot of couscous, we know that in our family, we all speak the same language.

Summer Couscous

Serves 4

1/4 cup olive oil

3 tablespoons red wine
vinegar

4 cloves garlic,
finely chopped

Zest of 1 orange

1/4 cup freshly squeezed
orange juice

1 1/2 teaspoons ground cumin

1 teaspoon kosher salt

1/8 teaspoon freshly ground
black pepper

1/8 teaspoon cayenne pepper

1 1/2 pounds boneless leg
of lamb, cut into
1 1/2-inch cubes

2 tomatoes, diced

1/2 cup coarsely chopped
mix of fresh mint, cilantro,
and parsley

1 cup water

1 cup couscous

1. Marinate: In a small bowl whisk together oil, vinegar, garlic, zest, juice, cumin, salt, and peppers. Pour half this marinade over the lamb chunks. Cover (or seal in a plastic bag) and marinate, 1 to 24 hours.

2. Toss: In a large bowl, toss tomatoes, herbs, and remaining marinade. Let rest at room temperature while you prepare the couscous.

3. Fluff: Bring water to a boil in a small saucepan. Add couscous. Stir. Cover. Remove from heat. Let rest 5 minutes. Fluff with a fork. Add to the tomato mix.

4. Grill: Heat the grill (or broiler) to high. Thread lamb onto 4 skewers (if using wooden skewers, first soak them in cold water). Grill until just done, 3 to 4 minutes per side for medium rare.

5. Serve: Mound couscous salad onto four plates. Add a skewer of lamb. Enjoy.

PROVENANCE: *Inspired by Pierre Franey.*

NOODLES *AND* SYMPATHY

Should disaster strike, make lasagna. You may not know the disconsolate well. You may not know his family. But you know the situation calls for lasagna.

Not that a square of noodles can compose the moving tribute or compile the stack of bittersweet memories. Lasagna offers something simpler: cheese-cushioned, sauce-soothed empathy.

You're aware, of course, that customs change. That the memorial service can now be celebrated in navy or burgundy, as well as black. That the trend favors hearty appreciation over outraged lament. And yet, in the somber days after a loss, condolence is still welcome in the form of lasagna.

Lasagna has long been happy to keep the large family cheese-stuffed. To anchor the hot white plates at the red-sauce restaurant. And yet, it's best known as the International Casserole of Mourning.

Work that suits it well. Lasagna is accommodating. It's patient with the far-fetched substitution. Tolerant of the expired timer. Perhaps even enhanced by the crispy top of neglect. Lasagna finishes its kitchen tour in a single pan. It's convenient to transport, heat, freeze, or ignore, all in the same container.

Lasagna is sturdy. It can loaf in the fridge for days, only to improve. It's hearty. One nutrient-dense square keeps the tearful on task all day. The lovesick may be too anxious to eat. But the heartsick are grateful for ballast.

Lasagna is calm. No strident arugula or showy venison scampers its terrain, expecting someone to admire its lean profile and strong flavors. Lasagna sticks with soothingly bland ricotta.

None of which sullies its reputation. Though lasagna is linked with distress, it carries no taboo. Lasagna is welcome—even expected—at the potluck, housewarming, and farewell party.

Maybe lasagna comforts because it shares so much with the pillow—soft, thick, and given to giving. Even the distraught who finds his freezer cramped to lasagna capacity will accept surplus. Commiseration loves company.

Lasagna

Serves 6

15 ounces ricotta cheese

3 tablespoons chopped fresh herbs such as basil, parsley, and thyme

1 clove garlic, chopped

Kosher salt and freshly ground black pepper

½ pound fresh mozzarella, grated

¼ pound Parmesan cheese, grated

Olive oil

3 cups tomato sauce, your favorite or mine (recipe follows)

½ pound lasagna noodles*

1. Prep: Defying convention, choose an 8 x 8-inch oven-safe pan (the off-duty brownie pan is perfect). Though lasagna traditionally fills a 13 x 9-inch pan, the noodle-to-surface-area ratio is so annoying that even the geometrist gives up in tears.

2. Mix: Stir together ricotta, herbs, and garlic. Season with salt and pepper. In a small bowl, toss mozzarella and Parmesan.

3. Layer: Lightly oil the pan. Spread ½ cup sauce across the bottom. Neatly lay in 3 noodles. Spread on ½ cup sauce. Spoon one-third of the ricotta mixture. Scatter on one-fourth of the grated cheeses. Make two more layers following the noodle, sauce, ricotta, grated cheese pattern. (For sturdy construction, alternate the noodle orientation from east-west to north-south.) End with a final layer of noodles, the remaining sauce, and grated cheese.

4. Bake: Cover with foil and slide into a 350-degree oven for 40 minutes. If you like a crunchy top, remove the foil during the last 15 minutes of baking. Let rest a few minutes. Serve hot or warm.

*Fresh lasagna noodles deserve gratitude, not precooking. Dried noodles should be boiled just until pliable, about 4 minutes. Drain. Rinse under cool water. Avoid "no cook" noodles.

Sweet Tomato Sauce

Makes about 3 cups

Melt 4 tablespoons unsalted butter in a medium skillet over medium-low heat. Add 1 finely chopped onion and cook until soft, 10 minutes. Pour in 1 (28-ounce) can whole tomatoes in juice (first run through the blender). Toss in 10 fresh basil leaves (slivered), and kosher salt and freshly ground black pepper. Cook, stirring now and then, 20 to 30 minutes. Purée.

PROVENANCE: *Sauce adapted from* Verdura *by Viana La Place*

THE JOY ⅇ𝒻 JOY

Early in my cooking career, I relied heavily on *Joy of Cooking*. Especially for banana bread. Not that it was hard to come by a banana bread recipe. Home cooks were always passing along 3 x 5 cards that forced the honest loaf into dried-apricot and wheat-germ smuggling.

Not *Joy*. *Joy's* banana bread rose high in the pan. It had a crisp crust and a tender crumb that achieved the ideal balance of levity and intensity. Not as compact as pound cake nor as frivolous as the biscuit. It had the perfect texture: banana bread texture.

One afternoon while on duty at the junior-high library, I got to discussing banana bread with the actual librarian. Demonstrating my reference skills, I turned to the cookbook shelf, pulled down *Joy*, and flipped to page 536. Not banana bread. Cottage cheese. This was not the *Joy* that presided over my mom's kitchen. This was another *Joy*. One with different ideas about banana bread.

Right there in front of Dewey Decimal tab 641.5 the truth was revealed to me: *Joy of Cooking* is not an immutable text, like the Ten Commandments. It changes.

Since then I've come to appreciate the nuances of *Joy of Cooking*. I like the way the copyright page dates a marriage. I respect 1953's forthright explanation of turtle soup, which begins: "Cut off the head of a snapping or soft-shelled turtle." I like 1975's knowing instructions for culturing yogurt and 1997's breezy way with balsamic. Some readers thought that edition suffered from too many chefs. But I like it for what it is—a shiny mirror mounted above the American stove.

Now we had a new bundle of *Joy*. The 75th anniversary edition sought to regain the warmth and candor of 1975, which, with its Brownies Cockaigne and Rombauer specials, read like a stack of 3 x 5 cards passed along from Irma S. Rombauer herself. I had assumed, vaguely, that Cockaigne was a family name, but by finally reading the author's note learned it's a mythic land of mythic importance to the Rombauer family.

Happily, the new *Joy* retained its staunch defense of the cocktail party. Unhappily, it lost patience with the lumpy gingerbread man. But the book revived quite a few old favorites, lightly edited for modern times, including Banana Bread Cockaigne.

Banana Bread

Makes 1 loaf

1. Blend until creamy:

⅓ cup vegetable shortening

½ cup sugar

¾ teaspoon finely grated lemon zest

2. Beat in:

1 egg, lightly beaten

3. Sift before measuring:

1¾ cups flour

4. Resift with:

1½ teaspoons baking powder

¼ teaspoon baking soda

5. Mash 2 or 3 ripe bananas to make:

1 cup banana pulp

Add the sifted ingredients in 3 parts to the sugar mixture alternately with the banana pulp. Beat the batter after each addition until smooth. Scrape into a buttered loaf pan, about 9 x 5 x 3 inches. Spread smooth.

6. Scatter on: ½ cup chopped walnuts

Bake at 350 degrees until brown on top and done in the center (poke with a tooth-pick; it should come out clean), about 50-55 minutes.

PROVENANCE: *Adapted from* Joy of Cooking, *1954 edition.*

A SIMPLE SOLUTION

Simple can be simply dreadful. Simple propaganda lurks on the magazine cover, best-seller table, and annoying pop-up promotion: Declutter, deacquisition, desist. Mottos that are supposed to relieve the over-worked and overwhelmed. But don't.

Not that you would fall for the sweeping clean-sweep suggested by one site: Toss the obsolete sweater, software, and spouse. You'd never attempt the

15-minute kitchen, closet, or career renovation. But you frown with interest over one novel thought: breezy brunch.

Dispensing with hard-boiled skepticism, you try over-easy. Striving for simple, you don't scramble to dust or mop. You poach a tablecloth from the iron-later rumple. You barely crack a cookbook. With sunny-side-up optimism, you settle for two recipes: frittata, the same one you've been puffing for, well, ever. And potato, cut and crisped.

You puff egg. You crisp potato. You wave your guests inside. They sit. They study rumple and puff and crisp, at some remove. Soon you find yourself back in the kitchen, hurrying English muffin from freezer to toaster. Simply humiliating.

Later, when you declutter enough to locate that simple-minded magazine, you de-acquisition it. Savagely.

You realize you like complicated. Maybe not bacon-on-a-swing complicated. Not spear-it-and-cure-it-yourself complicated. But at very least the carefully selected and beautifully composed cheese-plate complicated.

With gravlax, perhaps. Each sliver curled into a pink ribbon promoting smoked-salmon awareness. Reclining on a spotty backdrop of lemon slices. Accompanied by a handsome smoked trout, swimming happily across its freshwater pond, tangling now and then with a translucently thin tomato slice or a delicate ring of red onion. A thicket of salt-poached asparagus undulates below. Distractions dart here and there: a few robust olives, a couple of fiery jalapeños and a handful of tiny tomatoes, some sliced, some whole, peppered and shiny with lemon-sharp vinaigrette.

Warm bagels, of course. A cool salad, perhaps. And wedges of tortilla española— that masterpiece of ordinary staples rendered extraordinary. Tender potato disks and melted onions layered into eggs fend off the perils of a light lunch.

A heap of strawberries rounds things out, along with a deep bowl of crème fraîche and a wide, sunny lemon tart.

Not breezy. Downright cloudy with complication. Affording its own simplicity: nothing left over to de-acquisition.

Tortilla Española*

Serves 4

2 pounds waxy potatoes (such as Yukon Gold), peeled

2¼ teaspoons kosher salt

1½ cups olive oil

2 onions, chopped

5 cloves garlic, chopped

6 eggs

⅛ teaspoon freshly ground black pepper

1. Slice: Using a mandoline or a sharp knife and patience, slice the potatoes into ⅛-inch disks. Toss with 2 teaspoons salt.

2. Soften: Heat half the oil in a well-seasoned (or nonstick) 8-inch skillet. Add the onions and garlic. Cook until soft, but not browned, about 8 minutes.

3. Sizzle: At the same time, heat half the oil in another medium skillet. Slide in potatoes. Sizzle over medium heat until tender, about 10 minutes.

4. Drain: Set a sieve over a bowl. Drain onions and potatoes. (Later you can strain and save the delicious oil for other projects.)

5. Rest: In a large bowl, beat eggs, remaining ¼ teaspoon salt, and pepper. Add drained potatoes, onion, and garlic and mix gently. Let rest 10 minutes.

6. Set: Heat 1 tablespoon reserved oil in the 8-inch skillet over medium heat. Pour in the potato-and-egg mixture. Cook, shaking now and then, until the eggs are set at the edges and the tortilla easily slips around in the pan, about 8 minutes.

7. Flip: Set a wide, flat plate upside down over the pan. Holding pan and plate securely together, flip tortilla onto plate. Set the pan back on the heat. Add 1 tablespoon reserved oil. Slide the tortilla back into pan (uncooked side down). Tuck the edges under to achieve the Frisbee look.

8. Test: Cook until a toothpick stabbed in the center comes out clean, about 5 minutes. Slide onto a platter and cool at least 10 minutes. Serve warm or room temperature, cut into wedges.

*Tortilla, as in "little cake," in this case a cake of potato and egg, not tortilla as in the taco wrapper.

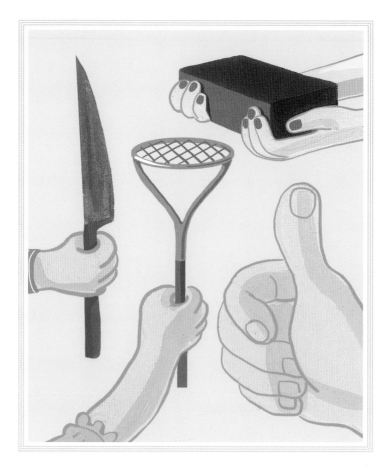

CHEZ NOUS

Family dinner is alleged to bolster SAT scores, lower blood pressure, and foster world peace. Which seems likely, if hard to track. At our table, no one has ever administered a standardized test, blood screen, or peace prize. Still, we persist in eating dinner, every night. After all, what's the alternative?

One lazy weekend we changed things up. "Let's all cook together," Noah demanded. "Everyone makes one dish." Ingenious—coming as it did from the sole member of the kitchen brigade who had yet to master toast. Noah called mashed potatoes. Hannah settled on Brussels sprouts. Bob took chicken under a brick. I offered to expedite.

My youngest mashed with abandon. My big girl worked the big knife. My husband found a 45-minute recipe, then found 45 minutes of distraction in the basement. Sighing, I expedited the chicken into the pan and applied the brick.

Eventually we all sat down to a family-cooked family dinner. The legumier pronounced his work scrumptious. The saucier declared her sprouts a triumph. The dad de cuisine, persistent perfectionist, critiqued "his" chicken, which he felt should have been squished flatter, cooked longer, and finished crispier. Close enough, I decided, to high-scoring, low-pressure, and peaceful.

Chicks 'n' Bricks

Serves 2 adults and 2 children

1 (3-pound) chicken

3 tablespoons olive oil

2 tablespoons fresh
lemon juice

2 teaspoons fresh
thyme leaves

1 teaspoon fresh
rosemary leaves

1 clove garlic, smashed

1 teaspoon kosher salt

¼ teaspoon freshly ground
black pepper

1. **Smash:** Set the chicken, breast-side down, on a cutting board. Using poultry shears, cut along each side of the backbone. Remove and discard (or freeze) backbone. Flip the chicken over, open, and flatten by pressing with the heel of your hand. Soak 1 minute in a pot of cold salted water. Rinse and pat dry.

2. **Marinate:** Mix 2 tablespoons oil with remaining ingredients. Rub marinade into the chicken, then slip chicken and any remaining marinade into a zip-top bag. Chill 1 hour or more.

3. **Crisp:** Heat remaining oil in a large heavy skillet (cast-iron would be ideal) over medium. Settle chicken in hot pan, skin-side down. Weight down with two bricks wrapped in foil, side by side. Let sizzle, undisturbed, until skin is deep brown and chicken is half cooked, about 20 minutes. Flip chicken. Do not weight this side with bricks—that would sog the crisp crust. Let sizzle until meat is cooked through and the inner thigh registers 165 degrees, about 20 more minutes. Munch hot or warm.

SCOUT'S HONOR

The girl seeking wide horizons is advised to join the Girl Scouts. I wasn't really the military type, but thought it might merit the risks. Join up. Wear a uniform. Promise to be loyal, useful, friendly, courteous, obedient, thrifty, cheerful, and clean. Eventually, they'd assign me cookie detail. By then I'd have security clearance. I would access the recipe for the Thin Mint.

I visited my local recruiting office, next to the principal's suite. Only to learn that at seven the girl isn't eligible for Girl Scouts. She has to serve in a lesser unit, the Brownies, and endure the humiliation of the brown uniform.

Our troop trained in the Multipurpose Room. Our sergeant wore a bunny-pink cardigan and spoke in a bunny-soft whisper. Nothing like what I'd seen on M*A*S*H.

Our first drill had us on the floor in a circle, legs crossed. We each received a supply kit: one sour, empty, 8-ounce milk carton; one handful of bunny-pink cotton balls; one glue bottle. Our task: glue balls to carton, add eyes, admire bunny-pink bunny. No one mentioned the Thin Mint.

I accepted an honorable discharge.

Still, I pressed on with my mission. At cookie season I placed my Thin Mint order with an enlisted girl. I paged through cookbooks. I experimented with crushed candy cane and chocolate bar.

I got distracted by cookies of higher rank. The Oreo, commander of the mass-produced forces. The chocolate chip, general of the home-baked services. The madeleine, admiral of the literary fleet.

One Chicago afternoon I dropped by Angel Food Bakery, lured by chef Stephanie Samuels' collection of Easy-Bake Ovens. There in the case stood a row of Thin Mints. Not rank-and-file Thin Mints, but ones with a lump of sumptuous ganache slipped between cocoa wafer and chocolate coat.

I requisitioned the recipe. Samuels didn't inspect my uniform or perform a badge count. Accepting that enthusiasm for chocolate and mint and crunch conferred sufficient rank, she passed over the document. I crammed the recipe into my jeans pocket. I always knew I belonged in civvies.

Thick and Thin Mints

Makes about 100 2-inch cookies

10 tablespoons (1 stick plus 2 tablespoons) unsalted butter, softened

1 cup sugar

1 egg

1 teaspoon vanilla extract

2 teaspoons peppermint extract

1½ cups flour

5 tablespoons Dutch-process cocoa powder

½ teaspoon baking soda

⅛ teaspoon fine salt

1 pound semisweet chocolate, chopped

1 cup heavy whipping cream

1 pound bittersweet chocolate, chopped

2 tablespoons vegetable oil

1. Fluff: Use a stand mixer fitted with the paddle attachment to cream butter and sugar until pale and fluffy. Beat in egg, vanilla extract, and 1 teaspoon peppermint extract.

2. Mix: Sift in flour, cocoa, soda, and salt. Mix thoroughly.

3. Chill: Pat into four disks. Wrap in plastic and chill at least 2 hours.

4. Roll: On a well-floured surface, roll out one dough disk to ⅛-inch thin. Punch out 2-inch circles with a cookie cutter. Repeat with remaining dough, rerolling once.

5. Bake: Settle rounds on a parchment-paper-lined baking sheet, 1 inch apart. Prick each with a fork. Slide into a 350-degree oven and bake until set, 10 to 12 minutes. Cool.

6. Whisk: Tumble semisweet chocolate into a medium bowl. Bring cream to a boil; pour over chocolate. Let rest, 5 minutes. Whisk smooth. Add remaining 1 teaspoon peppermint extract. Let this mint ganache cool.

7. Fill: Pile ganache into a zip-top bag. Snip one corner. Squeeze a squiggle of ganache down the center of each cookie. Let set.

8. Melt: Heap bittersweet chocolate into a saucepan. Melt over low heat with vegetable oil. Let this chocolate coating cool slightly.

9. Coat: Holding one cookie by its edges, dip, ganache-side down, in coating. Flip cookie and set it on its flat side. Repeat, dipping all cookies. Chill. Serve cold or room temperature.

SLICE *of* LIFE

We packed lightly for the trip home. Sweaters. Boots. And the standard half-empty satchel of good intentions. We'd meant to wrap up a 50-year Cognac. My parents had that many miles on their marriage.

The baby cousins toddled from blocks to high chair chanting, "No, no, no." The teenagers slumped by the screen sulking, "No no no." The mid-sized shuttled between the two, asking, "Now now now?"

We cooked. We ate. We kicked the soccer ball. We looked at art and looked up friends. We loafed.

My childhood home was once shelter to two parents, two brothers, three cats, two goats, one dog, uncounted goldfish, and the itinerant rabbit or graduate student. Now it held two grandparents and many, many things.

We'd be cooking and need a stockpot. We'd pry open a cabinet, spelunk its darkest corners and stumble on some neglected curiosity. A fish-shaped fish flipper. Or a wooden bread bowl, circa 1972. Barely used. It was a throwback to the days of honey whole-wheat. "Remember when we used to bake bread?" Mom asked. She handed me the bowl. "Yours."

Maybe I'll put it to work. Like everyone, I'm crazy about the recipe that calls for no fancy ingredients, just time. Stir, ignore, and bake up a crusty loaf that looks fresh off the red-eye from Paris.

One day, maybe when my marriage has earned a decent Cognac, I'll pass off the bowl to my girl, the one stranded between the frowning little cousins and the sullen big ones. The one trying to cajole both sets into a game of checkers. "Remember when we used to bake bread?" I'll ask. "Here," I'll say: "Yours."

Ricotta-Stuffed Focaccia

No-knead bread, in all its simplicity, is explained in *Artisan Bread in Five Minutes a Day* by Jeff Hertzberg and Zoë François. Here I use the book's Simple Bread Dough to bake a puff (like a giant pita), then split it and fill it with ricotta. The construction was inspired by Avec, in Chicago.

Serves 4 as an appetizer

1 pound Simple Bread
    Dough (recipe follows)

Flour

Olive oil

1 cup ricotta cheese

1 ounce Taleggio cheese

2 teaspoons fresh
    rosemary leaves

1 teaspoon fresh
    thyme leaves

Truffle-scented salt

1. Roll: Sprinkle a little flour over refrigerated dough. Grab a 1-pound hunk, about the size of a grapefruit. Sprinkle with a bit more flour. Quickly smooth the top over and tuck ragged ends under, forming a ball. Set it on a lightly floured work surface. Roll with a lightly floured rolling pin into a 12-inch circle, ⅛-inch thick.

2. Bake: Brush a baking sheet with olive oil. Roll dough around the rolling pin and unroll it onto the baking sheet. Brush dough with a little olive oil and slide into a 500-degree oven. Bake until golden and puffed, about 7 minutes.

3. Swirl: Meanwhile, swirl ricotta, Taleggio, and herbs together in the food processor.

4. Fill: Use a serrated knife to split the pizza puff along its perimeter, separating top from bottom, English-muffin style. Be careful of escaping steam. Spread bottom with ricotta mixture. Return top, pressing gently to adhere layers.

5. Serve: Brush top with olive oil. Sprinkle on truffle salt. Use a pizza cutter to slice into small squares. Serve warm.

Simple Bread Dough

Makes 4 pounds

3 cups lukewarm water

1½ tablespoons active
   dry yeast

1½ tablespoons kosher salt

6½ cups flour

1. **Mix:** In a large bowl mix water, yeast, and salt. Add all the flour. Stir until moist, about 1 minute. No kneading necessary.

2. **Rest:** Cover (not airtight) and let dough rise at room temperature until it begins to collapse, about 2 hours (or ignore up to 5 hours). Use dough now or refrigerate (covered, not airtight) up to 14 days.

LUCKY CHARMS

ood luck lurks in the unlikely corner. My children rely on backward pajamas, stray ladybugs, first stars. I depend on a rear-view mirror mummy who keeps my passengers safe and driving record clean. I also believe any fortune-cookie fortune I like. The one magnet-mashed to the fridge swears I'll get everything I want.

Still, it's good to have back up. Luck snaps from the wishbone. It twists through long-life noodles. It clinks in coin-shaped carrots. Luck clings thick to black-eyed peas.

I learned this at a party dominated by a platter of peas, staring their black-eyed stare. "Good luck," the hostess insisted. After a bowl or two I knew I wanted the recipe. As my fortune promises, I got it.

My scientific side wondered about the pea's power. After some study I concluded that the luck emanated, precisely, from bacon fat. Good indeed.

Good-Luck Peas

Serves a small party

½ pound dried
    black-eyed peas

½ pound bacon, frozen
    and diced

8 jalapeño peppers,
    stemmed and seeded

2 cloves garlic

2 stalks celery, cut up

1 onion, cut up

½ bell pepper, any color,
    cut up

1½ cups canned
    crushed tomatoes

2 cups chicken broth

Ingredients cont'd

1. Soak: Rinse beans, pulling out any suspicious-looking specks. Scrape into a medium pot and douse with cold water to cover by 2 inches. Bring to a boil. Cover. Turn off heat. Let soak 45 minutes.

2. Crisp: Heat a medium Dutch oven over medium. When hot, scatter in bacon and cook, stirring, until crisp and brown, about 4 minutes. Scoop out and drain on paper towels. Carefully pour bacon fat into a heatproof measuring cup. Set aside.

3. Soften: Toss jalapeños, garlic, celery, onion, and bell pepper into the food processor and pulse to bits. Return 1 tablespoon bacon fat to the pan. Heat over medium. Add chopped vegetables and cook soft, about 5 minutes.

4. Simmer: Pour in tomatoes, broth, pepper sauce, salt, pepper, sugar, and nutmeg. Drain and rinse

1 tablespoon red pepper
sauce (such as Tabasco)

1 teaspoon kosher salt

1 teaspoon freshly ground
black pepper

1 teaspoon sugar

A few grates of nutmeg

3 tablespoons flour

soaked peas. Add to sauce. Simmer uncovered, stirring occasionally, until flavorful, 45 minutes.

5. Thicken: Make a rough roux by stirring flour into remaining 3 or so tablespoons bacon fat. Stir this mixture into the peas and cook until thick, about 5 minutes. Cool slightly (better yet, refrigerate and gently reheat the next day). Scatter on reserved bacon.

6. Serve: Makes an excellent warm dip for sturdy chips or, heaped alongside rice, a lucky version of that southern classic, Hoppin' John.

PROVENANCE: *Adapted from* Best of the Best From Texas *by way of my friend Mary Keen.*

Chapter 4: Shake

Everything about my life surprised me. I couldn't believe we lived in Baltimore. I couldn't believe I worked from home. I couldn't believe I got breast cancer.

My first thought was: We have to renovate.

When we'd moved into our house, our plan was to redo the worn-out bathrooms, the crumbling kitchen, and the uninhabitable third floor. A year and a half later, our house still had "lots of potential."

Once I figured out I was in for lots of treatment, I figured we'd need a live-in sitter. And to live in, she'd need somewhere to live. So, while I cycled through surgery, chemo, radiation, and reconstruction, I managed the renovation of the third floor. It took a long time and came out somewhat lopsided. But then, so did all that reconstruction.

The night before my first surgery Amy brought over an amulet. A friend of her sister's had worn it during her surgery. As did Amy. As would I. It helped.

In the beginning, Rachel offered to set up a dinner delivery round robin. I told her not to bother. Alison warned I'd miss six weeks of work. I doubted it. Mom worried about the summer trip to Italy. It was only January; I assured her we'd make it.

We still felt new in town. Friends came from Berkeley and Boulder and Brooklyn to hold my hand. They sent flowers and books and frozen peas. Thanks to Rachel, our Baltimore friends (and colleagues and neighbors and mere acquaintances) made us dinner, every night.

By the time I felt steady enough to send the amulet on to Lavea, the au pair arrived.

Early in my food-writing days, I learned that creating recipes and feeding a family were different tasks. One I did during the day, with pencil and measuring tape and timer. The other I did in the evening, with conversation or a glass of wine. One called for lots of feedback. The other did not.

Once in a while (say, when I was behind schedule), we'd end up testing a dish at the dinner table. That happened the au pair's first night. Everyone took a bite of potatoes and jumped in—too oily, too salty, too brown. Cynthia, fresh from Costa Rica, wore a look that needed no translation.

A year after my diagnosis, I returned to work. The *Tribune* put my picture on the front page. What a welcome home.

DOWN TIME

lost a lot that year. Some body parts. Ones largely considered decorative and yet—I had thought—mine. Also my hair. My patience. My habit of wandering the kitchen tied into an apron.

I gained a lot that year. Time with old friends. Time for new friends. Gratitude for understanding colleagues and generous neighbors. Even my dog's best friend's human made us dinner, a paella so delicious it kept my husband smiling for a week.

I expanded my pillow collection. I scowled at bad movies and smirked at bad jokes and shrugged at bad thoughts. Superstition, I decided, neither causes nor cures. I carried on a passionate affair with my laptop. I brought it to bed and never let it leave.

Mostly I hoped for the best.

It wasn't much of a culinary vacation. I ate soup in the hospital and buttered toast back home. I ate ice cubes at chemo and popsicles back home. I ate nothing at radiation and nothing microwaved back home. I ate many, many little white tablets.

I served my children mac 'n' cheese, which they found neglectful. I served my children fabulous, friend-made meals—venison chili, corn chowder, lentil stew— which they boycotted. They wanted made-by-me.

Following orders, I drank a lot of water. Following habit, I drank a lot of coffee. Following treatment, I drank a lot of Champagne.

Then I made that paella.

Paella is simple fare complicated by superstition. Never cooked indoors, only out. Never by women, only men. Never in a skillet, only a paella pan. Never for dinner, only lunch.

Surveying my midafternoon kitchen I found no bonfire, no man, no pan. I shrugged and gave the recipe a try. I chopped and grated and stirred. I pushed around the rice and saffron and sausage. My paella steamed hot and fragrant and soggily overcooked. I set it on the table, hoping for the best. My children found it fantastic: It was accompanied by me, in apron.

Garden-Party Paella

This recipe is designed to be cooked in a thin outdoor paella pan (about 17 inches across), on a kettle grill (at least 21 inches), outside. Lacking pan, grill, or outdoors, use a wide, heavy skillet on the stove.

Serves 8

½ cup olive oil

1 pound medium shrimp, peeled and deveined (tails left on is a nice look) under a bag of ice

Bag A:

6 ounces fresh chorizo sausage, casing removed (or smoked chorizo sausage, sliced)

1 onion, chopped

4 cloves garlic, chopped

2 red bell peppers, chopped

Bag B:

1 (14-ounce) can plum tomatoes, with juice, run through the blender

2 tablespoons chopped fresh parsley

1 tablespoon sugar

1 teaspoon kosher salt

1 teaspoon ground turmeric

½ teaspoon saffron threads

½ teaspoon dried oregano

½ teaspoon smoked paprika

¼ teaspoon freshly ground black pepper

1 bay leaf

1 sprig fresh rosemary

1. **Pack:** You will be working outside, so pack accordingly. Leave shrimp and clams in the fridge until you need them. Arrange all the other ingredients on a tray. Bring along a wooden spatula, an extra plate, some foil, extra salt, and smoked paprika. Slip the phone, set to timer mode, in a pocket.

2. **Ignite:** Set a chimney starter on the lower grate of a kettle grill. Use it to light a stack of charcoal chunks or briquettes. Let burn until the top is light gray with ash, about 30 minutes. Pull on insulated barbeque mitts and carefully pour hot charcoal onto the grate. Use sturdy tools to spread out coals. Return the top grate. Set a wide outdoor paella pan on top.

3. **Sizzle:** Pour oil into the pan. When hot, add the shrimp and cook, stirring with the wooden spatula, until just curled and pink, about 3 minutes. Scoop out shrimp onto the plate, season with some salt and paprika. Cover loosely with foil and set aside.

4. **Soften:** Slide contents of Bag A into the pan. Cook, stirring, until sausage is cooked and crumbled and onion softened, about 10 minutes.

5. **Thicken:** Slide in contents of Bag B. Cook until much of the liquid has disappeared, about 10 minutes. This sofrito of softened vegetables will flavor the rice.

6. **Plump:** Stir in rice. Pour in 4 cups hot broth. Stir. From here on out, no stirring. Traditional paella is cooked in a single thin layer, forming a nice brown bottom crust. Let cook, 15 minutes. Sprinkle on ham;

2 cups short- or medium-
grain rice (Spanish Bomba
is traditional, but Italian
Arborio works nicely)

6 cups chicken broth, hot,
in a thermos

2 cups diced cooked ham

16 small clams, scrubbed,
in a colander, under
a bag of ice

1 lemon, cut into wedges

press into rice with the back of the spatula. Cook 10 minutes. Taste rice. If it's dry, drizzle on about 1 cup remaining broth. Keep cooking, uncovered, until rice turns tender, about 10 minutes.

7. Steam: Nestle clams into the rice, hinge-side down. Drizzle in about 1 cup remaining broth. Scatter on cooked shrimp. Cover pan tightly with foil. Cover grill and cook until clams steam open and shrimp are hot, about 5 minutes. Discard bay leaf and rosemary. Spritz everything with lemon. Heave pan onto the table. In the paella tradition, hand out forks; no plates necessary. Dig in.

FOREIGN EXCHANGE

Au pair, the agency explained, means on par. As in equal. The girl who showed up, wobbily supported by spiked heels and broken English, was not our equal. She was far more capable. For instance, she woke at dawn. Packed the lunchbox, located missing sock and violin, played a vicious game of hide-and-seek, and made coffee. She was a marvel.

In return we offered her room, board, stipend, and a chance to study our national habits. She was duly stunned by the eight-lane expressway, the wide-open terrain of the megastore, leafless winter tree, and peanut butter. Especially peanut butter. On toast, apple, tortilla, fork, or finger.

We introduced her to other novelties. Craisin. Bagel. Leftover. "Leff-obar?" she lilted. "This is American food?"

The leftover, we explained, isn't simply left over. It's not until a meal has been constructed from the building blocks of previous culinary achievements that a dish rises to the level of leftover. Consider the classics: Dagwood sandwich. Chicken pot pie. Meatloaf.

Nor is every leftover mere happy happenstance. Like the outlet mall and the remaindered bookstore, the leftover industry deals in duplicity. There are whole cookbooks devoted to the promise of "cook once, eat all week." Whole families, as Calvin Trillin would have it, that eat nothing but. Whole holidays designed as prelude to turkey-on-rye.

"In my country," the au pair frowned, "we have no leff-obar."

Then one morning, culture was exchanged, right in our kitchen. Faced with a tubful of remaindered roast turkey, the au pair paired old with new and made something novel: the turkey empanada.

The hot pocket, crisp on the outside, savory and juicy inside, achieved the highest standard of leftover—not merely on par with the original, but even more capable. The girl in heels looked pleased, patting reheated turkey into a fresh circle of masa. Surely it qualified her for citizenship.

Cross-Cultural Empanada

Makes 10

Vegetable oil

¼ cup finely chopped
red pepper

¼ cup finely chopped onion

2 tablespoons finely
chopped fresh cilantro

1 tablespoon finely
chopped celery

1 clove garlic, chopped

2 cups shredded cooked
turkey

1 tablespoon Salsa Lizano or
steak sauce

1 teaspoon kosher salt

1 pinch turmeric

3 cups instant corn masa

2 to 2½ cups water

Shredded cabbage, optional

1. Soften: In a medium saucepan, heat 2 tablespoons oil over medium heat. Add pepper, onion, cilantro, celery, and garlic. Cook until fragrant, about 2 minutes.

2. Sizzle: Add turkey, sauce, ½ teaspoon salt, and turmeric. Cook until sticky, about 5 minutes. Let cool.

3. Knead: Measure masa and remaining ½ teaspoon salt into a medium mixing bowl. Add water slowly, kneading the mixture with your hands, until dough feels like fresh play dough. Divide and roll into 10 balls. Cover with a kitchen towel.

4. Roll: Snip off the business end of a quart-sized zip-top bag. Cut along the sides and unfold it. Roll one ball of dough between your palms for several seconds. Place the dough ball on the plastic ex-bag. Pat and turn until the circle of dough is 6 inches in diameter. Use flat fingers of one hand for the patting, and curved fingers of the other hand to shape the edge.

5. Fill: Spread 1 to 2 heaping tablespoons of turkey mixture across the diameter of the circle. Use the plastic to lift and fold the dough into a semicircle. Press gently to seal the edges. Repeat with remaining dough and filling, keeping finished empanadas covered with a clean kitchen towel.

6. Fry: Pour oil into a medium skillet to a depth of ¼ inch. Heat over medium-high. Fry empanadas two at a time until crisp and golden, 2 minutes per side. Slice open on seam and stuff in cabbage, if you like. Munch while hot.

ON THE LOOSE

Teens run away. They have their reasons. At fourteen, Grace and I ran away because her parents wouldn't let us smash the foundation of their home.

We had spent many an after-school afternoon at the historical society, tracing the path of the underground railroad. For reasons that escape me now, we were convinced the railroad once stopped in her basement. We were certain that if we smashed the right stones, we'd uncover evidence.

Our way of running away was to walk to Hancher Auditorium and watch Merce Cunningham tangle up on stage. Then we walked to Nicole's.

Nicole had been to Europe; she could pronounce carbonara and pancetta. She boiled a cauldron of spaghetti and heaved it onto the Formica. She pelted the noodles with bits of bacon. Then, to my amazement, she cracked in an egg. This was not a recipe found in the *Betty Crocker's Cookbook for Boys and Girls*.

We stabbed and twirled. The tangle tasted both daring and reassuring. Like running away, then calling home.

Runaway Pasta

Serves 6

2 eggs*

½ cup grated
   Romano cheese

½ cup grated Parmigiano-
   Reggiano cheese

Freshly ground black pepper

2 tablespoons chopped
   fresh parsley

3 tablespoons olive oil

4 cloves garlic, smashed

½ pound pancetta, diced

¼ cup dry white wine

1 pound spaghetti

1. Whisk: Crack eggs into a small bowl and whisk briefly. Stir in cheeses, pepper, and parsley.

2. Toast: Pour oil into a small skillet. Settle garlic in oil; toast over medium-high heat until golden, 5 minutes. Discard garlic.

3. Crisp: Tumble pancetta into the fragrant oil and cook until plump and a bit crisp at the edges, 5 minutes.

4. Sizzle: Carefully pour in wine. Sizzle 1 minute.

5. Boil: Meanwhile, cook the spaghetti in boiling salted water until tender but firm. Drain. Heap into a serving bowl.

6. Coat: Scrape the pancetta and surrounding sauces onto the spaghetti. Toss. Pour in egg mixture and toss energetically, until all the strands glow glossy. Serve small portions topped with more pepper.

*If you harbor raw-egg concerns, look for a carton stamped "pasteurized."

THE WAY THINGS WORK

Some little nubby snapped off the food processor the last time it got a really good scrub. Nothing important, just a white plastic notch that had no function. Other than to make the machine go.

Which seems unreasonable. I grew up with a desperately heavy Mixmaster that routinely dropped its lug nut into the batter bowl, barely breaking stride. We'd retrieve the spare part later, baked into banana muffin or birthday cake.

These days appliances want all their parts attached in "integrated" ways that won't detach. One nubby on the lam and the whole works, well, won't.

I could order a new nubby. That is, if I could turn up the number for that kitchen hospital, the one where the triage nurse gets on the phone and takes vitals: capacity, model, complaint. He asks in a voice worn weary if the feed-tube and sleeve assembly is locked onto the work bowl. He prescribes some clamp or screw or toggle that might help—if I knew how to perform open-Cuisinart surgery.

It's a stark choice: Nub replacement. Or replacement.

That's the way things work. Consider dinner. The modern child isn't willing to do the hard labor of lifting all the peas from the risotto or segregating the corn kernels from the succotash. She simply pushes away the plate and switches to a replacement meal of PB&J, yogurt, or shredded cheese.

Even the grownup eschews egg sandwich and pockets instead the high-protein soy bar. A processed product called, ominously, meal replacement. Meant, no doubt, for the feed tube.

My friend Ann, who spends her workday repairing desperately ill babies, outsmarts both picky child and harried adult. She stocks her stockpot with replacement-meal replacement: tiny lentils and chunky potatoes simmered to a companionable mash. High-protein, low workload, and—unlike soy powder—delicious.

Lentils make an excellent replacement for breakfast. Or lunch. Or dinner. Or steak, when fending off the offended vegetarian. The recipe helps the harried forgo processed food and the cook forgo food processor. Making it irreplaceable.

Light-Work Lentils

Serves 4

1 cup French green lentils

1 carrot

1 celery stalk

1 waxy potato, such as
   Yukon Gold

2 cloves garlic

1 bay leaf

1½ tablespoons olive oil

1 teaspoon red wine vinegar

½ teaspoon (or so)
   kosher salt

Freshly ground black pepper

4 ounces soft goat cheese,
   optional

1. **Rinse:** Pick out any suspicious specks from the lentils. Rinse thoroughly with cold water. Scrape into a medium saucepan.

2. **Chop:** Dice the carrot, celery, and potato into ½-inch cubes. Coarsely chop garlic. Add vegetables and bay leaf to the saucepan.

3. **Simmer:** Pour in cold water to cover lentils by at least 2 inches. Simmer, covered, until lentils are tender, about 20 to 25 minutes.

4. **Dress:** Drain in a colander. Scrape into a serving bowl. Dress with olive oil, vinegar, salt, and pepper. Serve hot or warm (or even cold) with cheese crumbled on top, if you like.

BATTLE CREEK

Dessert was a hotly contested course in our household. The younger generation thought it should conclude every meal. The older generation thought not. Fortunately one patch of territory remained peaceable: breakfast. No one advanced the dessert offensive before noon. Or so we thought.

One evening we were decamped at the local osteria. The enlisted boy and girl, invoking the restaurant exemption, ordered ice cream sandwiches. The uniformed server delivered an oval of pistachio gelato nestled inside a sugar-dusted bun. Along with news: "In Italy," she reported, "we eat this for breakfast."

The parents conceded that components of the dish—bread and eggs and milk—might qualify as breakfast. They considered the pistachio: its rosy armor, green intensity, and floral flavor. Its tightly sealed hull ripens by cracking into a grin.

The remainder of the evening saw the infantry mapping out its battle strategy and grinning. The parents, white napkins in hand, prepared to surrender.

Pistachio Ice-Cream Sandwiches

Serves 4

1¼ cups raw shelled
  pistachios

1½ cups whole milk

1½ cups heavy
  whipping cream

5 egg yolks

¾ cup sugar

¼ teaspoon kosher salt

2 tablespoons chopped
  roasted salted pistachios

4 brioche or other
  soft sweet rolls

1. **Toast:** Spread nuts on a rimmed baking sheet. Slide into a 350-degree oven and toast, shaking once or twice, until fragrant and crisp, 10 minutes. Cool. Slide nuts into a colander and rub them against the holes, loosening and losing skins. Chop nuts coarsely.

2. **Steep:** In a medium saucepan heat milk, cream, and toasted pistachios just to boiling. Remove from heat, cover, and let steep 15 minutes.

3. **Beat:** In a medium bowl briefly whisk together yolks, ¼ cup sugar, and salt.

4. **Thicken:** Stir remaining ½ cup sugar into the cream mixture. Slowly pour hot cream over yolks, whisking constantly. Return to the pan and cook over medium-low heat, whisking, until 175 degrees and thick enough to lightly coat a spoon, about 15 minutes.

5. **Cool:** Set pan in an ice bath (a bowl partially filled with ice water) and stir until cool, a few minutes. Cover and refrigerate 4 to 24 hours. Strain into a clean bowl. Discard nuts. Churn in an ice-cream maker. Add the salted pistachios in the last minute. Pack into an airtight container. Press a piece of plastic wrap against ice cream. Cover and freeze firm.

6. **Fill:** Split rolls, scoop in pistachio ice cream. Start your day happy.

STICKY SITUATION

I renovated the kitchen one Saturday morning while Bob was out. Actually, it was his idea. Grabbing grocery list and car key, he shouted over his shoulder: "Fix the fridge."

He had a point. The bar that holds the condiments in check had lost its grip and with a great twang of excitement, mayo and mustard and salsa were on the loose, capering across the floor.

I resettled the refugees in the interior and let the fridge door chill. It seemed to appreciate the break. Each time I tugged the handle, it snapped to with nose-smacking speed. The sauces seemed to be having a nice time socializing with the yogurts and the peanut butters. I thought we could get along fine without repair.

Then Bob made one of his heroic resupply expeditions, and I realized we needed every speck of shelf space. So I got out the tools: scissors and duct tape.

Ordinarily, I consider duct tape cheating. But in this case I was simply reconstructing an assemblage that had come with our house. A restoration of sorts.

I paused to reflect on my work. And on duct tape, strong enough to seal gun turret, flexible enough to repair rocket ship, if too adhesive for actual ductwork. The sticky-backed, fabric-bolstered heavyweight has gone on to a stellar second career in the quick-fix sector and a third in fashion, self-sticking into belt, wallet, clutch, and prom dress.

What I admire most about duct tape, however, is its affability, answering to "duct tape" or "duck tape" with equanimity.

Just when I was wrapping up my reverie, Bob returned with the groceries. I managed to fit everything snugly into the fridge. And planned, in appreciation, a feast of affable pasta sticky with duck.

Quick-Fix Pasta

Serves 6

4 prepared duck legs, confit*

1 carrot, chopped

1 onion, chopped

1 stalk celery, chopped

1 tablespoon chopped fresh
  thyme leaves

3 fresh sage leaves, chopped

1 cup red wine

2 cups chicken broth

3 tablespoons tomato paste

Kosher salt and freshly
  ground black pepper

1 pound pappardelle or
  other wide pasta

2 sprigs parsley, chopped

⅓ cup grated
  Parmesan cheese

1. Sear: Heat a large heavy skillet over medium-high. Add duck legs and cook until skin is nicely browned and pan is glossy with duck fat, 5 minutes. Lift out duck and set aside.

2. Brown: Turn down heat to medium. Add carrot, onion, celery, thyme, and sage and cook until sweet and lightly browned, 10 minutes.

3. Deglaze: Cautiously pour in wine, scraping any bits from the pan bottom. Stir in chicken broth and tomato paste. Simmer, uncovered, until mellowed and thickened, about 15 minutes. Season with salt and pepper.

4. Shred: Pull duck meat from bones; add to sauce and simmer until flavors meld, about 10 minutes.

5. Boil: Meanwhile, cook pasta tender but firm. Drain. Add to sauce. Stir gently. Let rest, covered, a few minutes.

6. Serve: Scoop into shallow bowls. Dust with chopped parsley and cheese.

*Purchase duck legs confit (duck legs preserved in fat and spices) at the meat counter (just ask) or from one of the fancy food stores. D'Artagnan is a good producer.

PROVENANCE: *I was inspired by the braised duck legs in* Wolfgang Puck Makes It Easy, *which I made considerably easier by switching to duck legs confit.*

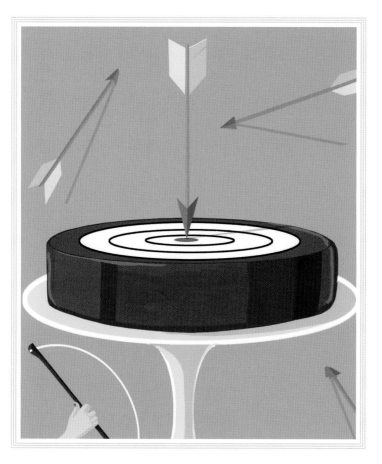

THE QUEST

As hostess, I keep many a sharp arrow in my quiver. Cheerful salad. Dependable vinaigrette. Triumphant roast. Should I snap a string, stumble mid-shot, or miss the mark, all will be pardoned by way of chocolate cake.

By cake I do not mean some imposing tower crusted with sugar roses. Nor the earnest layer cake. By cake I mean a stealth contraption, low and humble. A cake that's simple to prepare and simply adorned. So unassuming it might seem an afterthought, or French. Sliced and savored, its aim is true. Pure. Intense. Perfection.

At a young and careless age, I possessed such a recipe. I came by it so effortlessly—a typed sheet folded into a packet of photos and letters—that I did not grasp its value.

In the spartan splendor of my first apartment, I stirred together its few ingredients. My roommates salaamed. In my loft, with its off-label wiring and savage oven, I baked a charred rendition, one my first boss pronounced "unusual."

Then—predictably—I lost it. In the words of the ancient ballad, I would never have that recipe again. Oh, no.

Which is why I am doomed to search.

I've fallen for fake: the catalog come-on that promises bold flavor in a flimsy box. I've suffered confusion, presuming "flourless" to mean "good." I've puzzled over the molten mess served with spoon, and the powerful puck served with fork and saw.

I've pressed on, sifting flour, separating eggs, stirring ganache.

Eventually I came across a pleasing version simple enough to count as both afterthought and French. Not perfect, but nearly. I keep the recipe close at hand, armed for the dinner-party emergency.

And I maintain my mission. Over time, I've grown accustomed to the heroine's plight: to loss, to perseverence, and, endlessly, to hope.

Almost-Perfect Chocolate Cake
Serves 12

12 ounces bittersweet chocolate, chopped

11 tablespoons (1 stick plus 3 tablespoons) unsalted butter, cut up

¾ cup sugar

5 eggs, separated

⅓ cup flour

1 cup Chocolate Glaze (recipe follows)

1. **Melt:** In a large heavy saucepan set over low heat melt chocolate, butter, and sugar. Let cool.

2. **Mix:** Whisk egg yolks into the chocolate. Whisk in flour.

3. **Fluff:** Beat egg whites to firm peaks.

4. **Fold:** Vigorously mix one-third of the egg whites into the chocolate batter. Gently and thoroughly fold in remaining whites.

5. **Bake:** Pour batter into a buttered 9½-inch springform pan. Slide into a 350-degree oven and bake until the cake is firm and springy, about 35 minutes. Cool completely. Release cake and invert onto a 9½-inch cardboard or cake-pan round.

6. Glaze: Set cake (on its round) on a wire rack. Set rack over a rimmed baking sheet, to catch drips. Pour all the warm glaze into a big puddle on top. Use the back of an offset spatula to nudge glaze toward the edges, where it can drip becomingly down the sides. Let set a few minutes. Stun guests.

Chocolate Glaze

Makes about 1 cup

Chop 4 ounces semisweet chocolate and tumble into a medium bowl. Heat ½ cup heavy whipping cream to boiling. Pour hot cream over chocolate. Cover with a plate and let stand 5 minutes. With a soft spatula, gently stir smooth. Stir in 1 teaspoon cognac.

PROVENANCE: *Adapted from Patricia Wells' masterpiece,* Bistro Cooking. *I couldn't resist adding a ganache glaze.*

Nothing Cake

Almost-perfect chocolate cake can be adapted to Nothing Cake, when flour, butter, and cream are contraindicated (I find this approach handy at Passover). Simply switch butter to canola oil and flour to ground almonds (aka almond meal or flour). Serve plain or dusted with a little powdered sugar.

'ᴏᴏᴏᴏᴏ'

CLEAN SWEEP

The computer promised to sweep the office paperless. But mine tended toward papermore. Each list or scrap or crumple seemed so menacing, I dared not toss. Instead I filed, amassing eight massive cabinets of happily chatting detritus.

Then disaster struck. One day, moving men arrived. They rousted each quivering paper from its home and stuffed it in a box. At random. Obviously, the criminals should have been booked on the spot. Instead, I paid them.

Years later, the papers still cowered in their twenty-seven boxes. Then one weekend when the house was quiet opportunity struck. Fueled by Thai takeout, I spent two days filing.

I stacked up cartons of som tam, a bracing lime-spiked salad of shredded green papaya, carrot, cilantro, and shrimp. With savage disrespect for tax audit or scrapbook, I stacked up a twenty-two-box discard pile. It was so heavy with rancid poems and tender term papers and deeply personal check registers that it seemed indiscreet to let it linger in the alley. Poking at the shredded salad, I suddenly knew inspiration.

The truck arrived with EMS speed and in twenty minutes had munched the mess into fine confetti. It seemed to me the paperless office owed little to the computer. And much to its ingenius counterpart, the shredder.

Shredded Salad

Serves 4

1 clove garlic

3 tablespoons fresh lime juice

1½ tablespoons Asian fish sauce*

1 tablespoon sugar

1 small fresh Asian or serrano chili

Kosher salt

¼ pound small shrimp, peeled and deveined

1 small green papaya**

1 carrot

⅓ cup fresh cilantro leaves

2 tablespoon roasted peanuts

1. Whisk: Crush garlic with a mortar and pestle. Work in lime juice, fish sauce, and sugar. Snap on rubber gloves to seed and chop chili. Spike dressing with as much—or little—heat as you like.

2. Boil: Bring a small saucepan of water to a boil. Salt lightly. Add shrimp and cook until just done, about 1 minute. Drain and rinse under cool water. Halve shrimp the long way. In a large mixing bowl, toss shrimp and dressing.

3. Shred: Peel papaya. Slice in half and shake out seeds. Shred into fine strands (the food processor can be helpful). Measure 3 cups into the mixing bowl of shrimp. Peel and shred carrot and add, along with cilantro leaves. Toss well.

4. Serve: Coarsely chop peanuts. Sprinkle on salad. Crunch immediately.

*Available in the Asian foods aisle of many grocery stores and at specialty markets. I'm particularly fond of Golden Boy fish sauce for the eerie glowing baby on the label.

**Look for hard, deeply colored fruit marked "green papaya." (Inner flesh is white and slightly bitter, like the lovechild of a cucumber-horseradish romance.)

PROVENANCE: *Adapted from* Gourmet.

LARGER THAN LIFE

Men, rumor has it, respond to the visual. My research suggests they are attuned to the aural. Turned up to 11.

As a newlywed, I tried to persuade my newlyspouse that loud is just as good as deafening, that small is beautiful, that our decorating scheme need not reprise *2001: A Space Odyssey*. Bob held a wake for his megaspeakers.

Soon after, he met his contact in a parking lot in Kalamazoo and came home with two crates. After some lugging and scraping and swearing, our living room was dominated by a 200-pound eggplant-colored coffin. Actually, two.

The 200-pound eggplant-colored, coffin-shaped speaker pair cannot be ignored, camouflaged, or accessorized. I suggested we discuss the addition with each other. With an interior decorator. Or an attorney. Bob acquiesced to a trade-in, and eleven years later, made good.

Two cardboard boxes arrived air-freight. Each contained a charming one-eyed alien, easy on the eyes and ears. I was overjoyed. I cooked eggplant every day for a week. Slim, deep-purple glossies, spiked with ginger soy. Pale oval beauties crisped onto flatbread. Heavy clubs stewed into ratatouille.

Then, while I was charring a celebratory round of involtini, the UPS man knocked. I learned that the aliens had friends. And I learned a new phrase: surround sound.

Eggplant Involtini
Serves 4 as an appetizer

1 medium eggplant

Olive oil

2 cloves garlic

¼ cup loosely packed fresh parsley

¼ cup loosely packed fresh basil leaves

½ teaspoon kosher salt

¼ loaf white bread

¼ cup grated Parmesan cheese

2 ounces mild goat cheese

2 anchovies, drained

1 egg yolk

¼ cup pine nuts, toasted

¾ cup tomato sauce

1. Slice: Trim the stem off the eggplant. Slice lengthwise on a mandoline into thin slices. Discard the two skin-covered edges. Brush both sides of each slice with olive oil.

2. Char: Lightly oil a ridged griddle or skillet. Heat over medium-high. Char the eggplant, 1 minute per side.

3. Mix: With the food processor running, drop garlic down the chute, one clove at a time. Add parsley and basil and pulse to bits. Add ¼ teaspoon salt and the bread (in chunks or slices) and pulse to crumbs. Add parmesan cheese, goat cheese, anchovies, and egg yolk and pulse until just combined. Stir in nuts.

4. Roll: Stretch out 1 eggplant slice. Press on 1 tablespoon breadcrumb mixture. Roll from wide bottom to narrow top. Set into a small lightly oiled baking pan. Repeat with remaining eggplant slices. Sprinkle with ¼ teaspoon salt. Smooth on tomato sauce. Slide into a 300-degree oven and bake until hot, about 20 minutes. Serve warm.

FIRST AID

The hospital always struck me as a rarified destination. Turns out it's an easy vacation to book: Simply feel wretched and fix the physician with a meaningful glower. The guy with the stethoscope can handle the reservation. He might insist.

At check-in the receptionist wanted blood pressure, temperature, and weight. The accommodations were hardly accommodating: cramped room, cruel bed, drab décor. Activities were minimal: TV, for a price; pacing, free; needle sticks nonstop. Terrible food.

I stuck with the specialty of the house: lukewarm apple juice. And concluded that the hospital's greatest contribution to the culinary arts is the bendy straw. Its design is ingenious: It bends. It also returns to the upright position by way of crinkle action that can amuse the compromised for hours. It allows the supine to sip, minus the slosh.

Were the drink under transport actually cold and refreshing the straw might advance health science. I spent my stay working out the rotisserie-league recipe. I imagined brisk mint, sweet honey, tonic ginger, and bracing lemon, over ice. A lemonade that proffers not just lemon, but aid.

The sort of aid I needed most. I pocketed a spare straw and checked out. Next time, I'm going to Hawaii.

Lemon Aid

Serves 10

16 lemons

4 inches fresh ginger

1 small bunch fresh mint

2 cups water

1½ cups sugar

2 tablespoons mild honey

5 cups cold sparkling water, still water, or ginger ale

1. **Prep:** Zest 4 lemons. Squeeze all lemons; measure out 2½ cups juice. Peel ginger; slice into coins. Pluck mint leaves from stems. Save the prettiest leaves whole; coarsely chop the rest. Measure out ½ cup chopped mint, loosely packed.

2. **Simmer:** In a medium saucepan, stir together 2 cups water, sugar, honey, lemon zest, ginger, and chopped mint. Simmer 5 minutes. Pull off heat, cover, and let cool 1 hour.

3. Strain: Pour syrup through a fine-mesh sieve into a large pitcher; discard zest, ginger, and mint. Stir in juice. (Syrup can be stored, covered and chilled, for several days.)

4. Serve: Fill a tall glass with ice. Add several whole mint leaves. Half fill with syrup. Top off with an equal measure of sparkling water, still water, or ginger ale. Stir. Administer.

DO GEESE SEE GOD?

Sudoku amused many an armchair mathematician. Not me. I found it pleasing to herd the numbers around their corral during the minute post-takeoff and pre-pretzel. Then the whole enterprise turned grating.

Same for the crossword. I was fond of words, and knew quite a few cross ones. But taking a perfectly sturdy word, like "potato," and turning it sly, like "six-letter tuber," was downright annoying.

The palindrome, on the other hand, appealed. I respected a word so amiable it could be read frontways and backwards. Plus the palindrome conserved letters, which—who knew—might have been endangered.

The gateway palindrome read clever if mild: Mom. Dad. Ewe. It provoked a taste for the stronger stuff: Noon. Civic. Racecar. And lead to the practically profound: "Do geese see God?" The palindrome, like the bag of potato chips, was hard to put down. Once I stayed up all night locked in a palindrome smackdown.

I was equally fond of the palindrome's stock characters. Camus rarely wandered my mindscape. But I was happy to catch a glimpse of him in "Camus sees sumac." Napoleon strode by, boasting "Able was I, ere I saw Elba." I particularly liked Otis, of "Sit on a Potato Pan, Otis!"

I'd never met an actual Otis. Nor a designated potato pan. I imagined it as a flat, heavy device handy for preparing the galette or its cheesy cousin, the gratin.

The dish might have appealed to Camus, or Napoleon, being French. And to Otis, with his potato fixation. As well as Otto, Anna, Hannah, or Bob. And the reveler recovering from an all-night word binge. Potatoes were soothing that way.

Though the six-letter tubers themselves may well have quivered in their buttered dish. No doubt they wondered: "Won't I be bit now?"

Potato Pan

Serves 6 as a side dish

4 tablespoons (½ stick) unsalted butter

½ pound mushrooms, plain or fancy, sliced

1 tablespoon fresh thyme leaves

1 clove garlic, chopped

¼ cup dry white wine

Kosher salt and freshly ground black pepper

2 pounds waxy potatoes (such as Yukon Gold), thinly sliced

3 ounces Gruyère cheese, grated

½ cup heavy whipping cream

1. Brown: In a large skillet melt 3 tablespoons butter over medium-high heat. Add mushrooms and thyme and cook until beautifully browned, about 10 minutes. Add garlic and stir 1 minute. Add wine and sizzle 1 minute. Season with salt and pepper.

2. Boil: Settle potatoes in a large saucepan and cover with cold salted water. Simmer tender, stirring once or twice, about 10 minutes.

3. Mix: Stir cheese into cream.

4. Layer: Rub remaining tablespoon butter into the bottom and sides of a 9-inch potato pan or baking pan. Use a slotted spoon to scoop up half the potatoes and settle them in the pan. Season with salt and pepper. Cover with mushrooms. Pour in half the cream mixture. Cover with remaining potato slices. Season with salt and pepper. Pour in remaining cream mixture.

5. Crisp: Slide into a 375-degree oven and bake until golden on top and bubbling at the sides, about 40 minutes. Serve warm wedges right side up or upside down.

IN THEIR ELEMENT

My landscaper, being eight, brought a strong sense of style to his work. Eschewing clichés, like grass and flowers, he focused on a single ornamental feature: the hole.

His assistant, being a dog, would on occasion fling dirt from the center to the outlying heap. More often, he would straddle the heap and shoot the dirt back into the hole. This cycle kept boy and dog fully employed.

The hole served as the garden's focal point. Staring into it had a calming effect, especially when compared to staring at a bid from a grownup landscaper. Pacing its perimeter brought to mind the meditation circle. It's was also a handy cache for the rawhide bone, soggy ball, and chewable triceratops.

The hole attracted attention. Passersby peering over the fence commented on its capacious nature. They pondered its "meaning."

Midsummer, my landscaper added a feature. I had acquired an enormous plastic tub to water the dog. The landscaper offered to fill it. And empty it. Into the hole. Suddenly, we had a water element.

One soon brimming with boy and girl and dog and neighbor and friend and mud. I passed around watermelon. Each bright pink wedge rocking in its rind counted as 92 percent water. And 100 percent summer.

I decided to forgo the grownup landscaper. He'd probably want to tidy up, tamp down, and tend. But the crop in my back yard needed no encouragement to grow.

Melon Ice

Serves 6

2 ounces dark chocolate, chopped

⅛ teaspoon peppermint extract

6 limes

2½ pounds (with rind) seedless watermelon

½ cup sugar

6 tablespoons Lillet Blanc

1 pinch kosher salt

1. Melt: Tumble chocolate into a microwave-safe bowl and zap on low power until just melted, about 1 minute. Drop in peppermint and work smooth with a soft spatula. Scrape into a small zip-top bag.

2. Shape: Line a baking sheet with parchment paper. Snip a corner off the bag and squeeze drops of melted chocolate onto the paper, forming 60 or so seed shapes. Slide sheet into the freezer and let set, 5 minutes.

3. Slice: Cut each lime in half across its equator. Run a grapefruit knife around the interior rim, separating flesh from rind. Lift out flesh, leaving 12 lime shells.

4. Pulse: Scoop out watermelon flesh. Use the food processor to pulse to bits, along with flesh of one lime. (Save remaining lime middles for another project.) Press purée through a medium-mesh sieve into a quart-sized measuring cup. There should be about 2 cups juice. Stir in sugar, wine, and salt.

5. Swirl: Churn in an ice-cream maker. Slide most of the chocolate seeds into the melon ice on the last turn.

6. Freeze: Scoop ice into the lime shells. Sprinkle remaining chocolate seeds on top. Set filled limes on an empty ice-cube tray or into a muffin tin to prevent tipping. Cover with plastic wrap and freeze until firm, about 2 hours. Scoop up with a spoon inside or slurp Popsicle-style outside.

HAPPY BIRTHDAY

A birthday came my way. Not a fat one, round and menacing, just the ordinary sort that shows up, ready or not, once a year.

Many a birthday girl lingers by the pool or slurps fruity drinks or stumbles through karaoke. My idea of fun is a clean kitchen and no company save for butter, eggs, and marzipan.

I decided on a cake complicated in construction yet clean in design: the cube. I remembered the advice of pastry savant Mindy Segal: A good cake offers adventure—yielding crumb, nutty snap, billowing buttercream. I focused on a cake rich in contrast. One, like the year I hoped to have, studded with pleasant surprises.

I consulted Julia Child on layers. Dorie Greenspan on fluff. Alice Medrich on balance. And Martha Stewart on architecture. Alone with a shelf of cookbooks, I'm not one to go easy.

Two new friends eased the effort: brawny mixer, willing to muscle 14 cups of stickiness, and brawny cake stand, able to hoist 150 pounds of pastry. I whipped almond batter and hazelnut dacquoise and mocha buttercream. I stacked and slathered a weighty block. Then rolled marzipan thin, sliced it to ribbons and tied up my cake like the gift it was.

Friends dropped by. We drank Banyuls and forked up cake and laughed, a lot. I decided next time to revert to chocolate and to fewer, lighter layers. Fortunately, I've got a whole year to work out the details.

Big Fancy Almond Cake

This recipe is more involved than my usual. It's cut down, changed up, and simplified(!) from a wedding-cake recipe. It's not hard, but there are a lot of steps. Construct only if you're craving complicated (sometimes I do). There are plenty of simpler cakes here.

Makes one tall 9-inch cake

2 9-inch Almond Cakes (recipe follows)

3 9-inch layers Hazelnut Dacquoise (recipe follows)

2 quarts Chocolate Espresso Buttercream (recipe follows)

1. Slice: Slice each almond cake in half horizontally. With a serrated knife and some patience, it's not hard. If you're nervous about veering off course, measure out the midway point and mark it by poking in toothpicks. Use these as guides.

2. Construct: Set one cake layer, cut-side down, on a cake platter. Smooth on a thin coat of buttercream. Set a dacquoise layer on top. Smooth on more buttercream. Keep stacking cake/buttercream/dacquoise/buttercream until you get to the top. Now frost everything with that lovely buttercream. Voila!

Almond Cake

2 cups almond paste (buy this)

1⅛ pounds (4½ sticks) unsalted butter, softened

2 cups sugar

12 eggs

2 cups cake flour

1. Buzz: Settle almond paste, butter, and sugar in the food processor. Buzz smooth, about 1 minute.

2. Mix: Scrape almond mixture into the bowl of a stand mixer fitted with the paddle attachment. Crack in eggs. Beat at medium speed until smooth, about 3 minutes. Beat on high speed 15 seconds.

3. Fold: Pull bowl off its stand. Sift flour over the batter. Fold in gently.

4. Bake: Scrape batter into two buttered and floured 9-inch square baking pans. Slide pans into the center of a 325-degree oven and bake until golden and springy, about 55 minutes. Cool 10 minutes. Turn out onto a rack and cool completely.

Hazelnut Dacquoise

½ cup plus
   2 tablespoons sugar

½ cup blanched hazelnuts
   (see page 335)

1 tablespoon cornstarch

4 egg whites

⅛ teaspoon cream of tartar

1. Buzz: Tumble sugar and hazelnuts into the food processor. Pulse to grind. Scrape into a bowl. Sift cornstarch over nuts. Fold together with a soft spatula.

2. Fluff: Slide egg whites in the bowl of a stand mixer fitted with the whisk attachment. Measure in cream of tartar. Whisk on high speed to soft peaks. Continue to whisk, cascading in remaining 2 tablespoons sugar, to glossy peaks. Gently fold in ground hazelnuts.

3. Pipe: Scoop batter into a pastry bag fitted with a plain tip (or a zip-top bag, then snip the corner). Trace the outline of the 9-inch-square baking pan onto three sheets of parchment paper. Flip over paper (pencil smudge down) and set each on a baking sheet. Use as a guide to pipe the dacquoise batter into three 9-inch squares, each about ½ inch high. Smooth with an offset spatula.

4. Bake: Slide the pans into a 200-degree oven and bake for 7 hours (yes, 7 hours!) until firm, dry, and lightly colored. Cool.

Chocolate Espresso Buttercream

Makes about 2 quarts

Slide 8 egg whites into the bowl of a stand mixer. Measure in 2 cups sugar. Set this bowl over a pan of water over medium-high heat. Whisk until egg mixture is foamy and 165 degrees hot, about 5 minutes. Return bowl to the mixer and whisk on high speed into fluffy, glossy peaks, about 5 minutes. Make sure bowl is cool. Rub it with an ice cube if need be. Reduce speed to medium and add 1½ pounds (6 sticks) unsalted butter, softened, a few tablespoons at a time, whisking constantly. Whisk in 8 ounces bittersweet chocolate (70 percent), melted and cooled to room temperature. Flavor with 2 tablespoons brewed coffee mixed with 2 tablespoons espresso powder and 2 teaspoons vanilla extract.

PROVENANCE: *Adapted from* Baking With Julia *by Dorie Greenspan.*

AHEAD *of* THE CURVE

The average trend sped my direction, swerved, and kept right on going. Jeans had reached new heights, or depths—I was hazy on which. Molecular gastronomy was in. Or out. Nonetheless, I was ahead of the curve when it came to the goat.

At a tender age—so long ago that feta counted as foreign—I was seized by the desire to raise goats. Members of my family, my neighborhood, and my municipal court would come to ask: "Why?" To which I answered: "Because."

Echo and Erica grew quickly. They developed strong forelegs and strong wills. They were belligerent. They bellowed, in concert. They took in startling quantities of organic goat granola and returned a trickle of organic goat milk.

Which might have made delicious goat cheese. My brother Josh spent junior-high shop class sawing and gluing me a cheese press. I still had it, and I still hadn't used it.

I was so engaged in mixing granola and tossing alfalfa salad and scraping muck that I never cleared my agenda for boiling, straining, separating, pressing, aging, and brining. Though I wished I had. Goat cheese—soft or aged, herbed or plain—offered the thrill of a clean sharp bite.

After both lawsuits were settled and 4-H established a goat category, we spent a weekend at the county fair. Echo won the red ribbon, Erica won the blue. They were, after all, the county's only goats.

I felt proud. And so did Erica, who gave her ribbon a clean, sharp bite.

Chevre Corn Cakes
Serves 4

½ pound bacon, frozen and cut ½-inch thick crosswise

2 cups corn kernels shaved from 4 ears of corn

1 cup chopped onion

1 cup cornmeal

2 teaspoons baking powder

½ teaspoon kosher salt

½ teaspoon baking soda

1 pinch cayenne pepper

¾ cup buttermilk

1 egg

5 ounces mild goat cheese, crumbled

1 bunch scallions, white and tender green, sliced into thin rings

Canola oil

1. **Crisp:** Heat a large cast-iron pan over medium. When hot, scatter in bacon and cook, stirring, until crisp and brown, about 4 minutes. Scoop out and drain on paper towels. Pour off all but 2 tablespoons bacon fat.

2. **Soften:** Cook corn and onions in bacon fat over medium heat until onions turn golden, about 12 minutes.

3. **Mix:** In a large mixing bowl whisk together cornmeal, baking powder, salt, baking soda, and cayenne. In a large glass measuring cup, whisk together buttermilk and egg. Add half the cheese to buttermilk mixture. Pour over dry ingredients and stir gently but thoroughly. Stir in half the scallions and all the corn.

4. **Fry:** Coat the same skillet used for corn and onions with a thin film of oil and set over medium heat. When oil is quite hot, drop in ¼ cup batter for

each corn cake, leaving room for spreading. Cook golden brown, 2 minutes per side. Slip cakes onto a paper-towel lined baking sheet and keep warm under foil while frying the rest.

5. Serve: Top each cake with a spoonful of cheese and a sprinkle of bacon and scallions.

PROVENANCE: *Adapted from goat-cheese makers Capriole, regulars at Chicago's Green City Market and graduates of 4-H.*

FOND FAREWELL

Summer demands lazy: Sleep in, stay up. Sandwiched around the dedicated slouch. The season honors hammock, beach blanket, and ballpark bench. Still, it's good to have a goal, and mine is always the ice cream sandwich.

The ready-made, readily available from truck, cart, or poolside shack, defines the state of the art: gummy hole-pocked wafers squared off against vanillin-flavored ice milk. Authentic, in its artificial way, with scant room for improvement. And yet, I always try.

Like many a student, I long attempted to emulate the master. I smoothed vanilla-bean swirl between brownie bookends and shelved the mess next to the ice cubes. Cutting down the frostbitten block called for ice pick and cleaver. The hunks held a sticky, savage, inedible appeal.

Eventually it occurred to me that summer can be summed up by neither vanilla nor chocolate. The couple—famous for formal black-and-white attire, foreign accents, and long shelf life—works the social calendar year-round.

The dedicated summer sandwich should flaunt the dedicated summer fruit. And who is more dedicated than the plum? I poached and churned, producing a deep pink ice cream that lingered in memory—and on apron—for weeks.

One sticky afternoon I was struck by inspiration. Or by the impulse to poach someone else's inspiration: roasting.

I went scientific. I cooked down plum—along with its cousins apricot and almond—on the stovetop. The fruit melted quickly and swirled agreeably and then waited patiently in the freezer. It took control not to spoon up the control. An unauthorized taste test suggested it was good.

Then I made a batch in the oven. It took a whole hour to roast the fruit, and nothing much happened during the first 59 minutes. After the ding, I pulled out the pan and took a deep, intoxicating inhale. Even better.

I lined up four houseguests and four household regulars and handed each a spoonful of each. Everyone voted for the deeply colored, intensely flavored summer-sweet appeal of roasted.

Just under the deadline—on the last day of summer—I was finally prepared to vouch for my vacation. And—after a few more deeply delicious sandwiches—ready to trade scoop for sweater.

Summer Sandwich

Serves 8

1 pint Roasted Plumricot Ice
  Cream (recipe follows)

16 Ginger Wafers
  (recipe follows)

1. **Build:** Set 1 Ginger Wafer, bottom-side up, on a square of foil. Scoop on ¼ cup Roasted Plumricot Ice Cream. Top with another wafer, bottom-side down. Press gently. Wrap. Repeat with remaining wafers and ice cream.

2. **Freeze:** Freeze firm, several hours or overnight.

Roasted Plumricot Ice Cream

Makes 1 pint

4 plums

2 apricots

¾ cup sugar

⅓ cup heavy
  whipping cream

½ teaspoon vanilla extract

3 drops almond extract

1. **Roast:** Halve fruit and pull out stones. Set in a small baking dish, cut-sides up. Sprinkle with ¼ cup of the sugar. Cover tightly with foil. Slide into a 350-degree oven and roast until fruit has collapsed in a brilliant puddle, about 1 hour. Cool a bit.

2. **Swirl:** Scrape fruit and juices into the food processor or blender along with remaining ½ cup sugar, cream, and extracts; swirl smooth. Press through a medium-mesh sieve into a clean bowl. Set the bowl in an ice bath (a larger bowl partially filled with ice

water) and stir plum cream until no longer hot. Cover and chill completely.

3. Freeze: Churn in an ice-cream maker; pack into an airtight container. Press a piece of plastic wrap against ice cream. Cover and freeze firm.

Ginger Wafers

Makes 16 rectangles

¼ pound (1 stick) butter, softened

½ cup dark brown sugar

½ teaspoon vanilla extract

1 cup plus 2 tablespoons flour

4 teaspoons ground ginger

1 pinch of salt

1. Mix: Using a stand mixer fitted with the paddle attachment, set on medium-high, cream butter, sugar, and vanilla until fluffy, about 1 minute. On low speed work in flour, ginger, and salt until dough comes together, about 1 minute. Pat dough into 2 squares.

2. Roll: Sandwich 1 square between two sheets of parchment paper. Roll out, peel off top paper and trim, using a pastry wheel, to an 8 x 8-inch square. Slice into 8 rectangles, each 4 x 2 inches. Poke each a few times with a fork.

3. Chill: Slide dough, still on its bottom paper, onto a baking sheet and freeze firm, 30 minutes. Repeat with remaining dough.

4. Bake: Snap apart frozen wafers and separate a little on their parchment papers. Slide baking sheets into a 350-degree oven and bake until wafers begin to darken, about 15 to 17 minutes. Cool on the baking sheets.

A LOST ART

The damsel succumbs to distress. Perched at the raw bar, exploring a bowl of Madagascar shrimp, she is met with an unexpected herb.

Nothing so pedestrian as parsley, she muses. Nor so strident as anise. Stumped, she flails for help. The waiter rushes to the rescue and confides that her shrimp lounges in the company of chervil.

Chervil, she swoons. Once the worthy swore to uphold its code, to demonstrate kindness, munificence, and courtly courting. Whatever happened to chervil?

These days it's all basil. The sort of herb the fair cook can crush into pesto, pronto. Not one to spark dreams of daring rescue from drudgery.

Chervil descends, more or less, from the Latin for joy. Dried and crushed it brings to mind parsley, licorice, and celery. Yet sustains a mysterious undertaste that girds its reputation as healing, high-minded, and honorable.

Chervil, tarragon, parsley, and chive band together under the banner *fines herbes*, sworn to defend the good name of omelet, soup, or seafood. The same foursome (often joined by thyme, bay leaf, and sage) battles blandness as the bouquet garni.

The fair cook breathes in chervil's sweet scent and sighs. She imagines that in her Camelot—one where all meals are flavorful, all waiters courteous, and all dining companions dashing—everyone will practice, and partake of, more chervil.

Chervil Shrimp

Serves 4 as an appetizer

1 pound large shrimp

Kosher salt and freshly
  ground black pepper

2 teaspoons chopped fresh
  chervil

1 teaspoon chopped fresh
  parsley

1 teaspoon chopped fresh
  chives

1 teaspoon chopped fresh
  tarragon

¼ pound snap peas

3 tablespoons canola oil

1 tablespoon unsalted butter

Juice of 1 lemon

1. **Strip:** Peel and devein shrimp, leaving the tails intact. Season with salt and pepper.

2. **Prep:** Toss herbs together.

3. **Blanch:** Bring a small pot of water to a boil. Add snap peas and cook 1 minute. Drain and rinse.

4. **Sizzle:** Set a wide skillet over high heat until smoking hot. Pour in oil. Add seasoned shrimp and sear 30 seconds per side. Add butter and let brown, 1 minute. Toss in herbs and sprinkle with lemon juice. Add snap peas. Continue tossing until shrimp are just cooked through, about 1 minute. Serve hot or warm in small bowls.

PROVENANCE: *Adapted from Marcus Samuelsson's C-House Restaurant, Chicago.*

STEAMY SECRETS

The preteen knows what she needs. For instance: denim miniskirt with frayed hem, black leggings, white T-shirt, tight vest, and knee-high boots. She knows what she does not need: advice.

She knows she needs to attend her first middle-school dance. She knows it will be populated by girls in frayed miniskirts and by—significantly—boys. She is shocked to learn it will also be attended by her mother.

The preteen needs to sulk. For a week. She makes clear to her pillow and her best friend and her parents that she and her knee-high boots stand opposed. The mother knows her dance duties will be confined to the fringe. She knows doubt. Is she infringing on the sovereignty of the girl in the miniskirt?

Mother drives. Daughter pouts, takes five dollars and stomps toward the dance floor.

As chaperone, the mom is instructed to sit on a chair. In a hallway. In a basement below the dance floor. And to observe. She observes boys slinking toward the gym. She observes girls marching for the locker room. She observes wardrobe crises, whispering, and many a miniskirt.

After a time the mom abandons her post. She climbs the stairs and peers into the cafeteria, lit only by the glow of the vending machine. Boots thump, skirts jump in time to the din.

She emerges into the glare of the snack room and checks in with command-and-control: three moms dispensing potato chips. The noise shifts from stomping to shuffling. Boots wander in. One set, she realizes, belongs to her very own preteen. Mom feigns interest in a potato chip. The boots stomp her way. And stop. Girl pulls mother aside. And confides: "No one's asked me to slow dance."

After the hug, and the pep talk, and the potato chip, mom and daughter resume their posts.

On the way home, mom makes an offer: late-night noodles for a complete report. She stops at the sort of dumpling dispensary that, once snubbed by the low-carb crowd, has found new popularity.

In the company of steamy potstickers and sticky rice she gets the lowdown: One girl swung her hair around. The rest danced in a clump. One boy did the sprinkler. The rest barely moved. Three slow dances. Many fast dances. And a lot to think about—for mother and daughter alike. At least until the Valentine's Day mixer.

Asian Chicken Salad

Serves 4

½ pound skinless, boneless chicken breast

½ cup Ginger Salad Dressing (recipe follows)

Kosher salt

2 tablespoons vegetable oil

6 ounces flat Chinese noodles

2 teaspoons toasted sesame oil

5 ounces mixed salad greens

1. Marinate: Slide the chicken into a zip-top bag. Pour in half the dressing. Let rest 20 minutes at room temperature or refrigerate overnight.

2. Boil: Bring a large pot of water to a boil. Add a pinch of salt and 1 tablespoon vegetable oil. Add noodles and cook soft but still chewy, about 2 to 5 minutes (depending on noodle thickness). Drain (do not rinse). Toss with 1 teaspoon sesame oil.

3. Sear: Heat remaining 1 tablespoon vegetable oil in a skillet set over high heat. Add chicken and cook, basting with marinade frequently. Cook until just done, turning once, about 8 minutes.

4. Toss: Gently toss greens with noodles and the remaining dressing. Greens should wilt slightly in the warmth of the noodles. Arrange on a serving platter.

5. Glaze: Pull chicken off heat and slice thinly across the grain. Return slices to the hot pan. Pour in any remaining marinade, using the pan lid as a shield to protect against spatter. Working quickly so the chicken does not overcook, turn slices in the marinade until glazed.

6. Serve: Arrange chicken on top of salad and drizzle with remaining 1 teaspoon sesame oil. Serve at room temperature.

Ginger Salad Dressing

Makes about ½ cup

Whisk together: ¼ cup soy sauce, 3 tablespoons cider vinegar, 2 tablespoons toasted sesame oil, 2 tablespoons sugar, and 2 teaspoons finely grated fresh ginger.

PROVENANCE: *Adapted from* Modern Asian Flavors *by Richard Wong.*

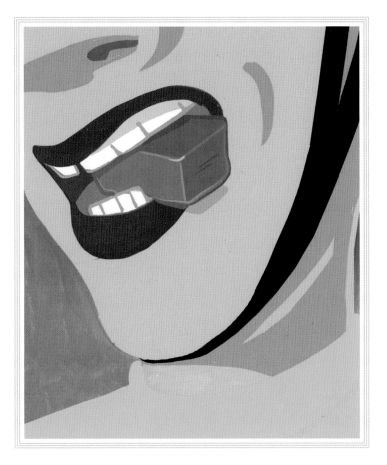

THE WORKOUT

Exercise is one of those habits I tried to avoid. Yet something came over me—humiliation, perhaps—that led me to take up bicycling. Not the pleasant coast-to-the-coffee-shop kind either. The sweaty bike-to-nowhere kind. In the morning.

Which shocked my family. Especially our local cyclist, the one committed to riding endlessly, every day, forever. At first Bob seemed skeptical. Then startled. Then scandalized to find me in bed reading *Bicycling* magazine. With interest.

I even listened to a lecture by a sports nutritionist. The sort of professional who, face-to-face with a steaming bowl of bouillabaisse, sees not life-enhancing stew but performance-enhancing molecules. In short: the enemy.

She explained that the athlete needs protein. But not too much protein. And carbs. But not too many carbs. And fluid. Though too much fluid can be fatal. The athlete needs recovery, she explained. This struck me as sound. The athlete needs a jolt of sugar and salt in order to right the internal chaos caused by sweat and stretch shorts and getting up early.

I remembered the salt caramel, hero of the sweet/salt workout. The way its sticky center sets off its salt crunch crust. The way its one-two punch pleases—over and over.

I set to work melting sugar and boiling cream and sprinkling salt and slicing squares and twisting tight a heap of salt caramels. Each offers the palate a stretch and strengthening routine. Each provides a chewy chunk of recovery. Armed with a pocketful, the amateur athlete might even enjoy her workout. At least until she recovers from the urge to exercise altogether.

Salt Caramel

Makes 64 small squares

¼ pound (1 stick) unsalted butter

½ cup sugar

½ cup light brown sugar

½ cup light corn syrup

1 cup heavy whipping cream

2 teaspoons vanilla extract

1 cup chopped pecans, optional

1¼ teaspoons flaky sea salt, such as Maldon

1. Focus: Candy making isn't hard, but it demands attention. Silence phone and banish dog. Multitasking abets disaster.

2. Calibrate: Clip a candy thermometer to the side of a small saucepan filled with water. Bring to a boil. When temperature stabilizes, check. If the thermometer registers 212 degrees Fahrenheit, great. If it's way off, toss. If it's slightly confused, take note. For instance, if it reads 2 degrees too high, add 2 degrees to the caramel's target temperature.

3. Prep: Keep that pan of hot water handy. Clip the thermometer to a large saucepan. Line an 8 x 8-inch baking pan with two lengths of parchment, crisscrossed. Melt butter and brush about 1 tablespoon onto the bottom and sides of the parchment-paper-lined pan. Set pan on a cooling rack. Keep the brush with the hot water.

4. Boil: Pour butter into the large saucepan along with both sugars, corn syrup, and cream. Bring mixture to a boil, stirring occasionally with a wooden spoon. Wash down any stray sugar with the brush dipped in hot water. Lower heat, keeping caramel at a steady boil, and continue cooking, stirring now and then, until temperature reaches 238 degrees (adjusted), 20 minutes.

5. Cool: Pull pan off heat. Carefully stir in vanilla, nuts, and 1 teaspoon salt. Pour into prepared pan; do not scrape out saucepan. Sprinkle caramel with remaining ¼ teaspoon salt. Let cool to room temperature, about 1 hour.

6. Cut: Lift out caramel by its parchment overhang. Peel off paper. Use a large knife to cut 1 x 1-inch squares. Wrap each in a twist of wax paper. Enjoy post-exercise, or whenever a sweet/salt hit appeals.

7. Clean: Fill saucepan with water to cover caramel residue. Bring to a boil. Scrape sides with a wooden spoon. Drain.

THE WAY IT CRUMBLES

Each tradition has its traditions and mine lacks cookie. Potato pancake, yes. Cookie, generally, no. So when my friend Michele suggested a holiday cookie exchange, I gave her an earnest blank look.

She explained: Each friend bakes a batch and brings it to a central cookie depository. In this case, her dining room. There the cookies are sampled and redistributed. Each baker arrives with one kind and leaves with many. Though new to the ritual, I easily picked up on its core value: winning.

I studied Michele's instructions with freshman intensity. I was to bake seven-dozen cookies. Divide five dozen into ten sets of six. Plate two dozen. And arrive hungry.

I paged through cookie cookbooks. Studied the recipes highlighted as holiday-approved. I considered gingerbread and peppermint, sprinkles and bars. I settled on my standard: two tiny shortbread rounds pressed against raspberry jam, which glistens through an even tinier cutout window. I picked moon and star.

This cookie takes time and patience. I generally assemble precious few, and offer them as valentines to precious fewer. This is not a seven-dozen sort of cookie. And yet, honoring the spirit of the cookie exchange, I felt it offered my best shot at Best.

I stirred and rolled and cut and baked and filled and cooled. I folded my cookies into brown paper packages and tied each up with string.

On exchange day, the contestants stood ready for review: chewy brown-sugar bar, chocolate-dipped chocolate chip, festive meringue, candy-speckled block. And one made by Michele herself, a plain shortbread sandwich, filled with jam. Like mine.

I bit. It offered a heartbreakingly tender texture and warm brown-butter flavor. It was, in the words of my eight-year-old cookie connoisseur, the best cookie in the world. So I settled for the consolation prize: Michele's recipe.

Heartbreaks

Makes about two dozen

2 cups flour

1 teaspoon baking soda

1/8 teaspoon fine salt

1/2 pound (2 sticks) unsalted butter

3/4 cup sugar

2 teaspoons vanilla extract

1/2 cup raspberry jam

1. Mix: Whisk together flour, soda, and salt.

2. Brown: Settle butter in a medium saucepan over medium heat. Let butter melt, foam, then brown, about 15 minutes. When specks lurking at the bottom turn caramel colored, pull pan off heat.

3. Mix: Stir in sugar, then flour mixture. Add vanilla. Set the pan aside and let the dough cool to room temperature, about 30 minutes. Do not refrigerate. You can leave it at room temperature up to several hours, if you like; the wait will make the dough a little easier to handle.

4. Roll: Pat dough into two disks. Roll each between two sheets of wax paper to 1/4 inch thick (note that 1/4 inch is about twice as thick as the average sugar cookie). Slide (still in wax paper) onto a baking sheet and freeze firm, 20 minutes.

5. Shape: Remove one sheet of dough from freezer. Peel wax paper off the top and pat back into place. Flip and peel off the other sheet of wax paper. Use a 1½-inch cookie cutter to punch out heart shapes. (If the dough cracks, let it sit at room temperature a few minutes. If a cookie breaks, don't fret. This is shortbread dough—just press the pieces back together. They will mend during baking.) Reroll scraps once. Repeat with remaining dough.

6. Bake: Set cookies on two parchment-paper-lined baking sheets. Slide into 325-degree oven and bake until just beginning to color, about 10 minutes. Slide the whole sheet of parchment onto a rack to cool. Cookies are very fragile at this point. Let them cool completely, without touching or otherwise disturbing. When you are ready to fill cookies (next step) use a frosting knife to lift each cookie. Handle gently.

7. Melt: Zap jam (right in the jar if you like) until spreadable, 1 minute. Stir to blend hot spots. Use a pastry brush to glaze flat side of one heart. Press on another heart, sandwich style. Assemble remaining sandwiches.

8. Resist: Settle hearts in an airtight container and sequester for two days. Don't cheat. Hearts will transform from crisp and tasty to tender and heartbreakingly delicious. They will also become less breakable. Share.

PROVENANCE: *I wrangled this recipe from my friend Michele Singer, who lifted it from Gourmet, which adapted it from food writer Celia Barbour. I've reworked the technique, but retained the enchanting texture.*

TALENT AGENT

Talent comes in many flavors. I admire the master of eyeliner, balance sheet, and garden shears. But counter with parking. Name a destination—traffic-clogged, yellow-curbed, signage-pocked—and I can locate an adjacent sliver of legal parking. This skill comes direct from a higher power. One day Aunt Ruth revealed to me her philosophy: Park smack in front. The next day I had the gift. I can park anywhere.

Boasting is immodest and imprudent. I try to convince the backseat crowd that hard work, practice, patience, and good manners pay off. But some skills simply alight.

Bob, for instance, possesses potent powers of ordering. Give him a menu—plain or fancy—and he will sleuth out the best dish. His technique involves careful study, much deliberation, and a pre-order interrogation that leaves the waiter pale and shaken.

After which the runner delivers me the dependable brown-butter ravioli or poached salmon, while Bob finds himself nose to nose with the home-run boudin blanc or the sizzling achiote shrimp that will remain seared into our collective memory for years. (He has an admirable corollary quality: He shares.)

Once Bob spent a hurried 14 hours in New York City during which he put in 13.5 hours at work and a few minutes munching walnut pesto crostini at a neighborhood wine bar.

He came home praising the pesto in such detail that I spent the next two days grinding walnuts and drizzling oil and chopping thyme. In aggravation, I googled the dish and discovered it had already been declared one of the year's best.

On snack break my ordering savant had found, in the words of the big-city restaurant sage, "the best spread for toasted bread since crunchy peanut butter."

And now he can spread it at home. Though I wouldn't mind the challenge of a road trip, negotiating Greenwich Avenue gridlock, locating number 52, and parking square in front.

Walnut Pesto Crostini

Serves 6

1 cup shelled walnuts

1 clove garlic

2 sun-dried tomato halves, packed in oil

2 teaspoons fresh thyme leaves

¼ cup freshly grated Parmesan cheese

Kosher salt

⅓ cup olive oil, plus a bit for bread

½ teaspoon sherry vinegar

1 loaf Italian bread

1. Toast: Spread walnuts on a baking sheet and slide into a 350-degree oven. Toast, shaking once or twice, until fragrant, crisp, and brown, about 13 minutes.

2. Degerm: Split garlic the long way and pull out any green shoot (the "germ").

3. Swirl: With food processor running, drop garlic down the chute. Add tomatoes and pulse to bits. Add walnuts, thyme, cheese, and ½ teaspoon salt. Pulse, none too finely. Stir in oil and vinegar.

4. Grill: Slice 12 pieces of bread. Coat a cast-iron skillet with a thin film of oil. Heat over medium-high. Add bread and toast till golden, 1 minute per side. Repeat with remaining slices.

5. Serve: Spread each slice of bread with a spoonful of pesto. Sprinkle with salt. Crunch happily.

PROVENANCE: *Inspired by New York City's Gottino, with a little help from the* New York Times.

CIRCLING BACK

The hula hoop came back. And front. Round and round. Also up, overhead. Down and step through. Backwards. Figure eight and other tricks fresh to the frontyard set.

Once, the hoop, like the jump rope, roller skate, or sidewalk chalk, eased the endless afternoon. It was not sport, nor art, nor, as the hoopers-come-lately had it, revolution.

Now there was slenderizing hoopercise. Steamy performance hoop. Competitive hooping. And devotional hooping convinced that giddy, spinning, sweet joy could turn the world around.

Hooping was big, and so was the hoop. No more flimsy pink plastic. Or flimsy purple plastic. The neohoop was custom-made of irrigation tubing, padded, and fancifully wrapped in electrical tape. It was huge, heavy, and high-priced.

The hoop group got together to freestyle, highstyle, and retrostyle, which would have been my style if I could have made the hoop to go around, not down.

I considered instead the stable, edible hoop. Not the greasy onion ring nor pudgy bagel. The doughnut, which was making its own comeback.

I mixed and rested and cut and fried. I thought happy doughnut thoughts. In my hooping days our family had a Doughnut Fairy, who on Sunday morning delivered a mixed baker's dozen. My homemade hoop resembled that elusive prize: Doughnut Thirteen. I glazed and bit and grinned. I wondered if giddy, spinning, sweet joy actually did count as revolution.

Sour Cream Doughnuts
Makes about 20

1 vanilla bean

2 eggs

1 cup sour cream

¾ cup whole milk

2 tablespoons butter, melted

½ teaspoon vanilla extract

4½ cups flour

1⅓ cup sugar

4 teaspoons baking powder

1 teaspoon fine salt

½ teaspoon freshly
   grated nutmeg

¼ teaspoon ground
   cinnamon

About 2 quarts vegetable oil

Glaze (recipe follows)

1. Whisk: Split vanilla bean the long way and scrape seeds into a large glass measuring cup. Add eggs, sour cream, milk, butter, and vanilla. Whisk together.

2. Mix: Sift flour, sugar, baking powder, salt, nutmeg, and cinnamon into the bowl of a stand mixer. Fit mixer with paddle attachment. Pour in sour cream mixture. Flick to slow speed. Dough will turn ragged, then lumpy, then thick. Increase speed to medium and beat smooth, no more than 2 minutes. Dough will be sticky.

3. Chill: Scrape down sides. Cover bowl with plastic wrap and refrigerate 2 hours.

4. Shape: Set half the chilled dough on a floured work surface, dust with flour, and pat to ⅜ inch thick. Use a 2½-inch round cutter and a 1-inch round cutter to punch out doughnut shapes. Set doughnuts and holes on a floured baking sheet. Repeat, rerolling scraps once.

5. Prep: Set a cooling rack over a baking sheet near the cooktop. Scrape glaze onto a plate.

6. Fry: Choose a heavy, deep pot for frying. Fill 2 inches deep with oil. Clip a candy thermometer to the side. Heat to 375 degrees. Use a slotted spoon to slide in 1 doughnut. It will sink, then rise. Once floating, fry golden brown, about 30 to 40 seconds. Flip and fry the other side golden brown. Lift out with a slotted spoon and rest on the rack. Break open doughnut and check that the center is cooked through. If not, lower heat, and increase time a smidge. Cook remaining doughnuts, four at a time, then holes.

7. Glaze: While still warm, dip each doughnut into glaze. Flip and rest glaze-side up on the rack. Best warm with coffee.

PROVENANCE: *Adapted from a recipe by Jory Downer, world champion baker and owner of Evanston's Bennison's Bakery.*

Glaze

Measure 1 cup of confectioners' sugar into a small bowl. Drizzle in 2 to 3 tablespoons brewed coffee, whisking to a thick glaze.

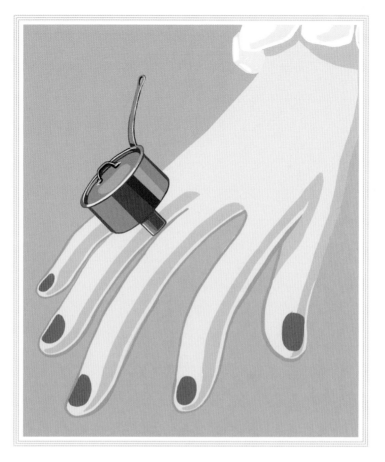

A FLING WITH BLING

The affair came on suddenly: intense, brief, and disastrous. Utterly predictable. What else could befall the happily married cook who steps out on her longtime cookware?

The casserole flaunted rugged good looks: glowing copper exterior, shining tin interior, sturdy brass handles secured with rivets. And a riveting accent. It was stamped "Made in Alsace."

I was a pragmatic cook, raised on Revere Ware. On my wedding day I graduated to All-Clad, choosing the stainless line for its machine-wash practicality. In early motherhood I relied on my cast-iron skillet and Dutch oven. Heavy but dependable.

I scoffed at the frivolous young cook who longed for copper.

But somehow this pan, with its 3-quart capacity, its promise of a "nonreactive" lining, and its half-off pickup line quickened my pulse. Maybe it wasn't too late for a fling with fancy.

I ignored friends' warnings. I didn't care that copper could only handle low heat and soft utensils. I believed everything the hang-tag told me. Even that the tender tin could take the tough stuff.

I crisped potatoes and swooned over my pan's steady hand. I grew reckless, risking metal spatula, brazenly high heat, daringly acidic ingredients. I cooked up a dramatic marinara. Served it triumphantly. And went to bed without doing the dishes.

In the morning, I found my handsome red pan pocked with green. I washed. I rinsed. I stared at the blotchy copper exterior and the scratched tin interior, worn through in menacing patches. I rushed to the cookshop. And met with a scalding scolding. "High heat? Spatula? Tomatoes? Wine!" The sales clerk smirked, "Maybe you can get it retinned."

But I knew I wouldn't. Instead I would go home and apologize to my All-Clad. I would haul out the heavy Dutch oven and fashion a simple stew from chicken and potatoes. I would serve it to my family, sadder but wiser.

Chicken Stew

Serves 4

2 pounds boneless, skinless chicken breast, cut into 4 pieces

Kosher salt and freshly ground black pepper

1 tablespoon finely chopped fresh rosemary leaves

2 tablespoons olive oil

8 cloves garlic, chopped

1 teaspoon saffron threads dissolved in a little warm water

1 teaspoon whole fennel seeds

1 (15-ounce) can whole tomatoes in juice, run through the blender

2 cups chicken broth

1 cup dry white wine

3 tablespoons anise liqueur such as Pernod

1 pound waxy potatoes, such as Yukon Gold, quartered

Rouille (recipe follows)

1. **Season:** Rub chicken with salt, pepper, and the rosemary.

2. **Brown:** In a large Dutch oven heat olive oil over medium heat. Brown chicken, about 4 minutes. Let rest on a plate.

3. **Simmer:** Lower heat to medium-low and add garlic, saffron, and fennel seeds. Stir, 30 seconds. Add tomatoes, broth, wine, liqueur, 1 teaspoon salt, and ½ teaspoon pepper. Stir, scraping up any browned bits. Simmer, partially covered, 15 minutes. Add chicken (along with any juices) and potatoes. Cook, partially covered, until tender, about 40 minutes.

4. **Serve:** Use two forks to shred meat into large chunks. Scoop stew into shallow bowls. Top with a spoonful of rouille. Savor.

Rouille

Use a mortar and pestle to smash 2 cloves garlic and 1½ teaspoons kosher salt into a paste. Scrape into a small mixing bowl. Whisk in 1 egg yolk (if you harbor raw-egg concerns, look for a carton stamped "pasteurized."). Slowly drizzle in ½ cup olive oil and ½ cup vegetable oil, whisking constantly into a thick sauce. Season with 1 ½ tablespoons lemon juice, ½ teaspoon crushed saffron threads, and ¼ teaspoon crushed red pepper flakes.

PROVENANCE: *Simplified from Ina Garten's* Barefoot Contessa Back to Basics.

CHICKEN CHIC

News arrived that chicken was in. Way in. The sister of a friend, resident of Los Angeles's most stylish enclave, confidant of our most stylish president, confirmed it. This trendmaster owned an actual chicken. Her chicken did not lounge in a pot, nor under a brick. It resided in a coop. It was the fully feathered, scratch-and-peck, nest-and-brood style chicken.

The chickenista was assured access to the latest egg. She believed in the happy chicken. As did her happy chicken. Who cackled her approval. At an early hour. An hour when the coddled residents of Los Angeles dream of hollandaise over sunny-side-up.

Which was how the sister of my friend discovered that her next-estate neighbor, the sort of taut personality covered relentlessly by the entertainment press, maintained a strong golf swing. And, even at the crack of dawn, accurate aim.

Devilish Eggs

Boiling eggs is an inexact art, affected by the size of the egg, the temperature of the fridge, and other factors. You may want to boil a test egg first to make sure you approve of the results. The finished egg should be cooked through, with a tender white and a set—neither sticky nor chalky—yolk.

Makes 12 stuffed egg halves

6 large eggs

3 tablespoons unsalted butter, softened

2 teaspoons Dijon mustard

Fine salt

1 lemon

Capers or caviar, optional

1. Boil: Set cold eggs in a single layer in a medium saucepan. Pour in cold water to cover by 1 inch. Bring just to a boil. Cover. Pull pan off heat. Let stand 16 minutes.

2. Cool: Scoop out eggs with a slotted spoon and submerge in a bowl of ice water. Rattle the eggs around in the bowl so they crack a bit. Cool 10 minutes. Crack gently all over and peel under cool running water, starting at the wide end.

3. Cut: Trim about ¼ inch white from each end. Cut in half crosswise. Pop yolks into a small bowl.

4. Smash: Add butter, mustard, and a pinch of salt to the yolks. Mash with a fork, thoroughly.

5. Fill: Set whites on a platter, open ends up. Sprinkle lightly with salt. Scoop yolk mixture into a zip-top bag, snip off one corner, and pipe yolks into whites.

6. Decorate: Zest long fine strips of lemon. Top each egg with curls of zest. If you like, fancy things up with a caper or two or a few grains of caviar. Enjoy in style.

FLOUR CHILD

When young, I nibbled at carrot cake. Not because I liked it. Who did? It was full of non-cake elements, like carrot, grated and grating. Raisin, wrinkled and resolute. Pineapple, soggy from the can. Walnut. Coconut. Safflower oil. Carrot cake achieved cake status only by virtue of its cream-cheese frosting. Bare, it counted as health bar. Or salad. Carrot cake didn't taste good. But it was packed with good intentions.

Carrot was a nonconformist cake. It took a stand: Cake didn't have to be tall and pretty and fluffy. Cake could be low and dense and nutritious. Cake didn't need to preen from a pedestal. It could be mixed and baked and served right in the lowly lasagna pan. With fingers. Carrot cake rebelled against the old-fashioned time-consuming cake recipe. It rebelled against the new-fashioned time-saving cake mix. Carrot cake, like the carrot itself, maintained links to the underground.

Carrot cake never missed a potluck. It stood on permanent display at the New Pioneer Food Co-op. It went well with guitar, consensus, and batik. And then it went away. Maybe people didn't stop eating carrot cake. But they stopped believing in carrot cake.

I hardly noticed. Like everyone else, I was busy smashing candy bars into ice cream. I followed the urban cookie struggles. I fretted over the murder- and suicide- and death-by-chocolate stalkings. I was amused by the cupcake parade with its tutu-pink frivolity, its bacon-and-blue-cheese intensity.

Sometimes I missed carrot cake. Sometimes I even missed potlucks and guitar-strumming and consensus-building. I decided to construct one. Not the original, though I had that recipe, smuggled in by Mom's grad-school co-conspirator Laurie Bedlington, who flirted it off a waiter at Things & Things' underground cafe. It was a marvel of time travel.

I constructed a new version mindful of old conventions, like sifting and creaming and folding. I dispensed with the dispensable, like sog and grater and flake. I retained the essential: carrot, now puréed smooth. Nut, toasted crisp. Cream cheese, whipped light. I mixed and stacked and frosted and cut. Breaking with tradition, I applied fork.

This cake yielded tender crumb, mild crunch, soft swirl. It was distinctly carrot, lightly gingered. Informed, but not overbearing. Free of bad habits, it honored good intentions. It tasted—deliciously—grown-up.

Grown-up Carrot Cake
Serves 12

1 pound carrots

½ pound (2 sticks) unsalted butter, softened

2⅔ cups sifted cake flour

2¼ teaspoons baking powder

¾ teaspoon ground ginger

½ teaspoon ground cinnamon

½ teaspoon fine salt

1¾ cups sugar

4 eggs, separated

Cream Cheese Buttercream (recipe follows)

½ cup pecan pieces, toasted

1. **Swirl:** Peel and trim carrots; cut into chunks. Tumble into a large saucepan. Cover with cold water. Boil tender, 20 minutes. Drain any remaining water. Tumble into the blender or food processor along with 1 tablespoon of the butter and swirl completely smooth. Measure out 1 cup purée. Cool.

2. **Mix:** Whisk together flour, baking powder, ginger, cinnamon, and salt.

3. **Beat:** Use a stand mixer fitted with the paddle attachment on high speed to fluff butter, 2 minutes. Cascade in all but 2 tablespoons sugar; fluff another 2 minutes. Beat in egg yolks, one at a time. Scoop in one-third of the flour; mix on low just until incorporated. Scoop in half the carrot purée; mix just until incorporated. Work in remaining doses of flour, carrot, flour until the batter glows a smooth pale orange.

4. Whip: Switching to the whisk attachment and a clean bowl, beat egg whites foamy. Cascade in remaining 2 tablespoons sugar, beat glossy. Use a soft spatula to fold whites gently and thoroughly into carrot batter.

5. Bake: Divide batter among three buttered and floured 9-inch cake pans. Slide into a 350-degree oven and bake until a toothpick poked in the center comes out clean, about 25 minutes. Cool 10 minutes. Turn out and cool completely.

6. Frost: Center one layer on a cake platter. Frost with Cream Cheese Buttercream. Scatter on half the pecans. Stack with a second layer of cake, buttercream, and pecans. Top with third cake layer. Smooth buttercream over top and sides. Decorate with a single fresh flower.

NOTE: Alternatively, use this recipe to make 24 standard-size cupcakes. Fill cups two-thirds full; bake about 15 to 17 minutes.

Cream Cheese Buttercream

Slide 4 egg whites in the bowl of a stand mixer. Using the whisk attachment, beat frothy, about 1 minute. Turn off mixer. Stir 1 cup sugar, ¼ cup water, and ½ teaspoon cream of tartar together in a small saucepan. Set over high heat and let boil without stirring until syrup reaches the soft-ball stage (240 degrees on a candy thermometer or when a bit of hot syrup dropped into a saucer of cool water forms a soft blob). Pour this syrup all at once into the mixer bowl. Whisk on high speed until fluffy, white, and completely cool, about 5 minutes. Make sure bowl is no longer hot (rub outside with an ice cube, if need be). Bit by bit, beat in ½ pound (2 sticks) unsalted butter, softened. Beat in 4 ounces softened cream cheese and 1 tablespoon vanilla extract. If buttercream seems too soft, chill about 15 minutes before spreading.

Chapter 5: Spread

Home seemed calmer: everyone was healthy and good, except Theo, ever the puppy, who remained healthy and bad. Work was a mess. The *Chicago Tribune* had collapsed into bankruptcy. The company was strangling its smaller papers, including the *Baltimore Sun*. Tired of firing for a living, Bob left.

The *Tribune*'s Sunday magazine, home to my column, was slated to fold. I thought my job was shot. But the editors decided to move Home on the Range into a new section called Sunday. Instead of two glossy pages with a glamorous food shot, I had a quarter-page "module," formatted to drop into any *Tribune* property. I had a tighter space, a smaller paycheck, and no safety net: no more recipe tester. On the upside, other papers started running the column, even the *Baltimore Sun*.

This was our new world: thinner papers, shared content, recession, and somewhere out there, two wars.

Bob took a job editing investigative stories at Bloomberg News and started commuting to Washington, D.C. I still commuted (via Internet) to Chicago. It didn't make sense to stay in Baltimore; it made less sense to leave. We had a school, a home, a life.

One that included local food. I read John Shields' *Chesapeake Bay Cooking*. I was a regular at our Saturday market, with its tender peaches and sweet corn. I wedged my way through the Sunday market under the expressway, a crush of hot doughnuts, pit beef, and black-eyed peas. I added oyster stew and cornbread stuffing to our Thanksgiving menu.

We planted wisteria. We learned to pound crabs. The night before Hannah's bat mitzvah, we served a menu that was strictly Baltimore, biscuits to rum-spiked Southsides. Maybe, unexpectedly, we had put down roots.

PRACTICE

I t was a perfect season. The Shamrocks won every game. And every playoff game. Until the championship game, which they lost.

The season was short and sweet.

On spring afternoons thirteen boys and one wiry girl practiced pitch and hit and run. They knelt: elbow on knee, chin on fist, eyes on Coach.

On summer evenings fourteen sets of parents practiced "Good eye" and "Good try" and "Good game." After which the players broke out the high-fives and chips.

My Shamrock wore his grass-stained white pants and sweat-stained green jersey, even to practice. He struck out. He dropped the ball. He stood shoulder to shoulder with Coach, eyes on the dirt. "Go at your own pace," Coach said. "Don't rush."

My player took to arriving early. He insisted on staying late. Once he missed an out and, thinking the game lost, crumbled into tears. "Keep a positive attitude," Coach said. "Stay strong." He never crossed home plate. But in the semifinals he hit a double that drove in two runs.

Afterward there was a party. With chips and burgers and hide-and-seek. Coach named my Shamrock Most Improved.

Then he served pie. One blueberry, one mixed berry, and one apple, with a baseball carved into each crust. A pastry so tender it verged on crumble, so strong it served up neat. In short: perfect.

Late that night, after my Shamrock fell asleep, I practiced pastry. Coach's recipe wasn't complicated. But it called for patience. "Go at your own pace," I recited. "Keep a positive attitude." In the morning I served mixed-berry pie to my player. Who declared it Most Improved.

Mixed-Berry Pie

Makes one 9-inch pie

1 disk Perfect Pastry
(recipe follows)

For crumble:

⅓ cup sugar

¼ cup rolled oats

3 tablespoons flour

¼ teaspoon fine salt

⅛ teaspoon grated nutmeg

4 tablespoons (½ stick)
unsalted butter, cut up

For filling:

2 cups whole raspberries

2 cups sliced strawberries

1½ cups whole blackberries

1½ cups whole blueberries

1 cup sugar

¼ teaspoon fine salt

Finely grated zest of 1 lemon

¼ cup cornstarch

1. Roll: Roll out pastry. Line the bottom of a 9-inch pie plate. Trim and crimp edges. Chill.

2. Pulse: For crumble, measure sugar, oats, flour, salt, and nutmeg into the food processor. Pulse to a fine powder. Add butter and pulse until largest lumps are pea-sized. Chill.

3. Macerate: Heap berries in a large bowl. Sprinkle with sugar and salt and mix gently with a soft spatula. Cover and let rest at room temperature, 1 hour. Berries will release some of their juices.

4. Thicken: Set a colander over a wide saucepan. Roll berries into the colander and let the juices drip into the saucepan. Return berries to their bowl along with the lemon zest. Dissolve cornstarch in a spoonful of water, then whisk this slurry into the berry juice. Set saucepan over medium heat and cook, whisking, until juice turns from cloudy and thin to brilliant and thick, about 2 minutes. Scrape thickened juice over berries. Mix gently.

5. Fill: Scrape berries and juices into the pastry-lined pie plate. Sprinkle on crumble.

6. Bake: Set pie on a rimmed baking sheet. Slide into a 400-degree oven and bake until golden, 25 minutes. Reduce heat to 350 and bake until crust is golden brown and juices bubble thick and purple, about 25 to 30 minutes. If the perimeter seems to be browning too quickly, shield with a pie halo (to make one fashion a hoop from crumpled foil). Cool completely, about 3 hours. Slice and serve.

Perfect Pastry

Lines one single-crust 9-inch pie plate

Measure into the food processor: 1¼ cups flour, 1 tablespoon sugar, ¼ teaspoon fine salt. Pulse to mix. Drop in 6 tablespoons cold unsalted butter, cut up. Pulse a few times. Drop in 3 tablespoons cold vegetable shortening (such as Crisco). Pulse until mixture looks crumbly, darkens slightly and clumps when squeezed. Turn out into a large mixing bowl. Drizzle in about 4 tablespoons cold water, mixing gently with a soft spatula, until pastry comes together. Pat into a disk. Wrap in wax paper and chill at least 1 hour.

MANIFOLD DESTINY

Nature nurtures bud and branch at some remove from civilization. Generally, a long remove. Which is why you spent summer strapped into a hot car, wishing for a cool breeze.

Mornings, you drove your dancer to dance camp and your naturalist to nature camp. Afternoons, you picked up. The backseat naturalist, armed with peashooter and pea, made his demands: "Don't drive so much. It's bad for the environment. The earth is going to explode. And we have to stop for a snow cone."

You sighed. You liked the earth. You arranged to carpool. You packed in one ballerina, three naturalists, and a dog. You spent more time, more crowded, in the car. You arrived home too cranky to cook.

Some weeks into this routine, you considered carbeque. "Cool," shouted your naturalist. "Isn't that when you crash into another car and they both explode?"

You chopped sunny tomato, basil, parsley, lemon, and garlic. You tossed in seaside shrimp and island feta. You folded this summer breeze into foil, and headed for the car.

To access the engine, you consulted the owner's manual. As opposed to the co-owner, who, had he known your plans, would have exploded. You figured the block-shaped hunk must be the engine block. You secured the foil packet with floral wire and snapped the hood shut. You started the engine.

You collected limp ballerina and sun-crisped naturalist. You drove home.

You popped the hood and pulled out the hot packet. Nothing seemed to have exploded. You served fragrant garlic shrimp to your happy campers, feeling cool as a snow cone.

High-Speed Shrimp

Serves 4

1 pound medium shrimp, peeled and deveined

3 plum tomatoes, chopped

4 ounces feta cheese, crumbled

2 tablespoons chopped fresh parsley

2 tablespoons chopped fresh basil

2 tablespoons olive oil

Finely grated zest of 1 lemon

1 clove garlic, finely chopped

1 teaspoon kosher salt

Freshly ground black pepper

1. Toss: Pile all ingredients into a medium mixing bowl; toss.

2. Wrap: Tumble half the shrimp mixture onto an 18-inch length of foil. Fold up into a neat 6-inch square packet, carefully folding free ends up and in to seal. Wrap in 3 more layers foil. Repeat with remaining shrimp, packing up a second packet.

3. Drive: Set both packets on the engine block and secure with wire. Put about 50 miles on the shrimp. Wear mitts to slide out. Unwrap and enjoy roadside.

4. Stay: For stationary shrimp, slip the foil packets into a 400-degree oven and bake until shrimp turn pink, curled and cooked through, about 35 minutes. (Can also be made in a 13 x 9-inch pan, covered in foil.)

PROVENANCE: *Inspired by a dish made by my friend Anne, who was inspired by* Real Simple *magazine, and adapted to highway conditions under the guidance of the carbeque classic* Manifold Destiny.

AROUND THE CAMPFIRE

The s'more exhibits many an engineering flaw. To wit: The exterior cracker measures square, while the interior marshmallow squishes round. This mismatch produces dangerously unsupported corners, which, when clamped between eager teeth, leverage open the sandwich. The cracker cracks along its fault line, resulting in dirt-encrusted s'more and tear-stained camper.

Worse, the s'more is built on a fallacy: that toasted marshmallow melts cold chocolate on contact. The sorry truth is this: It doesn't.

The scientist has attempted many a workaround, including pre-warming the chocolate-lined cracker fireside. Embedding chocolate in the marshmallow.

Wrapping fully composed sandwich in foil and tossing it in the fire. Even employing the microwave. These methods harbor defects too obvious and too heartbreaking to enumerate.

The S'more Security Administration has spent a summer investigating lapses in s'more security and has released these findings: The graham cracker should be reformatted round. The chocolate should be reworked soft. The prepackaged marshmallow remains unassailable.

The camper mindful of these safety measures will produce a stable, secure, and sticky s'more, which has the added benefit of tasting wonderful.

Secure S'mores

Makes 12

1 cup all-purpose flour

¼ cup whole-wheat flour

¾ teaspoon baking soda

1 pinch fine salt

⅛ teaspoon
    ground cinnamon

¼ pound (1 stick) unsalted
    butter, softened

2 tablespoons
    granulated sugar

2 tablespoons brown sugar

1 teaspoon honey

1 teaspoon vanilla extract

4 ounces semisweet
    chocolate, chopped

½ cup heavy
    whipping cream

12 marshmallows

1. Mix: Whisk together flours, baking soda, salt, and cinnamon. Using a stand mixer fitted with the paddle attachment on medium-high beat butter, sugars, honey, and vanilla fluffy with a mixer, about 2 minutes. Scoop dry ingredients into butter mixture; mix on low until combined. Beat until dough clumps, about 2 minutes.

2. Roll: Pat dough into a disk. Set between two sheets of wax paper and roll thin. Punch out twenty-four 2-inch circles, re-rolling scraps once. Set circles on two baking sheets; poke each twice with a fork. Slide into a 350-degree oven and bake until golden, about 10 minutes.

3. Melt: Tumble semisweet chocolate into a bowl. Heat cream to a boil; pour over chocolate. Cover, let rest 5 minutes. Whisk smooth. Let this ganache cool.

4. Build: For each s'more spread 2 crackers with ganache. Roast 1 marshmallow golden. Sandwich and chomp.

PROVENANCE: *Graham crackers adapted from the French Laundry.*

THE ROAD TRIP

The amusement park intends to amuse. I, however, refuse. The amusement park fills me with dread of winding road trip and wobbly roller coaster and wispy cotton candy. So when Hannah proposed an amusement excursion, I responded, meaningfully: no.

When she countered with joining a friend and her mom, I responded gratefully: yes.

The preteens planned an agenda that included many a fast and furious ride, followed by a fast and furious raid on the gift shop. This shop, indeed this amusement park, specializes in chocolate, which is the sort of amusement I understand. She padded her pocket with allowance and I covered lunch.

I passed the day amused by the silence that wafted through the house. Twelve hours later Hannah returned with sunburn and sack of loot. Endearingly, she presented Noah with a fat chocolate bar. Gamely she offered me a bottle of foil-wrapped chocolate drops. Sadly, she looked over the remaining bags of chocolate, in bricks, pucks, stacks, and mounds. She sighed: "Too bad I forgot to get something for Daddy."

I considered the lectures I might have delivered regarding prudence, budgeting, judgment. But realized I'd been spared the effort. Hannah, hands to belly, lay inert on her bed. I retired to heat some healing soup, thinking she didn't look the least bit amused.

Counterpoise Soup

Serves 6

1 tablespoon butter

1 tablespoon olive oil, plus
   more for drizzling

1 onion, chopped

5 cloves garlic, chopped

2 potatoes, chopped

1 teaspoon fresh rosemary

1 teaspoon fresh
   thyme leaves

6 cups chicken broth

Kosher salt and freshly
   ground black pepper

1 bunch watercress

1 lemon

2 tablespoons chopped
   fresh chives

1. **Soften:** In a wide saucepan melt butter into 1 tablespoon olive oil over medium heat. Tumble in onion and garlic; cook, stirring, until golden, 10 minutes. Stir in potatoes and herbs.

2. **Simmer:** Pour in broth. Simmer until potatoes turn tender, about 25 minutes. Cool (at least slightly).

3. **Wilt:** Swirl soup smooth. Return to the pot and reheat. Season with salt and pepper. Pluck leaves and tender branches from the watercress. Add to soup and cook until just wilted, about 3 minutes.

4. **Serve:** Ladle soup into small bowls. Sharpen flavors with a squeeze of lemon juice, a drizzle of olive oil, and a scattering of chives.

PROVENANCE: *Inspired by Nancy Silverton.*

THE STRUGGLE

Counting two children and 167 school days per year, I calculate I've composed one billion lunches. Not one of which has been thoroughly dispatched.

Excuses abound: Sandwich squishage. Tepid grapes. Classroom birthday, with cake. In the weekday struggle that pits nutrition against child, lunch loses.

I've attempted salade niçoise and checkerboard PB&J and poached chicken with pesto on baguette. I've also tried the opposite tack. Once I permitted my schoolgirl to purchase a vile plastic-wrapped contraption from the convenience case. I got a call from the teacher, certain I'd expired. Still, the plastic lunch came home, largely intact.

I bought into the fancy packaging fantasy, hiring Curious George or Wonder Woman as lunch escorts and welcoming Curious George or Wonder Woman home, still fiercely guarding hummus, carrot, and plum, ever so lightly mauled.

So, I surrendered. I served after-school snack. Snack had not huddled under Wonder Woman watch all morning, nor monkeyed around with Curious George all afternoon. It needn't be foil-secured or thermos-sealed or ice-pack protected. It came—significantly—with parental supervision.

Post-bus my children made quick work of fresh fruit, skim milk, and sweet treat. Because if they shunned fruit and milk, treat retreated. This equation contained the recommended daily dose of coercion and ensured snack success. Plus, they were hungry. They'd barely touched lunch.

Peanut Butter Cookies

Makes about 2 dozen 3-inch cookies

1¼ cups flour

1 teaspoon baking soda

¼ teaspoon fine salt

4 tablespoons (½ stick)
unsalted butter, softened

4 tablespoons lard*

½ cup granulated sugar

½ cup dark brown sugar

1 egg

½ cup crunchy peanut
butter

½ cup chopped roasted,
salted peanuts

1. Mix: Whisk together flour, baking soda, and salt.

2. Fluff: Beat together butter, lard, and both kinds of sugar. Beat in egg. Beat in peanut butter. Add flour mix and beat to combine. Beat in nuts.

3. Press: Scoop out balls using a 1¾-inch ice-cream scoop. Set on ungreased baking sheets. Dip a fork in sugar and use the back of the tines to gently press in a grid.

4. Bake: Slide into a 375-degree oven and bake until just barely golden, about 9 minutes (cookies will still be soft, but will firm up when they cool).

Available at the grocery store packaged like butter, lard gives these cookies a wonderful crumbly texture. If lard makes you squeamish, substitute butter.

JOIN THE CLUB

Cooking club is like book club, only there's no book. Making me well qualified to join. I always bring dessert, and I never read the book.

Our first theme was Middle East. The cuisine, not the conflict. I had been baking cherry pies all day and hewing to my principles—bring dessert, ignore assignment—I slid one into my cake caddy.

We ate couscous. We ate yogurt. We ate salad. And afterward, baklava. Sensing conflict, I took my cherry pie home. I amended my position to bring dessert, attempt assignment.

When the next email came around other cooks had volunteered for pasta, ratatouille, bruschetta. I figured we were going Italian. I took the sweet spot; I was always game for tiramisu.

Turned out the theme wasn't Italian. It was tomato. I considered marzipan, rolled round and colored tomato-red. I considered going out of town. Eventually I considered the assignment. After all, tomato is supposed to be a fruit.

Tomato tart seemed too much like pizza. Tomato granita seemed too much like disaster. I settled on caramelized tomato because (a) what isn't good caramelized? and (b) what isn't good over ice cream?

It worked. The hot tomatoes slid out of the skillet caramel sticky, citrus sweet, and mint bright, over ice cream. Though the tomato sundae might have been just as tasty, minus tomato.

Caramelized Tomato

Serves 4

6 plum tomatoes

1 orange

6 tablespoons sugar

2 tablespoons water

¼ cup orange liqueur

1 pint vanilla ice cream

Fresh mint leaves

1. Prep: Use a vegetable peeler to peel tomatoes. Quarter lengthwise. Pull out core and seeds. Rinse and set on a kitchen towel. Zest and squeeze orange.

2. Caramelize: Sprinkle sugar into a medium, heavy skillet. Pour in water. Heat over medium-high heat, swirling now and then, until sugar melts, caramelizes and turns amber, about 10 minutes. Remove from heat. Carefully pour in juice and zest.

3. Thicken: Bring syrup to a boil. Add tomatoes and liqueur. Strike a long fireplace match, stand back, and ignite. (Or don't, if you prefer.) Continue cooking, shaking the skillet, until flames subside and the sauce thickens, about 2 minutes.

4. Serve: Scoop ice cream into four shallow dishes. Spoon on tomatoes and hot syrup. Garnish with mint.

PROVENANCE: *Adapted from Lidiasitaly.com.*

A GOOD EGG

I met a chicken. She was the fluffy, pecking, chatty sort of chicken, keen on her afternoon snack of fresh thyme and stale graham cracker. I believe she said her name was Clark. Though, to be honest, I'm not sure I could distinguish her from her twenty-three compatriot Clarks. I admired her wholesome style, her sturdy coop, and her warm nesting box, complete with wholesome, sturdy, warm egg. Which I picked up, admired, and stole.

I did pay for the egg. But not in any way Clark might have appreciated.

I rinsed and dried and packed a dozen of the treasures home. I learned from my chicken-tending friend, Laura, that the fresh egg needs no refrigeration. I arranged my collection in a ceramic bowl, still-life style.

Then I cracked one into the frying pan.

I staged a taste test, pitting farm-fresh against grocery store against conve-
nience-case egg. Clark's egg ruled. Her white gleamed glossier and her yolk glistened brighter than the competition. Her egg was richly flavored and free of that
icky undertone I can only describe as eggy. I felt like driving back to the farm and
offering Clark an extra helping of corn mash. She was doing some great work out
there.

I tried to honor Clark's efforts. All week I whipped and scrambled. I constructed
the airy omelet, the tall souffle, and sunny lemon curd. Ceramic bowl empty, I placed
a call to the coop. Laura said Clark was in, and happy to handle a refill. That chicken
is a good egg.

Lemon Curd

Makes 2 cups

About 12 Meyer lemons
   (or substitute 5 standard
   lemons and 1 orange)

¾ cup sugar

¼ pound (1 stick) unsalted
   butter, cut up

4 eggs

1. Squeeze: Zest 2 lemons and cast the zest into a
large heavy saucepan. Squeeze fruit and measure
out ¾ cup juice. Add juice to the pan along with
sugar, butter, and eggs.

2. Whisk: Cook over medium heat, whisking constantly, until thick, about 5 minutes. Press through a
fine-mesh sieve into a clean bowl.

3. Serve: Pour warm or cold over fresh berries, pancakes, pound cake, or just about anything else.

Lemon Mousse

Serves 4

Whip 1 cup heavy whipping cream with 2 tablespoons sugar and ½ teaspoon vanilla
extract to sturdy peaks. Gently fold into 2 cups cooled Lemon Curd. Spoon over fresh
berries. Is there a better spring dessert?

GRATITUDE

Giving thanks is a lovely tradition, dating back to the early settlers, who joined the already settled for a feast of felled deer, boiled root, and spare oyster. As—more or less—do we. We counted our blessings, which, inexplicably, did not include dining-room chairs.

So close to the rocky shore of Thanksgiving, I could not compose both pleasing menu and pleasing dining room. I planned to settle my settlers on the sofa. Then remembered I had invited guests.

Out stalking the urban oyster, I sighted a second couch. It was a fine specimen: four legs, five pillows and a mound of fluff, stuffed into linen. I texted Mom: "White couch?" Provoking the rapid: "No." I had it delivered.

I settled on oyster stew. Its ocean scent recalled the turbulent voyage. Its smooth slurp soothed the furrowed brow. Its hot swirl of salt and sweet eased the guests into the daunting task ahead.

I gave thanks for our sweet and salty bounty and for those whose good advice I failed to follow. And I offered gratitude for cream-based bisque, which blended so nicely into white upholstery.

Oyster Stew

Serves 8 as a first course

4 ounces bacon,
 frozen and sliced
 crosswise into fine strips

2 tablespoons
 unsalted butter

½ cup chopped onion

½ cup chopped celery

2 cloves garlic, chopped

3 tablespoons flour

2 cups milk

2 cups heavy
 whipping cream

Kosher salt and freshly
 ground black pepper

¼ teaspoon cayenne pepper

1 pint (about 4 dozen)
 shucked oysters with
 their liquor

1. **Crisp:** Heat a large Dutch oven over medium. When hot, scatter in bacon and cook, stirring, until crisp and brown, about 4 minutes. Scoop out and drain on paper towels, leaving rendered fat in the pan.

2. **Soften:** Sizzle butter into bacon fat. Tumble in onion, celery, and garlic. Cook over medium until meltingly soft, 20 minutes.

3. **Thicken:** Stir flour into vegetables and cook 3 minutes. Heat milk and cream in a saucepan. Pour into vegetables and cook, stirring, until thickened, about 5 minutes.

4. **Season:** Strain soup into a clean pan; discard solids. Season with salt and both peppers. Heat until steaming, but not boiling. Add oysters and their strained liquor. Cook just until oysters plump and their edges begin to curl, 2 minutes. Serve in small cups, very hot, garnished with bacon shards.

A LAZY LOAF

A bundle showed up on my doorstep with a note attached. It read: "Amish Friendship Bread." I took in the baggie of sticky starter and, following the instructions, burped it and nursed it, like a foundling, on milk and flour and sugar.

On Day 10, the note insisted, I was to feed, divide, and mix. I added more flour, more milk, more sugar. But drew the line at "One large box of instant vanilla pudding." I'm not sure what's Amish or friendly or homemade about instant vanilla pudding, but I wasn't willing to find out. I mounded the mess in a pan, sprinkled on cinnamon sugar and slid it into the oven.

It came out moist and brown and terribly sweet.

I had been instructed to pour the remaining starter into four zip-top bags and give away three. Like all chain letters, this one appealed to my better nature: Share friendship! And to base fear: Neglect and the starter will die!

True, if not especially friendly. Bread starter can be conjured from flour and water and airborne yeast. The sour blob, like yogurt culture and kambucha mushroom, dooms the cook to a lifetime of tending.

But it's not necessary to quickbread. The cook can switch to baking soda, bolster her batter with sour cream, and bake a tender, tangy teabread. One she can share, or devour solo.

Standoffish Cinnamon Loaf

Makes 1 large loaf

2 teaspoons unsalted butter, melted

1 cup sugar

1½ teaspoons ground cinnamon

Fine salt and freshly ground black pepper

½ cup walnuts, toasted

¼ pound (1 stick) unsalted butter, softened

2 eggs

1 cup sour cream

1 teaspoon vanilla

1¾ cups flour

1 teaspoon baking soda

1. Mix: Brush a 9 x 5 x 3 loaf pan with the melted butter. Stir together ½ cup sugar, the cinnamon, a fat pinch of salt and a few grinds of pepper. Sprinkle 2 tablespoons cinnamon mixture over the bottom and sides of the pan.

2. Grind: Toss walnuts and remaining cinnamon mixture into the food processor. Grind fine.

3. Fold: Use a stand mixer fitted with the paddle attachment to cream softened butter and remaining ½ cup sugar. Crack in eggs, fluff. Measure in sour cream and vanilla, fluff. Whisk together flour, soda, and a pinch of salt. Sprinkle flour mixture over sour cream mixture; fold gently. Cast on half the walnut mix; fold once or twice, aiming for a marbled effect.

4. Bake: Scrape batter into prepared loaf pan. Top with remaining nut mixture. Slide into a 325-degree oven and bake until a toothpick poked in the center comes out clean, about 50 minutes. Cool a bit, turn out, slice, and savor, with or without friends.

GOOD AND BAD

Fried food has a terrible reputation. Greasy. Fatty. Fast. Which is unkind. The civil society expects its citizens to learn—and practice—tolerance.

Just because the tempura-battered onion, the slim-sliced potato, or the lamb-stuffed samosa does its tanning in the deep-fryer, that doesn't make it bad. The honest will concede that fried food can be good. Very good.

It's the standard double standard: The lovely and luscious get blamed for attracting attention. But the self-respecting fritter knows better. Treated considerately, the eggroll, beignet, or churro can cook up crisp, light, and quick.

An entire holiday honors fried food. Hanukkah celebrates many a miracle, including a remarkably steady supply of oil. In commemoration, the chosen choose to celebrate over the fried. Praise and sour cream alike are heaped on the oil-crisped potato pancake. Jam jams the middle of the deep-fried dough pillows called soufganiyot.

The plump pouf calls for careful crisping in oil neither scorching hot nor sogging cool. A steady sizzle will seal the outside and steam-puff the inside. The task can be eased by two tools: the reliable thermometer and the sturdy mnemonic device. Maintain an even 365 degrees, just another reminder that naughty can be nice—daily.

Soufganiyot
Makes 4 dozen

2¼ teaspoons (1 packet) active dry yeast

½ cup whole milk, lukewarm

¼ pound (1 stick) unsalted butter

1 vanilla bean

½ cup sugar

4 egg yolks

1 tablespoon brandy

½ teaspoon fine salt

½ teaspoon freshly grated nutmeg

2½ cups (or so) flour

Vegetable oil for frying

½ cup raspberry jam

Powdered sugar

1. Proof: Scatter yeast into a large mixing bowl. Pour in warm milk. Let rest.

2. Brown: Melt butter in a small saucepan over medium heat. Split vanilla bean the long way and scrape seeds into the pan. Add bean. Cook until butter browns, about 10 minutes. Let cool. Remove bean.

3. Mix: Stir into yeast mixture sugar, yolks, brown butter, brandy, salt, nutmeg, and 2½ cups flour. Dough will be sticky. Cover bowl with plastic wrap and let rise, 2 hours.

4. Cut: Dust dough with about 1 tablespoon flour. Turn out onto a floured surface. Pat into a square ½-inch thick. Use a pizza cutter to slice into 1-inch squares. Set dough squares on a floured baking sheet, cover with a kitchen towel and let rise, 1½ hours.

5. Fry: Pour oil into a deep heavy pan to a depth of 3 inches. Heat to 365 degrees. Add 1 dough square and cook until puffed and brown, about 1 to 2 minutes per side. Scoop out with a slotted spoon. Break open and check that the center is cooked through. If not, lower heat and increase time a smidge. Fry the rest, a few at a time. Drain on a rack set over a rimmed baking sheet.

6. Fill: Poke each puff with the tip of a knife. Spoon jam into a zip-top or pastry bag. Squeeze in 1 teaspoon jam per puff. Sprinkle with powdered sugar. Munch warm.

IN THE DOGHOUSE

My dog was an animal. He growled at the innocent. He barked at the friendly. He lunged at the next-door cat, releasing himself from my grip and my arm from its socket. He dined, eagerly. His taste ran toward freshly buttered bagel, freshly delivered babka, and freshly braised brisket. It was astonishing he survived such antics.

Originally, my father had served as reference for this dog. "The best family dog," he decreed, "is a Lab." We acquired a Lab. I tried not to hold it against him.

So when Dad said my dog needed help, I demurred. He suggested I try Australian dog training. A woman came to my house dressed as a duck. She recommended I change my dog's diet from kibble to gourmet kibble. And she suggested I learn to bark.

Which I did. The dog continued to growl at the innocent, bark at the friendly, and lunge at the cat. But my children's behavior changed dramatically. They took on the look of the perpetually mortified.

Then Dad came to visit. My dog seemed eager to show off new skills. He rushed the sofa, grasped a pillow and opened it, ziplock style. He made quick work of the rest, frosting the rug with a thick layer of feathers. Then he swallowed Dad's hearing aid.

I decided to give my bark a rest and focus on bite. I baked up a tray of Australian sausage rolls. They came out somewhat more American pig-in-a-blanket. Which, come to think of it, might make a good pet.

Sausage Roll
Makes 12

3 cooked beef bratwurst

1 package (about 1 pound) all-butter puff pastry, defrosted

1 egg, separated

1 tablespoon Dijon mustard

1 teaspoon water

1. **Grill:** Light the barbie (or broiler), and set on bratwurst. Grill, turning regularly, until well tattooed, about 5 minutes. Cool slightly. Quarter the long way.

2. **Roll:** Unfold puff pastry on a lightly floured surface and roll out to an 18 x 16-inch rectangle. Whisk together egg yolk and mustard; brush all over pastry. Cut pastry into 12 strips, 8 x 3 inches each.

3. **Wrap:** Roll up quartered brats in pastry strips (straight on or spiral), twisting ends.

4. **Bake:** Set sausage rolls on a parchment-paper-lined baking sheet. Whisk together egg white and water; brush each roll. Slide into a 400-degree oven. Bake until puffed and golden, about 15 minutes. Serve warm.

BLACK AND WHITE

Mixed marriage called for fortitude. Especially mine, which binds until death opinionated New Yorker and opinionated non-New Yorker. The door to our room is posted with the plea: "Mom and Dad, pleas don't fite."

Not that we sweat the shallow stuff, like Cubs versus Yankees or mortgage versus vacation. But when it comes to the deep, we don't budge. Like the cookie. Bob believes in the black-and-white, the oversize medallion conferred shrink-wrapped place of honor in deli, bakery, and sitcom. To the big-city child, it's the big cookie.

A position I respect but do not share. To me the black-and-white hardly qualifies as cookie. It isn't crisp, like the Oreo. Nor pliant, like the chocolate chip. Nor crumbly, like the peanut butter. It's spongy, like a sponge. The black-and-white comes coated with a plaster of wet, set confectioners' sugar, as smooth and tasty as wet, set plaster. It's the sort of cookie that inspires me to shrug. Or meddle.

Discouraged by the original's bland base, I baked a chewy, chocolate version. Bob found it scandalous. Disheartened by the sugar-sweet glaze, I painted a melted chocolate version, which Bob found dry. I dipped a ganache-coated version, which Bob found ridiculous.

Eventually I caved, settling for a traditional vanilla puck, pleasantly cakey. I smoothed on melted meringue, half bright white, half dark chocolate. It isn't the native New Yorker's black-and-white, but it honors the original's ethic of cooperation, as well as our own motto: Don't fite.

White-and-Black Cookies

Makes 24 big cookies

3 cups flour

¾ teaspoon fine salt

¼ teaspoon baking soda

½ pound (2 sticks) butter, softened

1⅓ cups sugar

2 eggs

2 teaspoons vanilla extract

½ cup sour cream

Two-Toned Icing (recipe follows)

1. Mix: Whisk together flour, salt, and baking soda.

2. Fluff: Using a stand mixer fitted with the paddle attachment set on medium-high, cream butter and sugar, until fluffy, about 3 minutes. Add eggs and vanilla, fluff 1 minute. Switch to low speed; mix in half the flour mixture. Mix in sour cream. Mix in remaining flour.

3. Shape: Scoop golf-ball-sized mounds of dough onto parchment-paper-lined baking pans. With wet fingers pat each ball into a 3-inch wide disk.

4. Bake: Slide 1 pan into the center of a 350-degree oven and bake until cookies turn golden at the edges and springy in the center, about 14 minutes. Repeat with remaining pans. Cool.

5. Decorate: Flip cookies to the flat side. Use a small offset spatula to frost in white and black. A semicircle of each color is traditional but not required. For a cooperative, marbled effect, use the tines of a fork to pull some dark icing to the light side and vice versa.

Two-Toned Icing

Crack 3 egg whites into the bowl of a stand mixer. Measure in 1 cup sugar. Set this bowl over a pan of simmering water. Whisk until egg mixture is 165 degrees hot, about 5 minutes. Return bowl to the mixer and whisk on high speed into fluffy, glossy peaks, about 5 minutes. Divide into two bowls. For white: Mix in 1 teaspoon vanilla extract and 1 to 2 tablespoons hot water, enough to calm the peaks into glossy, spreadable icing. For black: Mix in 2 ounces melted unsweetened chocolate and 1 to 2 tablespoons hot water or coffee, enough to achieve glossy, spreadable icing.

PROVENANCE: *Cookie dough adapted from* The All-American Cookie Book *by Nancy Baggett. Nontraditional icing may scandalize the New Yorker, but it will delight everyone else.*

IN DISGUISE

We had a vegetarian for dinner. He was amiable. And flexible. Not that he tolerated meat or seafood or fish. Or even broth that remembered meat or seafood or fish. But he was willing to endure egg and cheese. And happy to bring his own tofurkey.

Hardly necessary, I said. Or advisable, I thought. But he insisted. He's crazy about tofurkey.

I had nothing against tofu. (I had nothing against the stray vegetarian, either.) I liked creamy tofu cubed into miso soup or sturdy tofu cavorting through the broccoli stir-fry. But I was skeptical of food in disguise. And a block of tofu carved into roast-turkey pose seemed odd.

Though, as art, interesting. I cataloged my favorite food-shaped foods: The foil-wrapped chocolate "sardine" clamped into a twist-key can. The faux-mushroom meringue dusted with cocoa "spores." The roulade log, buttercream striated into bark. Maybe, I thought, I was guilty of carnivorous, dessertarian prejudice.

When the tofurkey was unveiled from its foil cloak, I was disappointed. It looked like a brown, shriveled cantaloupe, with gravy. Nothing like a turkey. "What would be the point of that?" the vegetarian asked. Something, I suppose, like the point of calling a ball of tofu tofurkey. But I let it go.

Afterward, I considered boiling down the tofu carcass into broth. But decided to go with mushroom, which offers a meaty mouthful, minus the masquerade.

Mushroom Broth

Makes 2 quarts

1 ounce dried porcini
  mushrooms

1 cup hot water

1½ tablespoons olive oil

1 onion, chopped

2 carrots, chopped

2 celery stalks, chopped

2 cloves garlic, chopped

6 sprigs fresh parsley,
  chopped

4 sprigs fresh thyme

3 fresh sage leaves

2 bay leaves

1 teaspoon kosher salt

9 cups cold water

1. Soak: Settle mushrooms in a small bowl. Douse with hot water. Let soak.

2. Caramelize: Heat oil in a large soup pot. Add onion and cook, stirring, over medium heat until deeply colored, about 20 minutes.

3. Soften: Tumble in carrots, celery, garlic, herbs, and salt. Cook, stirring, until softened 5 minutes.

4. Strain: Pour mushrooms through a coffee filter. Add liquid to the pot. Rinse mushrooms and add to the pot along with 9 cups water.

5. Simmer: Bring broth to a boil; simmer until deeply colored and fragrant, 45 minutes. Strain through a fine-mesh sieve. Makes a flavorful base for vegetable soups and an excellent start to French onion soup.

PROVENANCE: *Adapted from* The Greens Cookbook, *by Deborah Madison and Edward Espe Brown.*

SUGAR ICING

Skiing put me in mind of fluffy snow, sunny afternoons, and drifts of whipped cream adrift on hot chocolate. Invited to a mountain redoubt, I doubt not.

I had a working knowledge of the ski acquired in the west, which proved useless in the east.

I zipped into my jacket. And was remanded to the closet to layer in waffleweave underwear, underglove, and underhelmet balaclava.

The snow glistened like ice. Which it was. All day I shrieked down the ice-crusted mountain. I gasped at the ice-crusted air. I marveled at the ice pellets that pinged against my helmet, wriggled down my balaclava, and shot up my nose.

At last light I skidded to a stop and followed the scent of burnt sugar to a small log cabin. I clomped in line with the other skier-shaped ice pops and was handed a waffle.

This was no weak-willed waffle. This was a thick, hot confection studded with ice pellets, which turned out to be pearls of pearl sugar. I bit, and was warmed right down to my waffleweave.

Back home I tried to re-create the sugar waffle, staple of the Belgian street corner. I tinkered with its yeast-raised friendliness, its sugar-speckled graininess, its butter-bolstered tenderness. And though my home waffle delighted me, it never delivered the sheer bliss I had experienced on the mountain. Which might have been gratitude for having survived.

Sugar Waffles

Serves 10

Sponge:

5½ teaspoons active dry yeast

1 tablespoon sugar

¼ cup warm water

⅓ cup milk

1 egg, beaten

1 cup flour

Paste:

6 tablespoons flour

1 tablespoon sugar

¼ teaspoon baking powder

1 pinch salt

9 tablespoons (1 stick plus 1 tablespoon) unsalted butter, softened

1 teaspoon vanilla extract

½ cup pearl sugar*

1. Proof: To make sponge, measure yeast and sugar into a large bowl. Pour in warm water. Let stand until creamy, 5 minutes. Mix in milk and egg, then flour. Cover with plastic wrap and let sponge rise until doubled, about 20 minutes.

2. Mash: To make paste, mix flour, sugar, baking powder, and salt together in a medium bowl. Drop in butter and stir smooth. Gently stir in vanilla and pearl sugar.

3. Shape: Work paste into sponge to form a sticky dough. With floured hands divide dough into 10 balls. Set dough balls on a floured baking sheet. Flatten each slightly into a thick disk.

4. Bake: Heat a waffle iron to 350 degrees or the lowest setting. Settle one dough disk in each section and bake until just golden outside, still tender inside, about 3 minutes. Lift out. Repeat with remaining dough. In the Belgian tradition, serve warm and unadorned.

*Pearl sugar is available on the imported-foods shelves of fancy grocery stores and online through wafflecabin.com and other sites. Lacking pearl sugar, cut sugar cubes into quarters.

PROVENANCE: *Waffle Cabin's Ingrid Heyrman refused to divulge her secret formula for waffles, but she sent me a recipe from the 1996 cookbook "Everybody Eats Well in Belgium." This recipe is adapted from that.*

NEVER GETS OLD

New is nice, if fleeting.

New flashes crisp color, clean edge, sharp scent. Consider the brief brilliance of the fresh crayon, smooth lipstick, taut wallet. Consider the pearly string of zeroes aligned on the virgin odometer, the crinkle of paper-covered carpeting, the shiny plastic smell of new car.

The new owner inhales, yoga style, exhaling any disappointment over the low trade-in rate and lack of nav. One deep breath and the new owner knows pride, good posture, and dread.

Because the line between new and not-so-new is slim. Say, for instance, the new car owner idles in the grocery-store parking lot, waiting for a spot. She may be alarmed to discover that the minivan framed in the windshield is attempting to back into her smiling new grille. She may shift into reverse, admire the rearview cam, and navigate into a cinder-block wall. In this case, the line between new and not-so-new measures nine inches long, one inch wide, and a paint job deep. She sighs. Shifts into drive. And drives.

Back home the new owner unpacks a sack of oranges. With a sharp knife, she strips away the peel and pith, exposing the crisp color and sharp scent of citrus: perpetually fresh. She boils red wine into a sticky syrup, reveling in the knowledge that wine is best not-so-new. She douses new with old and savors the simple and simply delightful combination. Delicious, she thinks, licking her spoon, never gets old.

Oranges with Wine Sauce

Serves 8

1 bottle red wine (preferably inexpensive and Spanish)

1 cup plus 2 tablespoons sugar

1 stick cinnamon

8 cold oranges (or a mix of tangerines, tangelos, blood oranges, and oranges)

1. Reduce: Pour wine into a medium saucepan. Stir in 1 cup sugar and the cinnamon stick. Set over high heat and boil until reduced to 1 cup, about 20 minutes. Let cool.

2. Swirl: Zest 2 oranges. Buzz zest and remaining 2 tablespoons sugar in the food processor until fragrant, 2 minutes.

3. Slice: Lop off north and south poles of each orange. Cut away remaining peel and pith in long north-to-south strokes. Cutting between the strips of membrane, slice out wedges of orange. In the food trade these naked wedges are called "supremes." Slice wedges crosswise into triangles. Lift out any seeds as you work.

4. Serve: Settle triangles into 8 shallow bowls. Drizzle with wine syrup. Sprinkle with orange sugar.

PROVENANCE: *Adapted from a refreshing dessert served by my friend Debbie Kane, who adapted it from* Bon Appetit.

COMFORT FOOD

The needy need sustenance. So when the casserole contingent cornered me, I shrugged "sure." I was issued a 13 x 9-inch foil pan and orders: bake, freeze, and deliver. That's the sort of duty I can usually handle.

Then I read the recipe. It called for canned cream of mushroom soup, canned mushrooms, and dehydrated onion soup mix. The family burdened by bad job market, bad housing, or bad health need not be further demoralized by bad food. Troubles—big or small—call for the comfort of food that's real, and really good.

Claiming conscientious-objector status, I requested permission to pursue an alternative casserole: mac 'n' cheese. Honoring tradition, I stuck with the classic construction—elbow noodles paddling through Cheddar-bolstered béchamel. Given the deep-dish presentation, I decided to side with the crumb-top adherents.

Over the course of a cold and snowy week, I stocked my freezer with one rendition after another. I smoothed the sauce with less butter and more milk. I perked up the palate with Gruyère. And spiked the breadcrumbs with garlic.

The final version packed a creamy, steamy taste of home. Balm, I hope, to someone without a home.

Big Mac 'n' Cheese
Serves 12

2 tablespoons unsalted butter, melted

1 small clove garlic

¼ cup loosely packed fresh parsley leaves

1 (1-pound) Italian or country bread; split, soft middle pulled out (save crust for another project)

1 teaspoon kosher salt

1 pound elbow noodles

5 tablespoons unsalted butter, cubed

5 tablespoons flour

1 quart nonfat milk, warm

½ teaspoon freshly ground black pepper

⅛ teaspoon cayenne pepper

¼ teaspoon grated nutmeg

8 ounces (about 2 cups) Cheddar cheese, shredded

4 ounces (about 1 cup) Gruyère cheese, shredded

1. **Prep:** Set a 13 x 9-inch foil (or other) pan on a rimmed baking sheet. Brush bottom and sides of pan with some of the melted butter.

2. **Crumble:** Drop garlic down the chute of the spinning food processor and buzz it to bits. Drop in parsley leaves. Add bread; whirl into fluffy breadcrumbs. Drizzle in remaining melted butter and ¼ teaspoon salt. Pulse once or twice.

3. **Boil:** Bring a big pot of salted water to a boil. Add noodles and cook until firm but tender. Drain.

4. **Thicken:** Meanwhile, melt cubed butter in a large saucepan set over medium heat. Whisk in flour and let cook 2 minutes. Pour in milk and whisk thick, 7 minutes. Season the sauce with remaining ¾ teaspoon salt, both peppers, and nutmeg. Tumble in cheeses and stir smooth, about 2 minutes. Stir in noodles.

5. **Bake:** Scrape cheesy noodles into prepared pan. Pat bread crumbs across the top. (To save: Cover with foil and freeze. Uncover and bake at 375 degrees for 35 minutes.) Otherwise, bake at 375 degrees until golden and bubbling, about 20 minutes.

IN THE GAME

Food TV fails to impress. Sure those chefs can compose a complicated, beautiful, and delicious dish—times four—in less than sixty minutes. Sure they can do it under the scrutiny of three surly judges, one well-oiled host, and an incredulous home audience. Sure they can turn spinach, raisins, and a can of hominy into dessert. But that's nothing. Nothing compared to Average Mom.

In this competition, the contestant faces two hungry, overwrought judges and one harried, undercaffeinated host with a train to catch. Her challenge: To cook and plate three breakfasts, prep and pack two lunches, feed and walk one dog. In twenty-five minutes. With found ingredients. While pelted with bonus questions. Pre-shower.

For instance, while attempting to piece together a quesadilla from two neglect-crisped tortillas, cheese crumbs, and a banana, she may be asked to calculate the surface area of a cylinder. Should she shout "radius squared times pi times height," she will be disqualified. Because that formula yields volume, not surface.

And should she manage to pacify the dog and fill the lunchbox and check the homework and serve a wholesome whole grain breakfast and spell, correctly, muesli, she will have won. No matter how the judges rule.

Swiss Breakfast
Serves 2

Milk

Lemon

Apple

Rolled oats

Raisins

Blueberries

Slivered almonds

1. Curdle: Measure 3 tablespoons milk into each of two cereal bowls. Drizzle 2 teaspoons lemon juice into each. Milk will curdle; don't fret.

2. Grate: Set a box grater over a sheet of wax paper. Grate an apple (with peel) on the large holes. Scoop half the grated apple into each bowl.

3. Decorate: Sprinkle each serving with some rolled oats, a few raisins, a handful of blueberries, and a spoonful of slivered almonds. Good job.

SWEET RELIEF

Tax day, like most holidays, rolls around once a year—yet it always comes as a surprise. Like most, it calls for preparation. Which is to say three months of procrastination, followed by a single frantic night of hunting down and toting up. It calls for the sigh. The slump. And the snack.

Which is where many a taxpayer comes up short. He may be the sort to fell, stuff, and mount the wily receipt. He may slice and serve a brilliant electronic pie chart. He may text the accountant mercilessly. But no citizen of the United States of America need endure taxation without snackification. Isn't this why we tossed tea into the harbor?

The Internal Revenue Service recognizes two options. Intermittent Tax-Filing Incentive Snackification calls for the taxpayer to prepare a huge bowl of something sweet and salty and crunchy and set it a short reach from the 1040. He files and munches, until one or the other is done.

Culmination Tax-Filing Incentive Snackification calls for the taxpayer to prepare a huge bowl of something sweet and salty and crunchy and not touch it until he returns the return. One study found that Americans who checked off this box completed their tax preparation 72 percent faster than those using schedule A.

Of course, many a savvy taxpayer employs both Intermittent and Culmination Snackification on a single return. Which might qualify popcorn, almonds, and brown sugar for tax-deductible status.

Tax Crunch Crunch

Makes 1 big bowl

½ cup slivered almonds

3 tablespoons corn oil

¾ cup popcorn kernels

6 tablespoons unsalted butter, cut up

1 cup light brown sugar

¼ cup light corn syrup

2 tablespoons water

1¼ teaspoons fine salt

½ teaspoon baking soda

2 teaspoons vanilla extract

1. Toast: Shake almonds in a small heavy skillet over medium heat, until golden brown, about 5 minutes.

2. Pop: Stir together oil and popcorn in a large heavy pot. Cover, leaving lid a sliver ajar, and set over medium-high heat. Cook, shaking regularly, until popping sound slows, about 5 minutes. When quiet, tumble popped corn into a very large mixing bowl. Discard unpopped bachelors.

3. Thicken: Measure butter, sugar, corn syrup, water, and salt into a large saucepan. Set over medium-high heat and stir until mixture comes to a boil, about 4 minutes. Cook without stirring until caramel reaches 240 degrees, about 5 minutes. Pull off heat and stir in baking soda and vanilla. Caramel will foam up. Stir in nuts.

4. Mix: Pour hot caramel over the popped corn. Fold together with a soft spatula. Turn out onto two parchment-paper-lined rimmed baking sheets.

5. Bake: Slide sheets into a 250-degree oven and bake, stirring every 15 minutes, until crisp, 1 hour. Cool and crunch.

PROVENANCE: *Adapted from Ceiba restaurant, located not far from the Treasury Department in Washington, D.C.*

URBAN CRIME

Nature and nurture collude in the espalier. The tree with excellent posture and elegant outstretched limbs is as captivating as the ballerina holding her arms in second position—forever. The 3-D tree that thrives in two dimensions offers an Escher-esque appeal.

Many a plant strikes the unlikely pose. Consider rosemary twined into wreath form, the boxwood trimmed into topiary cone, the bonsai pruned into contemplative pose. Even the shaggy tomato plant rests its weary shoulders against a cage.

But training a deep-rooted tree calls for years of planning and pruning and tying and patience. Fortunately, the urban gardener need not practice planning and pruning and tying and patience. She can simply drop by the nursery and point.

Which I did. The tree's limbs were bent into "don't shoot" position and dotted, thrillingly, with pre-pears. They looked like berries, then grapes, and matured, over the warm months, into shapely fruit. Green at first, and then one sunny afternoon, gone. No note, nothing. I noticed a fat squirrel hurrying away, carrying something round and heavy. I think it was muttering, "Don't shoot."

I had meant to pick the first pear, to savor its curvy good looks, thin skin, and grainy bite. I had meant to peel and core and caramelize it, wrap it Escher-style, in a long strip of pastry, and bake it into a golden pear-shaped pie. It would have made a captivating dessert. Perhaps one best served with barbecued squirrel.

Upright Pear Pies
Serves 6

6 firm, ripe Bartlett pears

3 tablespoons
    unsalted butter

½ cup sugar, plus a little

Sturdy Pastry (recipe follows)

1 egg, lightly beaten with
    1 teaspoon water

Whipped cream, optional
    (page 291)

1. Peel: Use a vegetable peeler to peel pears, leaving stems intact. Working from the bottom, use an apple-corer to carve out the seeds and core, leaving pear otherwise whole.

2. Caramelize: Melt butter and ½ cup sugar in a wide skillet over medium heat. Add pears. Cook, turning pears gently with a wooden spatula, until syrup turns to caramel, about 15 minutes. Lower heat and continue to cook until pears are tattooed deep brown, about 15 minutes. Let cool.

3. Slice: Roll out pastry into a rectangle, ⅛-inch thin. Use a pizza cutter or pastry wheel to slice into long 1-inch wide strips.

4. Wrap: Brush pastry with beaten egg. Wrap each pear in pastry, bottom to top, mummy style. Decorate with leaves cut from pastry.

5. Bake: Set pears on a parchment-paper-lined baking sheet. Brush with egg wash and sprinkle lightly with a little sugar. Slide into a 375-degree oven and bake golden, 35 minutes. Serve warm, with or without whipped cream.

Sturdy Pastry

Wraps 6 pears

Measure 2 cups flour into a large bowl. Cut in 12 tablespoons unsalted butter. Whisk together 1 egg, 3 tablespoons cold water, 2 tablespoons sugar, and ¼ teaspoon salt. Drizzle egg over flour. Fold together with a soft spatula. Pat into a disk, wrap, and chill 1 hour.

'ᴄᴄᴄᴏᴏ'

PRESSED

The modern mom cares for her children incessantly. And for her parents intermittently. Sometimes she tends to both child and parent, at home and abroad, at the same time.

The sociologist likens her condition to that of a sandwich. Not a sandwich in the sense of easy and easily portable. A sandwich in the sense of squeezed from two sides. She is a pressed sandwich. Perhaps an oppressed sandwich. Occasionally a depressed sandwich. And yet, impressive.

The ordinary PB&J or egg salad on whole wheat goes squishy in the housing. Not so the panino, Cuban, grilled cheese, or crispy smoked duck with arugula and Manchego.

Such a sandwich may be built on a tender roll or sliced white. It takes heat from the griddle, grill, or skillet while enduring the weight of the press, pot, or heavy hand. It comes off the fire warmed through, cheese crusted, and nearly charred. And better for it.

Pressed Sandwich

Serves 4

1 small (½ pound) smoked duck breast*

1 handful baby arugula

1 tablespoon chopped red onion

Kosher salt and freshly ground black pepper

¼ pound Manchego (or other sheep's milk) cheese

1 (24-inch) baguette

2 tablespoons cherry preserves

1. **Render:** Pull fat off the duck breast; chop finely. Cast fatty bits into a large cast-iron skillet set over medium-high heat. Cook, stirring regularly, until fat coats pan and the bits have turned crunchy brown, about 10 minutes.

2. **Season:** Scoop crunchy bits into a bowl (set aside fat-slicked pan). Toss bits with arugula, red onion, salt, and pepper.

3. **Slice:** Carve duck meat into 8 thin slices. Slice cheese into 8 thin strips. Cut baguette into four 6-inch lengths; slice each in half horizontally. Open and pull out much of the bread's soft middle (save it for crumb duty another day).

4. **Compose:** Open 1 bread set. Spread sparingly with cherry preserves. Layer onto the bottom half: cheese, duck, arugula mix, duck, cheese. Top with cherry-spread top. Squish. Repeat with remaining ingredients, composing 4 sandwiches.

5. **Grill:** Heat duck-fat coated skillet over medium-high heat. Add sandwiches. Weight them down with another skillet, a full tea kettle, or another heavy object. Toast until bread is crispy and cheese melted, 2 minutes per side. Slice each sandwich in half on the diagonal. Make time to enjoy.

PROVENANCE: *Adapted from chow.com.*

*Often stocked in the sausage section. French importer D'Artagnan can be found at many markets and online. Otherwise, substitute smoked turkey breast for duck breast and olive oil for duck fat.

DUMPLING DIPLOMACY

My knowledge of Afghan culture could be stuffed into a dumpling. Cultural Crossroad. Hot and Cold. Proxy War. War War. But if civility convenes at the table, then my own peace plan starts in the kitchen.

I read up on Aushak, the dumpling darling of Afghanistan. Aushak may be boiled in a distant mountainscape, but they cook up as fragrant and familiar as ravioli.

Start with the leek—as common to the landlocked wilds there as to the kitchen garden here. Chop, spice, and soften over low heat. Heap the pungent mixture onto a dumpling skin. You can make the wrapper from flour and water and waiting and rolling and slicing. Or, taking advantage of crosscultural convenience, let the wonton wrapper serve as proxy. Fold, boil, and sauce twice: Once with a hot tomato ragu. Once with a cold yogurt swirl.

Hot and cold, thick and thin, cooked and raw work well together. Inspiration, perhaps, for us all.

Aushak

Aushak are traditionally served with both tomato meat sauce and yogurt sauce. This spring version calls for yogurt only. Green garlic or ramps would make good seasonal substitutes for the leeks.

Serves 4 as a first course

1 cup Greek yogurt

1 clove garlic, degermed and pressed

2 teaspoons chopped fresh mint leaves

1 to 2 teaspoons lime juice

1 teaspoon kosher salt

2 leeks

1 tablespoon olive oil

1 to 2 tablespoons water

¼ teaspoon cayenne pepper

20 wonton wrappers

1. Swirl: In a small bowl whisk together yogurt, garlic, mint, lime juice, and ½ teaspoon salt. Let sauce warm to room temperature.

2. Chop: Slice white and pale-green portion of leeks into long strips. Rinse and dry. Chop finely.

3. Soften: Heat oil in a medium skillet. Add leeks and cook over medium heat, adding water as needed, until tender and melded, about 20 minutes. Season with ½ teaspoon salt and cayenne pepper. Let cool.

4. Fold: Spoon 1 teaspoon leek mixture onto 1 wonton wrapper. Run a wet finger around the perim-

eter of the wrapper. Fold into a filled half-moon, triangle, or rectangle, pressing edges to seal. Repeat
with remaining wrappers.

5. Boil: Drop aushak in boiling, lightly salted water
and cook until tender and translucent, about 6 minutes. Scoop up with a slotted spoon and settle on
four plates. Spoon on a dollop of yogurt sauce.
Savor in peace.

SOUTHERN LIVING

Sarah's a straight arrow. The punctual, opinionated, pennywise type. Seat her next to a platter of miniature coconut cupcakes thick with cream-cheese frosting and the girl will munch not one, but two! So when she arrived for a southern-style garden party, I tempted her with a Southside.

The Southside is peculiar to Baltimore, which is peculiarly afflicted by summer. It's flush with lemon and lime and mint and rum. The native insists it shares nothing with the mojito (save lime and mint and rum).

Frankly, the cloudy Southside knows a cloudy pedigree. The cocktail historian traces its background to the South Side of Chicago, where its fruity flavor once masked the renegade rum's bathtub overtones.

The purist insists that the Southside can only be mixed by George Lee, one-time bartender at Baltimore's Elkridge Country Club, now eighty-something Southside entrepreneur. The local just gives him a call and he graciously drops by with a bot-tle. The interloper asks how to squeeze her own. To which he explains: "You can't."

Nonetheless, I've tried. My version may not duplicate Mr. Lee's sunshine-sweet elixir, but it's good for enduring summer.

Even Sarah declared it delicious. Which is saying a lot for someone who regularly downs one to two cocktails per year. The next night I saw Sarah at a big bash. She was wandering the edge of the dance floor looking forlorn. "No Southsides," she reported. I was proud of her: considering her second drink so soon. And I was proud of me, for pointing her toward wayward.

Southsides

Makes enough mix for about 8 drinks

2 cups water

2 cups sugar

6 lemons

6 limes

1 cup loosely packed mint leaves and stems

Club soda, chilled

Rum (Mount Gay is traditional)

1. Steep: Pour water and sugar into a medium saucepan. Zest 4 lemons; toss in zest. Bring to a boil, cover, and let simmer 3 minutes.

2. Juice: Squeeze all lemons and limes; measure out 2 cups (combined) juice. Pour juice into zest mixture.

3. Chill: Strain into a clean wide-mouthed glass jar. When cool add half the mint. Cover and chill.

4. Pour: For each drink settle a few of the remaining mint leaves in a tall 12-ounce glass. Fill with ice. Pour in 2 ounces Southside mix, 2 ounces rum, 2 ounces soda. Stir. Sip.

DO IT YOURSELF

The microwave went belly-up. Or, more specifically, door-open. Without the usual rejoinder of door-closed. After which it refused to zap.

Not that I cared. I liked to think I could raise tomato and eggplant and zucchini, build a bonfire, roast my crops, and machete them into ratatouille, right on the drab linoleum floor. I didn't need some high-speed light beam exciting the zucchini electrons into a frenzied state. I was good with DIY.

So when Noah announced, "Mom, the microwave door won't close," I shrugged and shoved it onto the deposed pile.

On dinner duty I dropped a cube of butter into the glass measuring cup, reached for the zap function and came up empty-handed. "No problem," I frowned. I pulled out a saucepan and melted the butter and poured it into the measuring cup, noting that the technique yielded the same quantity of melted butter, and a double helping of dishes. I scowled at the sponge.

Impatient, Noah opted for his own DIY. He slid a leftover grilled cheese from its carryout box. He stared at the congealed cheese sandwich, then at the empty square of counter space. He paused, then shouted, "Mo-om."

We considered reheating it in the oven, which seemed slow. We considered regrilling it on the stovetop, which seemed like overkill. We considered the barbecue, which seemed like a fire hazard. Finally we settled on the toaster, which made quick, crispy work of previously grilled cheese. "See," I smiled, "we don't need a microwave."

My cheese-streaked child didn't answer. He was busy tying each french fry into its own dental-floss harness, the better to lower it into the toaster. Maybe we do need a microwave.

End-of-Summer Ratatouille

Serves 8 per large eggplant

Eggplant

Onion

Bell pepper

Zucchini or yellow squash

Plum tomato

Kosher salt

Olive oil

Red wine vinegar

Garlic

Fresh basil

Freshly ground black pepper

1. Harvest: The late-summer garden is ripe with ratatouille-on-the-vine. Gather (from garden or grocery) eggplant, onion, pepper, zucchini, and tomato, roughly the same portion of each by weight.

2. Prep: Split vegetables in half the long way. Seed and core the tomatoes. Brush all vegetables with oil and sprinkle with salt. Let stand 20 minutes.

3. Grill: Grill vegetables over a medium-hot fire, turning once, until tender when squeezed. Figure about 25 minutes for squash, 20 for eggplant, onion, and pepper, 8 for tomato.

4. Marinate: When cool enough to handle, finely chop onion, pepper, and tomato. Coarsely chop zucchini and eggplant. Scoop all the vegetables into a large bowl along with any juice. Drizzle with oil (about ¼ cup for a 1-eggplant version) and a splash of vinegar. Season with a little chopped garlic and a lot of chopped basil. Grind on pepper and sprinkle with more salt, if you like. Refrigerate overnight. Serve warm. Reheats nicely in the microwave.

ORIGINAL SIN

Dishes are my specialty. In pursuit of the sandwich I may call upon salad spinner, cutting board, serrated knife, chef's knife, skillet, saucepan, wooden spoon, grater, peeler, plate, knife, spoon, and fork. Members of my household find this talent scary.

I know how disheartening the pileup can be. I empathize with the Swiss matron I once knew who would heave herself nightly from the dinner table with the prayer, "Du courage."

Honesty compels me to admit that this recipe calls for more time and more dishes than seems reasonable: about three days and the entire kitchen batterie. But then the culinary historian believes this to be the first ever tiramisu, the paleomisu, the original sin itself.

The retrograde recipe calls for four types of cream heaped over espresso-soaked ladyfingers, practically the only remnant retained by the modern one-bowl misu.

I did attempt restraint. I prepared half a dozen low-impact versions, with low-impact results. So here it is, the unapologetically fussy tiramisu. One worth the fuss.

High Impact Tiramisu
Serves 12

Zabaglione (recipe follows)

Pastry Cream (recipe follows)

Whipped Cream
  (recipe follows)

8 ounces mascarpone, at
  room temperature

1 package (24) ladyfingers

¾ cup cold espresso

2 tablespoon brandy

2 tablespoons sugar

¼ cup unsweetened
  cocoa powder

1. Mix: Stir together zabaglione and pastry cream in a large mixing bowl. Fold in whipped cream. Fold in softened mascarpone. Chill.

2. Layer: Arrange 12 ladyfingers in a single layer in a 9 x 9 x 2-inch pan. Mix espresso, brandy, and sugar in a small bowl. Brush ladyfingers with half the espresso mixture. Smooth on half the cream. Arrange a second layer of 12 ladyfingers. Brush with remaining espresso. Smooth on remaining cream. Dust with cocoa powder. Cover tightly and chill 1 to 3 days.

Zabaglione

5 egg yolks

½ cup sugar

½ cup sweet Marsala wine

1 teaspoon vanilla extract

Measure yolks, sugar, and wine into a mixing bowl. Swirl smooth with an immersion blender, 1 minute. Pour into the top of a double boiler set over medium-heat. Cook, whisking constantly, until hot and thickened, about 5 minutes. Pour into a clean bowl. Stir in vanilla. Cool, cover, and chill overnight.

Pastry Cream

½ cup sugar

⅓ cup flour

Finely grated zest of 1 lemon

3 egg yolks

2 cups whole milk

1 teaspoon vanilla extract

Measure sugar, flour, and zest into a heavy-bottomed saucepan. Add yolks and 1 cup milk. Swirl smooth with immersion blender, 1 minute. Set over low heat. Cook, whisking constantly, adding remaining milk a little at a time, until thick and smooth, about 10 minutes. Pour into a bowl. Stir in vanilla. Cool, cover, and chill overnight.

Whipped Cream

2 cups heavy
   whipping cream

¼ cup sugar

1 teaspoon vanilla extract

Whip cream, sugar, and vanilla to sturdy peaks. Chill.

PROVENANCE: *Adapted from the website of David Rosengarten, who adapted it from Baltimore baker Carminantonio Iannaccone.*

IN ABSENTIA

10/10/10 makes an impressive date, round and portentous. My mother and father were both born on 10/10, different years. It seemed a good day to celebrate. Besides, we had put off their fiftieth anniversary party for years.

Mom was thinking Chinese feast. Dad was thinking big band. The kids were thinking twenty-four-hour slideshow—one second for each of 86,400 family photographs.

One afternoon Dad noticed the landscape dim; he dialed 911. In the helicopter to the hospital, he charted the flight path in his head. Before bypass I asked if he was scared. He said: "No." He said not to worry; he might be out of touch for a while.

And then he went away. Maybe somewhere dark, somewhere beyond the reach of tube, of drip bag, of monitor crawl. Over weeks, then months, he would occasionally surface and smile or write a few words, and then dip down, back to wherever it was that he went.

Mom thought we should bring him home to warm bed and cold dog nose. The kids thought maybe another hospital. We got together to chart a plan.

We went to the museum to see Dad's work. He builds massive figures in clay, inhabitants of a dark and distant landscape. He prints enormous photographs, craggy rock faces that jut from the paper. We stood among those huge brooding forms, thinking how strong and keen he was. Wherever he was.

At night, we went to dinner with his students and his mentors and his friends. In the morning, we met with the medical director, the nursing service, the doctor on call.

In the afternoon, we tracked down the taco truck. We all liked the idea of the roving taco, on call. We ordered paper plates of pork carnitas and beef and chicken. There was a guy lingering by the picnic table; he needed a ride to the VA. Mom paid his cab fare.

The moment wasn't big and round and portentous. We didn't have Dad home, or better, or back from his travels. But we did have lunch with friends in the shade. And for a few minutes, it kept our worries away.

Papas Tacos

Serves 4

1 cup shredded
   romaine lettuce

¼ cup fresh cilantro leaves

2 scallions, white and tender
   green, cut into matchsticks

1 tablespoon freshly
   squeezed lime juice

Kosher salt

2 strips bacon, frozen and
   thinly sliced crosswise

1 clove garlic, finely chopped

1 teaspoon ground cumin

1 teaspoon dried oregano

1 large (29-ounce) can pinto
   beans, drained and rinsed

1 cup (or so) chicken broth
   or water

3 tablespoons peanut
   or corn oil

2 medium (9 ounces total)
   red potatoes, unpeeled,
   cut into matchsticks

Freshly ground black pepper

8 small corn tortillas

2 ounces (½ cup) crumbled
   queso fresco

Guacamole (recipe follows)

1. **Toss:** Heap together lettuce, cilantro, scallion, and lime juice in a bowl; toss. Season with a little salt.

2. **Crisp:** Heat a large cast-iron pan over medium. When hot, scatter in bacon and cook, stirring, until crisp and brown, about 4 minutes. Scoop out and drain on paper towels, leaving rendered fat in the pan.

3. **Mash:** Reduce heat under skillet to medium-low. Add garlic, cumin, and oregano to the bacon fat. Stir fragrant, 30 seconds. Add beans and broth. Cook, stirring and mashing, until thick, about 15 minutes. Add more broth if need be. Taste for salt.

4. **Fry:** Dry potatoes with a clean kitchen towel. In a separate skillet, heat oil over medium high. Add potatoes and fry until crisp and brown, about 7 minutes. Drain on paper towels. Season with salt and pepper. Toss with bacon.

5. **Steam:** Wrap tortillas in a clean, damp kitchen towel. Microwave until hot, about 2 minutes.

6. **Stack:** Set 2 tortillas (stacked up) on each of four plates. Spread with beans. Sprinkle with cheese. Pile on lettuce. Top with a spoonful of guacamole. Shower with potatoes. Munch.

Guacamole

Makes about 1 cup

Mash 1 clove garlic and 1 teaspoon salt together with a mortar and pestle (a Mexican molcajete would be traditional). Peel and pit 2 ripe avocados; mash in. Work in freshly squeezed juice of 1 lime.

CIRCULAR
REASONING

The sages claim that what goes around comes around. Which sounds sound.

I pulled the last recycling bag from the box, then slid the empty box into the bag, awestruck by the circle of life.

I remained captivated by the garden, where the seed grew into tomato, the tomato devolved into compost, the compost nourished the new tomato. Considering the neglect I applied to the garden, I found this cycle reassuring.

At times I wondered about the outer reaches of centrifugal force. I considered Theo scrabbling in a tight circle, in pursuit of his fleeing tail. What if he managed to catch and down it? Would he disappear? I gazed at the frantic ball of fur and claws, thrilled by the possibility.

In the kitchen, I spun my own frantic circle, churning cream into butter and producing buttermilk. Essential to the mashed potato. Which requires butter. Eerie.

At the table, face-to-face with the mashed potato mound, I felt awe. The butter/buttermilk/buttered potato cycle struck me as profound. Or at least profoundly delicious. The sages must have a word for this compact pleasure. Perhaps it's karma.

Endless Mashed Potatoes

Serves 12

2 cups heavy
    whipping cream

Fine salt

12 Russet potatoes, peeled
    and quartered

1. Churn: Pour cream into a butter churn, quart-sized glass jar fitted with a clean marble, or large mixing bowl. Churn (or shake or stir) as cream thickens, clumps, and turns to butter, about 20 minutes. This is an excellent job to hand to anyone underfoot in the kitchen.

2. Knead: Lift out butter and run under cool water, kneading gently, to release any trapped buttermilk. Heap into a bowl. Mash in 1 pinch (about $\frac{1}{16}$ teaspoon) salt. Cover and set aside. Strain buttermilk into a large serving bowl. Set the bowl near the stovetop to warm.

3. Boil: Settle potatoes in a large pot. Pour in cold salted water to cover by 1 inch. Simmer until fork-tender, about 15 minutes. Drain. Return potatoes to pot and pot to stove. Shake gently over medium heat until potatoes look dry, 1 minute.

4. Fluff: Set a potato ricer over the bowl of buttermilk. Run potatoes through ricer into bowl. Fluff with a fork. Immediately serve big scoops topped with fresh butter.

TIME MANAGEMENT

Should you find your home slovenly, your work overwhelming, and your hair appalling, you must throw a dinner party. It's the only remedy.

You can continue shoving laundry from here to there, paperwork from in to out, and hair from up to down. But more of the same gets you more of the same. You need something startling on the schedule: guests expecting to be entertained.

It's smart management. You remain hazy on the seven habits of highly effective people. But you're certain that eight is dinner at eight.

Know that the dinner party is not dinner. Dinner is the meal you compile night after night for yourself or your family or the occasional drop-in. Its guiding principles are nutrition, news, and did-you-finish-your-homework? It may be good or simply good enough.

The dinner party aims higher. You strive to turn out something striking and serve it up beautifully. You expect sparkling conversation, savory camaraderie, and sweet conviviality.

Perhaps it's mere vanity, writ delicious. But the impulse to please can be harnessed and turned—in the words of the superhero—to the cause of good.

The dinner party demands that you draw up a guest list and think of something to cook and find the tablecloth. Thought-provoking, time-consuming work. Distractions—like carpool or job—must be executed with brutal efficiency. The party eradicates both dilly and dally.

The dinner party demands you conform to certain social conventions. It's de rigueur that the guest be able to navigate the path from front door to sofa unencumbered by hazardous debris. If this means you must engage the vacuum cleaner, so be it. It's for a good cause.

Likewise hair. You can serve dinner in a swim cap. But the ambiance will be more relaxed if you and your hair agree on appropriate behavior well before hors d'oeuvres. You may need to consult a professional. Do what you must.

Best of all, the dinner party comes with rewards. You can happily check off the to-do list, incentivized, as the MBA would have it, by the promise of a sumptuous evening ahead. You know for certain there will be good company, delicious food, and a comfortable setting. Even if your own home strikes you, in party mode, as eerily clean, calm, and cheerful.

Calm Soup

Serves eight, happily

5 quarts fish stock
(make ahead, or better
yet buy this)

2 pound scallops

1 pound cod, cubed

1 cup dry white wine

2 pounds live mussels

1½ pounds lobsterette tails
or whole king prawns

1 pound monkfish
or John Dory, cubed

2 tablespoons each finely
chopped fresh thyme,
parsley, tarragon, and mint

½ cup heavy
whipping cream

Kosher salt

1. Simmer: Pour the fish stock into a large pot. Tumble in 1 pound scallops and all the cod cubes. Simmer until liquid is reduced by half, about 45 minutes. Let rest 20 minutes. The seafood is overcooked, but you don't care. You're after the intoxicating metal-scented broth that's left behind. Scoop out and dispense with scallops and cod (perhaps by impressing a cat).

2. Poach: Add the wine and turn up the heat. When hot, slip in the mussels and poach until they open, about 2 minutes. Scoop out mussels with a slotted spoon. Scrape out meat with a teaspoon and set aside in a bowl. Discard shells. Slip in the lobsterette and poach until just done, about 3 minutes. Scoop out lobsterette with a slotted spoon. Use a fork to pull out meat; add to the bowl with the cooked mussels. Discard shells. Add remaining 1 pound scallops and cook until just done, about 2 minutes. Scoop out scallops with a slotted spoon and add to the bowl of poached seafood. Add monkfish and cook until just done, about 4 minutes. Scoop out and add to the bowl.

3. Strain: Pour hot liquid through a cheesecloth-lined colander. Chill, if you're working ahead, or keep hot if you're on deadline.

4. Sort: Portion out the seafood into 8 wide bowls. Sprinkle with herbs.

5. Relax: Now time is suspended. The fish and seafood are perfectly done and safe from the peril

Recipe cont'd

of overcooking. The soup is hot and flavorful, but can hold, covered, over a low flame. Have a drink. Mingle.

6. **Serve:** Once you've lured your guests to the table with a simple salad, turn up the heat under the soup. Thicken with cream, season with salt. Ladle hot soup over the fish. Pass a basket of crunchy grilled bread and shallot butter. You've conquered the sea without breaking a sweat.

PROVENANCE: *Adapted from The FishGuy Market, Chicago.*

GOOD WILL TOWARD CRACKERS

The holidays called for the holiday party, and the holiday party called for toffee. The imported kind, coated with dark chocolate and dusted with praline. And the domestic kind, compiled from chocolate chip and saltine. Saltine toffee was thrillingly Cinderella: the lowly soup cracker exalted to party confection. Plus it was crazy delicious.

The secret ingredient was too compelling for actual secrecy. The hostess allowed her guest one bite before demanding: "Turn it over!" There, suspended in butter and brown sugar, floated the familiar hole-pocked cracker. Smirking.

The saltine didn't merely serve as thrifty butter extender, as handy where's-the-thermometer crispiness insurance. The soda cracker offered light layers and salty crunch to flirt with buttery sweet.

It wasn't the only cracker up to the task. In spring, many a hostess retrofitted her Christmas toffee for Passover duty with matzoh. The technique worked equally well with the rice cracker and the pita chip and—no doubt—the boxes they came in. What, dipped in butter and slathered in chocolate, emerged unimproved?

During the holiday season, as in all seasons, the hostess longed for peace on earth. She gazed at her toffees of many backgrounds. Surely this was a good place to start.

Saltine Toffee

Makes 36 bars

14 tablespoons (1 stick plus 6 tablespoons) unsalted butter

35 saltine crackers

1 cup dark brown sugar

12 ounces (2 cups) semisweet chocolate chips

1 cup chopped pecans, toasted

1. Organize: Line a 15 x 10-inch rimmed baking sheet with parchment paper, allowing for some overhang. Melt butter in a large saucepan. Brush parchment with a little of the butter. Line up crackers on buttered parchment, touching but not overlapping.

2. Thicken: Whisk brown sugar into remaining butter. Set over medium-high heat. Bring to a boil; cook until thick, about 2 minutes. Pour evenly over crackers.

3. Bake: Slide into a 400-degree oven and bake until brown and bubbly, about 6 minutes. Carefully remove from oven.

4. Gild: Scatter molten surface with chocolate chips. Let melt, 5 minutes. Use an offset spatula to spread chocolate. Cast on nuts; gently press into chocolate.

5. Cool: Freeze until firm, about 30 minutes.

6. Cut: Lift parchment by its overhang, and set toffee (paper and all) on a cutting surface. Slice into 18 squares, then into 36 triangles.

7. Confiscate: Take these to a party or risk toffee overload.

THE COLD SNAP

The kitchen should meet regularly with chicken. It's the dish that scents home homey. Especially chicken pot pie. The familiar mix of chicken and vegetables lolling in savory sauce, snuggled under a pastry blanket, brings to mind warm bed, good novel, and no need to budge. Hot pie improves cold weather.

Unless the sauce clings too intently. Then the whole contraption goes gloppy.

Achieving thick but not suffocating, creamy but not heavy is the pie maker's endless conundrum. I've tinkered with bases based on cream, half-and-half, and milk, finally settling on an all-broth approach. It whelms, instead of overwhelms, its pie compatriots.

Then there's the vegetable tussle. Factions in my household remain staunchly antipea. They square off against the pro-potato insurgents, caught in the crossfire of the celery-root snipers.

After a cold snap during which we subsisted on nothing but pot pie, I found I could rearrange the ingredients, anagram style, and come up with something familiar but fresh. This pie takes winter seriously; it's full of full-flavored browned mushrooms, onion, garlic, and carrot, and bolstered by port. It gets crunch from bacon and snap from sugar snap peas. All under cover of puff pastry. Hot from the oven, it makes you never want to leave your kitchen. Or chicken.

Winter Pot Pie

Serves 6

4 strips bacon, frozen and thinly sliced crosswise

8 ounces button mushrooms, halved

1 onion, quartered and sliced

3 carrots, sliced into coins

Kosher salt and freshly ground black pepper

1 clove garlic, chopped

1 teaspoon chopped fresh thyme (or ½ teaspoon dried)

2 tablespoons port wine

2 cups shredded rotisserie chicken

3 ounces sugar snap peas, thinly sliced crosswise

5 tablespoons unsalted butter

5 tablespoons flour

2½ cups chicken broth

A few grates of nutmeg

1 package (about 1 pound) all-butter puff pastry, defrosted

1 egg beaten with 1 teaspoon water, optional

1. **Crisp:** Heat a large cast-iron skillet over medium. When hot, scatter in bacon and cook, stirring, until crisp and brown, about 4 minutes. Scoop out and drain on paper towels, leaving rendered fat in the skillet.

2. **Brown:** Add mushrooms, onion, and carrots to the skillet with the rendered bacon fat. Season with salt and pepper. Cook until mushrooms are beautifully browned, 10 minutes. Add garlic and thyme; cook 1 minute. Deglaze with port. Scrape into a large bowl. Mix in chicken and snap peas.

3. **Thicken:** Melt butter over medium heat (feel free to use the same skillet, but note that cast-iron will tint the sauce an odd gray). Whisk in flour, cook 1 minute. Slowly add broth, whisking thick, 5 minutes. Season with salt, pepper, and nutmeg. Pour sauce over chicken and mix.

4. **Fill:** Scrape chicken mixture into a deep 9-inch pie plate (or other oven-safe pan). Cast on bacon. Cover with pastry; snip in a vent. Brush with beaten egg (or don't, for a more rustic look).

5. **Bake:** Slide into a 400-degree oven and bake until top is crisp and middle bubbles, 25 minutes. Dig in while warm.

KEEPER

Salt cod is a Christmas specialty somewhere. So at Christmastime I bought a brick. I stuck it in the back of the fridge, remembering that it's supposed to keep forever. Sometime later, actually about a year or so later, I read up on salt cod and pulled out the box.

Back when cod was plentiful and refrigeration sparse, the resourceful let salt, sun, and wind preserve the fish for eternity, or nearly.

The fish planks were packed into wooden boxes and shipped to places where people liked salt cod. Which is to say Spain. It remains wildly popular there, and with good reason, considering how many Spanish specialties involve salt cod revived with olive oil, garlic, and potatoes. One cookbook on my shelf details "Salt Cod Worship."

It lists a few caveats. It's important to secure the good stuff: the thick center cut that cooks up flaky and moist. I was thinking my year-old box of dried tails ranked as the not-so-good stuff.

I rehydrated the cod over several days. I poached it and flaked it and rolled it into little salt-cod cakes spiked with lemon and garlic and potato. They were good, but nothing to revere.

Times change. Now refrigeration is plentiful and cod sparse. Salt cod, once a necessity, now counts as—and costs like—a luxury. The cook who can't land the good dried stuff is advised to substitute fresh.

So I fried up a batch of fresh cod fritters spiked with lemon and garlic and potato. If there had been any left, they might have inspired worship.

Cod Fritters

Makes about 2 dozen

1 pound waxy potatoes (such as Yukon Gold), unpeeled

½ pound fresh cod, bones removed

1 cup Quickie Aioli (recipe follows)

1 tablespoon finely chopped fresh parsley

1 egg, beaten

Kosher salt

Olive oil, for frying

Lemon wedges

1. Boil: Cover potatoes with salted cold water in a large saucepan. Bring to a boil, reduce to a simmer and cook tender, about 30 minutes. Drain and cool.

2. Simmer: Cover cod with cold water in a large skillet. Bring just to a simmer; simmer 1 minute. Cover and let stand 2 minutes. Drain and flake.

3. Mix: Grate potatoes on the large holes of a box grater; discard peel (which will be left behind). Use a fork to gently mix in flaked cod, 2 tablespoons aioli, parsley, egg, and a little salt. Chill.

4. Shape: Roll 1½-inch balls. Flatten 1 side, shaping a dome.

5. Fry: Pour oil to a depth of 1 inch in a large heavy skillet. Heat to 360 degrees. Fry a few at a time, 1 minute per side. Serve warm with lemon and remaining aioli.

PROVENANCE: *Adapted from* The New Spanish Table *by Anya von Bremzen*

Quickie Aioli

Makes about 1 cup

Whisk together 1 cup mayonnaise, 2 tablespoons freshly squeezed lemon juice, 4 crushed cloves garlic, and 3 tablespoons olive oil. Chill.

FLIGHTS *of* FANCY

Trudging along concourse B, en route from Gate Here to Gate There, I was struck by a mirage. It's not unprecedented. Some people routinely conjure up the worst-case scenario. That way they've always got an escape plan—or a panic attack—handy. Not me. I routinely conjure up the best-case scenario. That way, I've always got distraction—or disappointment—handy. Reality rarely measures up.

So I wasn't entirely shocked by this unlikely scenario. There I was, travel-weary and trudging. And there it was: my favorite restaurant, transported to O'Hare, shrunk down, and sped up.

I smirked. My fantasies are so predictable. As if Rick Bayless would take Frontera, squeeze it down to a few tables and rework the menu to suit the fast-food format. As if he would take his signature dishes—pulled pork, slow-cooked ribs, smoky garlic shrimp—fit a serving onto a roll, and crisp up a portable feast.

I ordered the chorizo and poblano torta, wheeled my way to a seat and bit. It was everything I like, on a roll.

To figure out if you're dreaming you're supposed to try to wake up, or pinch yourself, or, if you're stuck in a futuristic action flick, spin a top. I noticed the guy at the next table had tomatillo salsa dripping from mustache to business suit. That seemed pretty realistic. Also, a loudspeaker announced my flight.

Still, I needed proof. So before I left, I ordered the rest of the menu, to go.

Chorizo Torta

Makes 4 big sandwiches

1 large (4-ounce) poblano pepper

1 pound fresh Mexican chorizo, casing removed

1 white onion, chopped

4 crusty Mexican bolillos or other sandwich rolls, about 6 inches long

4 tablespoons (½ stick) unsalted butter, softened

½ teaspoon dried oregano

4 ounces (1 cup) shredded Monterey Jack

4 ounces (1 cup) shredded sharp white Cheddar cheese

Tomatillo salsa

1. **Char:** Roast the pepper over a hot grill or under a broiler, turning regularly, until blistered and blackened, about 10 minutes. Rub off skin. Pull out and discard the stem and seeds. Chop.

2. **Brown:** Cook chorizo in a large dry skillet over medium heat, breaking it up with a wooden spoon, 5 minutes. Add the onion and oregano. Cook until onion has softened and sausage is done, about 5 minutes. Stir in chopped pepper.

3. **Compile:** Split rolls. Spread the outside with butter. Toss the cheeses together. Divide chorizo mixture onto the bottom half of each roll. Top with the shredded cheese. Close up sandwich.

4. **Crisp:** Squish and crisp in a panini press or on a medium-hot griddle, weighted down with a heavy skillet. Cook until browned outside and melty inside, about 7 minutes (flip once, if using griddle). Slice each sandwich in half on the diagonal. Serve the tomatillo salsa, for dipping.

PROVENANCE: *Rick Bayless supplied this recipe, which I adapted.*

A FISH STORY

Noah, my young scientist, submitted many an unlikely report. To wit: "Bees guts come out when they sting." And: "Men get hit by lightning more often than women." And: "A rabbit's teeth never stop growing." Most of which I, as distracted mother, filed under "Mmm, hmm."

My young scientist also claimed that a whale sporting a ten-foot-long horn prowled the Arctic. Hard to believe. Yet, unbelievably, true.

My scientist summoned evidence: The online photo album, the online encyclopedia entry, the online wilderness documentary. Proving that the splotchy white whale with the single, straight, spiral-twisted horn did indeed glide the glacial waters. Narwhal, unicorn of the deep, had this over the unicorn of the field: it was real.

Noah savored this moment. "You never believe me," he said. "But I'm always right."

He called up an animated short in which the single-horned narwhal danced to a jaunty tune that rhymed "ocean" with "commotion." "Narwhal, narwhal," it boasted, "inventor of the shishkebob."

This got my attention. Frankly, the culinary habits of the narwhal were hard to pin down, given that it lived in ice pack and dined at a depth of 4,000 feet, in darkness. No one had ever seen it prepare lunch. So the record is unclear on whether the whale kebobed its prey.

Still, it seemed fitting to credit the tusked whale with the ingenious idea of skewering fish. Just as it seemed fitting to credit the niceties of marinating, browning, and serving over crispy noodles to the species distracted mom. I was the one who routinely tried to rhyme "Just try some" with "Awesome."

Fish Kebobs

Serves 6

½ cup olive oil

3 tablespoons freshly squeezed lemon juice

1 clove garlic, finely chopped

1 tablespoon chopped fresh sage leaves

2 teaspoons chopped fresh thyme leaves

Kosher salt

1½ pounds mahi mahi, cut into 1-inch cubes

30 cherry tomatoes

6 scallions, white and tender green, cut into 1-inch lengths

18 whole fresh sage leaves

Freshly ground black pepper

1 pound linguine

2 tablespoons unsalted butter

1. Marinate: Whisk together oil, lemon juice, garlic, sage, thyme, and 1 teaspoon salt. Pour over fish cubes. Cover and chill, 1 hour.

2. Skewer: Thread fish cubes, tomatoes, scallions, and whole sage leaves onto 6 metal or soaked bamboo skewers (set aside marinade). Season with pepper and a little more salt.

3. Grill: Heat a ridged griddle over medium-high heat. Grill until fish is nicely browned on all sides, about 10 minutes.

4. Boil: Meanwhile, boil linguine until tender. Drain.

5. Sauce: Heat remaining marinade (the empty noodle pot will do nicely) to a boil. Boil 1 minute. Add butter. When melted, add cooked noodles. Toss. (If you like crispy noodles, scrape the sauced noodles into a wide skillet and set over medium heat, shaking now and then until browned on the bottom, 5 minutes. Cut into 6 wedges and serve crispy-side up.)

6. Serve: Divide soft or crisp noodles onto six plates, add a kebob to each. Enjoy.

SWEET SUCCESS

German chocolate is an aggravating cake. It's not German (it's named after Sam German). It's barely chocolate (it relies on the low-wattage "sweet chocolate" German developed). It's filled with a sticky mix of pecan and coconut flake, which goes on gloppy and goes down chewy. And it lacks frosting.

The playwright who introduces a gun in the first act is advised to fire it before curtain. Likewise the pastry chef who calls for a four-yolk filling ought to finish up with a four-white frosting. Any recipe that calls it quits — leaving cake bare and whites sloshing in the fridge—should be shredded.

I figured I could bake a German chocolate cake with a deeper, darker outlook. I'd lose the flakes, but retain the coconut lilt. I'd crisp the nuts and fluff the filling. I'd lavish the cake with a lightly salted caramel frosting. Sort of a plate-and-fork candy bar.

My plan worked. Though it took sixteen pounds of butter, sixteen trying afternoons, and fifteen failures.

The nutty expedition deepened my respect for the pastry chef, who must balance delicious and doable. I even came to appreciate that guy German, and the southern cooks who turned his baking bar famous. They knew the combo of chocolate, coconut, and pecan could become a classic.

Intensive German Chocolate Cake

Makes 1 glamorously tall 9-inch cake

2 cups cake flour

6 tablespoons unsweetened natural (not Dutch-process) cocoa

1 teaspoon baking soda

¾ teaspoon fine salt

¼ pound (1 stick) unsalted butter, softened

2½ cups dark brown sugar

2 teaspoons vanilla extract

4 eggs

4 ounces unsweetened chocolate, melted

1 cup buttermilk

¾ cup boiling water

2 cups Pecan Filling (recipe follows)

1 quart Caramel Buttercream (recipe follows)

1. Mix: Whisk together flour, cocoa, soda, and salt.

2. Fluff: Using a stand mixer fitted with the paddle attachment set on medium high, beat butter, sugar, and vanilla fluffy. Add eggs one at a time, beating fluffy after each. Mix in chocolate. Scoop in one-third the flour; mix on low just until incorporated. Pour in half the buttermilk; mix just until incorporated. Work in remaining doses of flour, buttermilk, and flour. Thin batter with the boiling water.

3. Bake: Pour into two 9-inch cake pans, buttered and lined with parchment paper. Slide into a 350-degree oven and bake until a toothpick poked in the center comes out clean, about 28 minutes. Cool 10 minutes. Turn out onto a rack and cool completely.

4. Stack: Slice layers in half horizontally. Set one thin layer on a cake platter, cut-side down. Spread on one-third the pecan filling. Continue filling and stacking. Cover top and sides of cake with caramel buttercream. Slice and serve.

Pecan Filling

Makes about 2 cups

¼ pound (1 stick) unsalted butter

1 cup dark brown sugar

¼ cup coconut milk (shake before measuring)

¼ cup heavy whipping cream

¼ teaspoon salt

4 egg yolks

2¼ cups toasted chopped pecans

1. Melt: Melt butter in a medium saucepan over medium heat. Stir in, in order: brown sugar, coconut milk, cream, salt, and yolks.

2. Thicken: Cook, stirring, until thickened, about 10 minutes. Set aside to cool.

3. Fluff: Use a stand mixer fitted with the paddle attachment to beat fluffy. Stir in pecans by hand.

Caramel Buttercream

Makes about 1 quart

1¼ cups sugar

2 tablespoons water

⅛ teaspoon fine salt

½ cup heavy whipping cream

4 egg whites

½ pound (2 sticks) unsalted butter, softened

1. Caramelize: Stir together ½ cup sugar, the water, and salt in a medium saucepan. Bring to a boil. Let bubble without stirring until syrup starts to color, about 3 minutes. Reduce heat to medium and watch closely; stir to a dark amber, about 2 minutes. Pull pan off heat and carefully stir in cream. Pour this caramel into a heatproof glass measuring cup and let cool.

2. Fluff: Slide egg whites into the bowl of a stand mixer. Measure in remaining ¾ cup sugar. Set this bowl over a pan of simmering water. Whisk until egg mixture is foamy and 160 degrees, about 5 minutes. Return bowl to the mixer and whisk on high speed into fluffy, glossy peaks, about 5 minutes. Make sure bowl is no longer hot (rub the outside of the bowl with an ice cube if need be). Reduce speed to medium and add butter, a few tablespoons at a time, whisking constantly. Beat in reserved caramel.

TO MARKET

The farmers' market affords the city dweller a taste of fresh. I piled up basil and arugula abundance, plotting the feast-to-be. Choosing basil and arugula was hungry work, so I perused the already ready: spring roll, crêpe, falafel, curry, samosa, and croissant. Also, that bread.

Hannah and Noah craved Ethiopian bread—not spongy injera—but whole-wheat flatbread rolled around some sort of golden ginger/garlic smash. I was sure it was made from something exotic, imported from somewhere exotic, like Ethiopia. In hopes of keeping lunchbox and children filled, I took to waking early each Saturday and rushing the Ethiopian stand.

Then one afternoon, while strolling the other market, the one with the fluorescent lighting and the Top 40 soundtrack, I came across a sack of yellow split peas. I'd never noticed these peas before. And yet, some telepathic message beamed from pea to me affirmed that these yellow lumps were the very soul of that stuffed bread.

I knew that the split pea, like its brethren lentil and chickpea, was a hardworking legume, full of wholesome attributes. Unlike the bean, it needed no presoak, no slow simmer. Stewed in a pot, it was the bedrock of the English pottage, or porridge. In Ethiopia, I learned, they called it kik.

I took home the yellow peas and cooked them up with ginger and garlic and cardamom. They steamed thick and savory; they begged for flatbread. I was relieved to discover that kik, with its ginger kick, was easy to pronounce, easy to cook, and easy to come by. Next Saturday, I was sleeping in.

Kik (Peas Porridge)

Serves 8

4 tablespoons (½ stick) unsalted butter

¼ cup chopped onion

¼ cup chopped carrot

¼ cup chopped celery

2 tablespoons grated fresh ginger, plus a little

4 cloves garlic, chopped

½ teaspoon ground cardamom

Kosher salt and freshly ground black pepper

1 pound yellow peas, rinsed and sorted

8 cups chicken broth, vegetable broth, or water

Olive oil

Lemon

1. **Soften:** Melt butter over medium heat in a large soup pot. Add onion, carrot, celery, ginger, and garlic. Season with cardamom, salt, and pepper. Cook, stirring now and then, until vegetables turn soft and fragrant, about 12 minutes. Stir in peas.

2. **Simmer:** Pour in broth or water. Bring to a boil, skimming foam from the surface. Lower to a simmer, partially cover and cook, stirring once in a while, until thick and creamy (adding more liquid if need be). Times vary, depending on the peas, but plan on about 1 hour.

3. **Season:** Taste. Add salt and pepper, if you like, or even another teaspoon grated ginger. Serve, drizzled with a little olive oil and a spritz of lemon. Works as a side dish, as a dip for crunchy vegetables and pita chips, or rolled into whole-wheat lavash or other flatbread.

SEPARATE BUT EQUAL

Some daydream of the tropical beach or the movie-star tryst. I always like to picture the handsome profile of an eight-burner cooktop.

In real life I have a roomy kitchen. Despite its dowdy looks, dim lighting, and duct-taped repairs, it works. The off-kilter cooktop keeps on cooking and the jetliner-loud dishwasher keeps on washing. So, I persevere. And I sketch floorplans.

I find inspiration among friends, shamelessly unfurling the measuring tape mid-meal. I study the cookspaces of Martha and Ina with concentration others reserve for the Talmud. I'm particularly keen on the kosher kitchen, with its separation of milk and meat. Not that I keep kosher. Every time I visit my brother-in-law, who does, he has to resanctify all the utensils I've inadvertently sullied.

Here's what I want: the double kitchen. One half savory, one half sweet.

Consider the wooden spoon. After a shift working ratatouille or bouillabaisse, there's no amount of scrubbing that can lift the garlic scent or saffron tint. Spoon to cake batter, I cringe.

In my double kitchen, there's one tub of wooden spoons and soft spatulas and offset knives all color-coded sweet, one color-coded savory. My blueprints spec two refrigerators. No lemon mousse bunking with the kimchee. No stinky cheese corrupting the coconut cake.

Ovens too. Stew in one, tart in the other. No burnt sugar marring the pork roast. No shallot aroma wafting over the crème brûlée.

My kitchen will be ruled by the doctrine of separate but equal. No mingling. No fraternizing. No mixing it up. In the gleaming double kitchen of my dreams there will be two places for everything and everything in two places. I'll rule this double kingdom, despotic and happy.

At least until I'm faced with a recipe that calls for equal doses of sugar and spice. The maple-sweet, cayenne-hot scallop, say. Then I'll have to sketch an annex.

Sweet and Spicy Scallops
Serves 6

1 orange

¼ cup maple syrup

1 teaspoon kosher salt

¼ teaspoon cayenne pepper

1½ pounds large fresh
  sea scallops

2 strips bacon, frozen
  and cut crosswise into
  ½-inch tabs

Lollipop sticks, optional
  (available at craft stores)

1. Juice: Zest and juice orange. Stir together 1 teaspoon zest, ½ cup juice, the maple syrup, ½ teaspoon salt and the cayenne pepper.

2. Slice: Cut thick scallops into disks ½ inch thick. Pat dry. Season with the remaining ½ teaspoon of salt.

3. Crisp: Heat a large cast-iron skillet over medium. When hot, scatter in bacon and cook, stirring, until crisp and brown, about 4 minutes. Scoop out and drain on paper towels, leaving rendered fat in the skillet. Munch on chips.

4. Sear: Heat bacon fat over medium-high heat. Dot with scallops and let sizzle (without moving) until nicely browned, about 2 minutes. Flip and brown the other side, about 2 minutes. Use a spatula to lift scallops onto a plate.

5. Reduce: Carefully pour juice mixture into skillet. Stir over medium heat until thick, about 5 minutes. Return scallops to pan and stir until sticky with sauce, 1 minute.

6. Serve: Nice as an appetizer. If you're having a cocktail party, skewer each scallop on a lollipop stick.

RISE AND SHINE

Baking soda and baking powder have a lot in common. The two share the same first name, live on the same shelf, and hold the same job: hoisting baked goods. Hot, heavy, and dangerous work. And indispensable to the cause of fluffy pancake or tender scone.

There are those in the pantry who look down on the powdery pair, who insist that height, loft, levity can only be achieved via whipped egg or warm yeast. Still, the home cook knows that the chemical leavener makes quick work of quickbread.

Assuming she chooses the right one.

The cook casts her mind back to Chemistry, which, with its beaker and formula and apron, held a kitchen-like charm. She recalls that baking soda is nothing but sodium bicarbonate. Alone, it does nothing. Mixed with vinegar or another acidic ally, it bubbles. The buttermilk biscuit and sour-cream coffee cake get their lift from baking soda.

Baking powder also contains sodium bicarbonate, premixed with an acidic kick-start (or two). It can go it alone in cake batter or cookie dough, no need for sour yogurt or tart lemon. Its brawny "double action" means it's laced with two catalysts—one that starts cold, one that kicks in when hot. Battering batter with the old one-two.

The home cook keeps these talents in mind, never presuming that one can sub for the other. She knows that the scone—like the rest of us—needs many a problem-solving tool. Including the modern approach: collaboration.

Take-a-Stroll Scones

Makes 8

1 cup plus
  2 tablespoons flour

¾ cup rolled oats

¼ cup plus 1 tablespoon
  light brown sugar

1 teaspoon ground cinnamon

1 teaspoon baking powder

1 teaspoon baking soda

¼ teaspoon fine salt

¼ pound (1 stick) cold
  unsalted butter, cut up

½ cup dried cranberries
  (or other dried fruit,
  chopped)

2 tablespoons roasted,
  salted pumpkin seeds

¾ cup heavy
  whipping cream

1. **Mix:** Measure flour, oats, ¼ cup brown sugar, the cinnamon, baking powder, baking soda, and salt into the food processor. Pulse a few times.

2. **Cut:** Drop in butter chunks. Pulse several times, cutting butter down to pea-sized (or smaller) bits.

3. **Fold:** Turn out into a large mixing bowl. Fold in dried fruit and seeds. Drizzle on cream, folding with a soft spatula, until dough clumps (you may not need all the cream).

4. **Pat:** Turn out dough (still a clumpy mess) onto a parchment-paper-lined baking sheet. Pat into a 1½ inch-thick disk, about 8 inches across. Brush the top with a little of the remaining cream and sprinkle with the remaining 1 tablespoon brown sugar. Using a long, heavy knife, slice dough circle, pizza-style, into 8 wedges. Separate slightly.

5. **Bake:** Slide into a 375-degree oven and bake until set and golden, about 15 minutes. Delicious warm or room temperature.

PROVENANCE: *Inspired by the Take-a-Hike Scone once served at Chicago's Bleeding Heart Bakery. This version drops the vegan convictions but retains the wholesome outlook.*

THE PERFECT PLAN

My clothes and I are not getting along. I expect them to do their job—look alert, zip, and button. They expect to do nothing but lounge in the closet. When it comes to basic duties, like zip and button, they downright refuse.

As their employer, I find this attitude unreasonable. Where's the imagination? The broad thinking? The stretch? Not, apparently, in my wardrobe.

I could submit to something truly humiliating, like shopping. Or volunteering for that TV show where they throw away all your clothes.

Instead, I've joined a plan. It's fun, sort of. You write down everything you eat. There's a friendly computer program that offers encouragement like: "Have some fruit!" And: "Try soup!" It converts the dishes into points and the points into goals and the goals into—something. I lose interest after I list all the delicious things I plan to consume.

Like dessert, an important part of any food plan.

Recently I put together a lovely bowl of raspberries. After a taste, I decided they could be sweetened by a soak in simple syrup and white wine. And softened with a swirl of crème fraîche. And perked up with a scoop of ice cream and a couple of tender almond cookies, glazed with jam.

The final composition glowed pretty and pink and pleasing. I'm quite certain it will meet with the approval of my plan because (a) it's fruit and (b) it's soup. My plan is to savor every bite.

Dessert Soup

Serves 8

1½ cups water

1½ cups sugar

18 ounces (3 small packages) raspberries

½ cup Crème Fraîche (page 384)

1 small (375 ml) bottle white dessert wine, such as Sauternes or Muscat

Crème fraîche ice cream (or substitute vanilla ice cream)

Fresh mint leaves

Almond cookies (buy these or follow recipe below)

1. Smash: Heat water and sugar in a large saucepan over high heat. Reduce heat a little and let bubble, 3 minutes. Tumble in 12 ounces berries. Cook, mashing with a spoon, until berries fall apart, about 3 minutes.

2. Chill: Strain berry mixture through a fine-mesh sieve into a glass bowl. Discard seeds. Whisk in crème fraîche. Pour in wine. Add remaining whole berries. Cover and chill overnight.

3. Serve: Ladle soup into 8 small chilled bowls. To each add a small scoop ice cream, a few mint leaves, and an almond-cookie "crouton."

Almond Cookies

Makes about 36 3-inch cookies

Cream together ½ pound (2 sticks) unsalted butter and ⅔ cup sugar. Beat in 1 egg, ½ teaspoon vanilla extract and ¼ teaspoon almond extract. Mix in 2½ cups sifted flour and ½ teaspoon fine salt. Divide in two. Settle each half between two sheets of wax paper and roll ⅛-inch thin. Freeze at least 15 minutes. When ready to bake, peel off both sheets of wax paper; punch out spring shapes (flowers, say) with a cookie cutter. Set cookies on a parchment-paper-lined baking sheet and slide into a 350-degree oven. Bake until edges just begin to turn golden, about 8 minutes. Glaze with melted raspberry jam, if you're feeling fancy.

PRIORITIZE

Recently a tartine winked at me from a bakery case. I'm ashamed to say I didn't wink back.

I had just finished an elaborate New York City lunch. I had a train to catch. It didn't seem the time to take on a tartine, even one lounging on rustic whole wheat. The sandwich, all open-faced innocence and creamy ricotta, didn't look like it would take lightly to travel.

I should have run a few laps around Soho. Or skipped the train. I should have maintained a lighter grip on my schedule and tighter grip on my priorities.

Because that sandwich haunted me. Back home, I thought about it. Was its whole-wheat slab soft or crisp? Was its ricotta plain or spiced? Were those roasted greens garlic-spiked? And that streak of caramel! Daring.

Finally I tracked down the tartine's creator, New York bakery genius Maury Rubin. He generously explained his tartine technique, which is more of an approach than a recipe: good bread, sweet caramel, fresh ricotta, and a shake of the Japanese red peppers called shichimi. Apparently I'd hallucinated the greens.

I tried Rubin's recipe (which he credits to City Bakery savory chef Ilene Rosen). I decided I preferred the bread pan-crisped and the ricotta spread thin. I moved the caramel from the bottom to the top. And I installed my formerly imaginary garlic-spiked greens.

It was a good lesson in the mechanics of sandwich building. And in the importance of knowing what's important. Which, come to think of it, are about the same thing.

Ricotta Tartine

Makes 1 open-faced sandwich per slice of bread

Olive oil

Kosher salt

Rustic whole wheat country bread, sliced

Whole-milk ricotta cheese

Roasted Broccolini (recipe follows)

Shichimi red pepper mix*

Caramel sauce (homemade or not), optional

1 Sizzle: Heat a thin layer of olive oil and a pinch of salt in a heavy skillet over medium-high heat. For each tartine, sizzle 1 slice of bread in the oil until golden brown, about 1 minute per side. Settle on a plate.

2. Build: Spread with a thin layer of ricotta. Scatter on roasted broccolini. Shake on a little shichimi. If you like, drizzle with a spoonful of caramel. Munch warm.

*A Japanese blend of red pepper, orange peel, and other spices, available in the Asian foods aisle of many grocery stores and at specialty markets. If you don't have any handy, a pinch of red or black pepper will do.

PROVENANCE: *Inspired by Birdbath Bakery in New York City.*

Roasted Broccolini

Makes about 2 cups

Slice 1 bunch broccolini into bite-sized pieces. Toss with 2 tablespoons olive oil and 1 clove chopped garlic. Season with kosher salt and freshly ground black pepper. Spread out on a parchment-paper-lined rimmed baking sheet. Slide into a 425-degree oven and roast until deliciously browned, about 8 minutes. Toss with 1 teaspoon lemon juice.

THE GOLDEN RULE

T he chickpea, a hardy perennial, grows in a sturdy pod called a tin. The standard cultivar matures at 15 to 15.5 ounces. The dwarf variety tops out at 10 ounces. Crack open either can to reveal the same interior: a cluster of creamy, pale, round nubs.

The chickpea thrives in any growing zone. It is native to the canned-bean section, often raised in alternating beds with the kidney bean, the pork-and-bean hybrid, or soup. It can be harvested in any season and stored indefinitely. It's a dependable crop.

The protein-and-mineral-packed pea can buck-up curry, amuse salad, fry up as falafel ball, or collapse into hummus.

Prompting the innocent to ask: Why? Hummus flourishes almost anywhere. It's abundant in the cooler case, hard by the baba ganoush.

Still, the home cook who takes on the task of shucking the can of chickpeas, seasoning the nubs with bright lemon, subtle tahini, and strong garlic, will be rewarded. Smashing elemental chickpea into complex hummus, she will know the homesteader's pride. Scooping the cool mix onto hot pita, she will know the pleasure of heirloom hummus: thick, rich, and lightly spiced. Even better, believe it or not, than the stuff in the tub.

Hummus

Makes about 2 cups

2 cloves garlic, degermed

1 (15-ounce) can chickpeas, drained and rinsed

6 tablespoons freshly squeezed lemon juice

2 tablespoons tahini

2 tablespoons water

1 teaspoon fine salt

¼ teaspoon cayenne pepper

4 slices preserved lemon*, rinsed, optional, but very good

With the food processor running, drop garlic down the chute. Stop; add remaining ingredients. Process smooth. Chill.

*Lemon peel preserved in brine. Lives near the pickles at fancy-food shops.

THE RULES

The dietician insists on more fiber, less sugar. The food pyramid instructs more fruit, less butter. Michael Pollan decrees more vegetables, less meat. And though such rules annoy me, I maintain my own. To wit: Never dine above or below grade. Cuts down on the disappointment invariably served at the basement-level dive and the hotel-top tavern. In the kitchen my rules rule out raisins, gelatin, and food coloring. Except under emergency conditions.

So when I set out to make Country Captain, I foresaw few regulatory issues. Country Captain is chicken stew, seasoned with curry. It could be called chicken curry, but it's not. It traces its heritage to the Savannah and Charleston spice trade. Very old school.

The recipe does call for currants, creepingly close to raisins. But because they're smaller, cuter, and more British, I gave them a pass. I forgot that Bob maintains his own dietary restrictions: no structures jutting more than two inches off the plate. And no cloves. Apparently my curry mix harbored cloves.

I tried again with a custom curry, only to learn that Bob lives by this law: no skin on chicken in stew. I could see his point; it gets soggy. On my third date with the captain, Bob announced a sweeping injunction: "I don't like this dish."

Fighting words. I reworked Country Captain from stew to stack (one just under the two-inch restriction): sticky rice, golden chicken, fragrant vegetables, crunchy toppings. I served the ex-stew as Captain Crunch. Which my local captain devoured, happily.

Captain Crunch

Serves 6

¼ cup flour

2 tablespoons plus 1 teaspoon curry powder

2 teaspoons kosher salt

1 teaspoon freshly ground black pepper

2 pounds boneless skinless chicken thighs, halved

4 slices bacon, frozen and thinly sliced crosswise

1 onion, chopped

1 red pepper, chopped

2 cloves garlic, finely chopped

¼ cup dry red wine

1 pint grape tomatoes, halved

About 3 cups cooked sticky rice

Currants

Slivered almonds, toasted

1. Season: Combine flour, 2 tablespoons curry powder, 1 teaspoon salt, and ½ teaspoon pepper. Rub spice mixture into chicken. Set seasoned chicken on a rack, pieces not touching; let rest 15 minutes.

2. Crisp: Heat a large cast-iron skillet over medium. When hot, scatter in bacon, and cook, stirring, until crisp and brown, about 4 minutes. Scoop out and drain on paper towels, leaving rendered fat in the skillet.

3. Brown: Add chicken to the hot bacon fat. Sizzle over medium-high heat, turning once, until nicely browned outside and cooked through inside, about 12 minutes. Scoop out chicken and cover loosely with foil.

4. Soften: Add onion, red pepper, and garlic to the pan. Season with remaining 1 teaspoon curry powder, 1 teaspoon salt, and ½ teaspoon pepper. Cook until soft and fragrant, about 7 minutes. Deglaze with wine. Add tomatoes and cook until tomatoes soften, but still hold their shape, about 5 minutes.

5. Serve: For each serving, scoop some rice into a shallow bowl. Arrange a few pieces of chicken on rice. Top with a scoop of the vegetable mixture. Let guests garnish with toasted almonds, currants, and crunchy bacon, if they like.

MOMS *of* A FEATHER

spent the week in a tree. I was lured there by an email from Mom. Click here, swoop eighty feet up a cottonwood, to an eagle's nest in Decorah, Iowa. The eaglecam captures an eagle couple tending to their three eaglets, 24/7.

Sweet, I thought. I watched reruns of the birdlets hatching. I checked the live action again. Soon I couldn't leave the screen. I never knew when the eagle dad might drop by with a fresh fish or the eagle mom might tuck the flock under her feathers. After which, my workday would be done, but not my work.

I told some mom friends. It made us miss those just-hatched days when we were stuck in the nest, doing nothing but fluffing and tucking and feeding, weary consternation creased between our beady eyes.

I told my editor. Maybe if he took to birdwatching, he wouldn't notice that I hadn't filed my story on lumpia. He clicked, chirped "aw," and asked after my story.

So I'll be brief: Lumpia are Filipino egg rolls, wrapped in thin pastry. They probably have an interesting history, and I'd look it up, but my browser is busy; the mom eagle is ripping up trout tartare and stuffing it into hungry beaks.

Lumpia are stuffed with pork and ginger, rolled and fried into crisp sticks. The sort that might come in handy to an eagle parent who endures an unseasonable snowstorm that had me up half the night checking on the cold little eaglets. When everything thawed, everyone was fine (except me: I was short on sleep); the eagles reinforced the nest with a stick or two.

Anyway, lumpia aren't sticks. They're snacks. And quite a bit tastier than shredded squirrel, I imagine. I might work up a recipe for that, as soon as the eaglets learn to fly.

Lumpia (Filipino Egg Rolls)
Makes 25

2 cups shredded
    Napa cabbage

1 pound ground pork

6 scallions, white and tender
    green chopped

¼ cup shredded carrots

2 tablespoons grated fresh
    ginger

2 tablespoons soy sauce,
    plus more for dipping

2 cloves garlic, chopped

1 package (25 count) lumpia
    wrappers*, defrosted

Canola oil

*Available with frozen foods in some grocery stores or at Asian markets, or substitute egg-roll wrappers.

1. **Mix:** Gently combine cabbage, pork, scallions, carrots, ginger, 2 tablespoons soy sauce, and the garlic in a bowl.

2. **Roll:** Set one wrapper on a work surface. Imagine the round wrapper as a clock face. Scoop on 2 tablespoons filling, spreading it straight from 4 to 8, leaving a 1-inch border bare. Fold in the edges (at 4 and 8) and fold up the bottom (at 6). Keep rolling into a fat cigar. Brush a little water on the loose flap (at 12); press to seal closed. Repeat with remaining lumpia.

3. **Fry:** Pour oil into a heavy pot to a depth of at least 1 inch. Heat over medium-high heat to 350 degrees. Add lumpia, a few at a time; cook to a deep, crispy brown, 4 to 5 minutes. Drain on paper towels. Slice in half on the diagonal; serve with soy sauce, for dipping.

Chapter 6:
Let Rise

Now we had a high school actress, dancer, journalist. We had a middle school scientist, ceramicist, shortstop. Parenting seemed more hands-off and daughtering more hands-on. We were all growing up.

Even Baltimore. Following the success of Cindy Wolf and Spike Gjerde, local chefs cooked up new restaurants. Young talent tricked out food trucks, spun sassy ice cream, and—finally, blessedly—brewed some serious coffee.

Bob still liked gritty: cornmeal, ground almonds, crumble. Hannah sought startle: spicy, sushi, seafood. Noah relied on reliable: potatoes, steak, ketchup. We all developed a taste for adventure. We traveled more. We took the train to New York to see plays and slurp noodles. We celebrated Noah's bar mitzvah in Israel, stopping first to introduce Hannah and Noah, my own Madeline and Pepito, to Paris.

I tried to learn the lingo of fangirl and *South Park*. I drove circles around the city, car floor crusted with leotards and protein bars. I flew circles to and from Denver, carry-on stuffed with bedside distractions for Dad.

Everything seemed to move both slowly and quickly. Already it was time to pack away the blocks, to box up the picture books. Who knew this recipe, the one that had seemed so long and savory, was really so short and sweet?

IN THE DARK

The day travels a standard arc, pajamas to pajamas. There's the lift of coffee, the lull of work, the jostle of the ballerina-and-ballplayer-shuttle. There's the calm of dinner prep and the oasis of dinner dispatch. Homework struggles, bedtime struggles, bed.

All assisted by the tool set that comes standard on the base model: sight, sound, scent, intuition, touch, and taste. Especially taste. The path from alarm-off to alarm-on is scattered with incentives—early morning buttered toast, late afternoon latte, midnight truffle—like crumbs across the forest floor.

Even so, I didn't know that taste rides its own crests and troughs. I made this discovery one night when the agenda was full and the refrigerator empty. I was up packing for a trip, trying to download a novel and upload the clothes. Periodically I'd stop to check on the moon. It was supposed to do something—lurch, or go dim—and I had sworn to wake my junior astronomer for the spectacle.

I looked through closets, looked at the moon, looked for a snack. Finally I settled for simple: honey on spoon. I stepped outside and in the extra-dark dark, swallowed sunshine.

I might have presumed the 2 a.m. taste bud tired, or tired of work. Instead, I got an extraordinarily precise report. I could taste the honey: golden, lightly lemon. And the contributing flower: delicate, pale purple. And the on-duty bee: burly, earnest. And his state of mind: pensive.

As was I. Perhaps I missed many such flashes of enlightenment, letting the daily jumble execute a full eclipse.

Honey Butter
Makes 1 cup

½ pound (2 sticks) unsalted butter, softened

¼ cup honey

1 tablespoon finely chopped fresh rosemary, optional

Kosher salt and freshly ground pepper

1. Mix: Using a stand mixer fitted with the paddle attachment, beat all ingredients until smooth.

2. Roll: Use soft honey butter immediately, or mound onto a stretch of parchment paper. Roll into a sausage shape. Chill.

3. Smear: Good slathered on almost anything, especially grilled corn, fish or shrimp; hot biscuits, or crackers awaiting cheese duty. Without the rosemary, nice on toast or scone.

Crème brûlée needs no embellishment. The smooth cream under the crazed crust offers cold and hot, soft and sharp, plain and fancy. In a cup.

While traveling I came across crème brûlée enhanced with halva. Traditionally the simple French dessert doesn't share a continent, much less a ramekin, with the simple Middle Eastern candy.

The combo intrigued me. Crème brûlée owes its dense texture and rich reputation to cream and sugar set thick over low heat. Halva owes its crumbly texture and jagged bite to sesame and sugar compressed at high heat.

Combining creamy this with crumbly that might undermine both enterprises. Yet miraculously it has the opposite effect—producing a dish that dishes out the best of two worlds. Which might also be the point of travel.

Halva Crème Brûlée

Makes 6

2 cups heavy
   whipping cream

½ cup halva, not coated*

6 egg yolks

⅔ cup plus
   6 teaspoons sugar

1. Bubble: Measure cream into a large saucepan. Crumble in halva. Simmer, whisking constantly, until thick, about 1 minute.

2. Fluff: Whip the yolks with ⅔ cup sugar, using a stand mixer and whisk attachment, until thick and pale, about 2 minutes. Reduce speed to low. Pour in hot cream, whisking constantly. Strain through a fine-mesh sieve into a clean quart-sized measuring cup.

3. Bake: Arrange 6 ramekins in a deep baking pan (the kind handy for lasagna). Pour about ½ cup cream mixture into each ramekin. Add hot water to the baking pan to a depth of 1 inch. Slide into a 325-degree oven and bake until just set, about 25 minutes. Cool. Chill.

4. Serve: Sprinkle each crème with 1 teaspoon sugar. If you've got a kitchen torch, you know your mission. Otherwise, set ramekins on a rimmed baking sheet

and slide under the broiler just until sugar melts, about 1 minute. Chill again and serve.

*Available in the imported foods aisle of many grocery stores and at specialty markets. Use any flavor that comes without a chocolate coating—plain, marble, nut—though nut chunks won't make it into the final dish.

‘OOOOO’

A FRENCH LESSON

Two French girls came to visit. They brought comic books, in French. They brought foie gras, in tins. They brought homework: a notebook full of questions about our native habits.

We played Twister, tangling into knots of right and left, *droit et gauche*. We watched "*Les Simpson*." We identified local wildlife: the squirrel.

Their school-group itinerary listed landmarks: Lincoln Memorial, Liberty Bell, National Mall. They wanted to visit bowling alley, movieplex, shopping mall.

We cooked local: meatball, fried chicken, PB&J. We learned that even in France school lunch is scorned.

On the last night, they remembered the homework. The two girls worked their neat cursive against page after page: How many pupils attend your host school? What is the state motto? What leisure-time activities does your host family pursue?

We scraped our way through all the questions and all the leaves of two fat artichokes. When we got to the heart, we got a vocabulary lesson. "*Coeur d'artichaut*," said one of the girls. "That's what we call someone who's shy."

We said our good-byes, hearts heavy, and no longer shy.

Artichoke Omelet

Serves: 1

1 good-sized heavy artichoke

Unsalted butter

Canola oil

Kosher salt and freshly
  ground black pepper

1 tablespoon freshly grated
  Parmesan cheese

1 tablespoon snipped
  fresh chives

1 tablespoon chopped
  fresh parsley

1 teaspoon chopped
  fresh mint

Finely grated zest of 1 lemon

2 eggs

1. **Trim:** Using a serrated knife, cut away the top third of the artichoke and all but ½ inch of its stem. Snap off outer leaves until only pale green leaves are exposed. Use a vegetable peeler to smooth stem and ridges. Cut artichoke into quarters (stem to leaf). Use a small sharp knife to cut out the fuzzy choke; discard. Slice artichoke quarters into thin (⅛-inch) crescents.

2. **Crisp:** Heat about 1 tablespoon butter and 1 tablespoon oil in a small heavy skillet. Add artichoke crescents in batches and fry crisp and golden, about 2 minutes per side. Set aside artichokes. Season with salt and pepper.

3. **Mix:** Toss together cheese, herbs, and lemon zest in a small bowl. Whisk together eggs and a pinch of salt in a separate bowl.

4. **Puff:** Wipe out skillet. Add 1 teaspoon butter and 1 teaspoon oil; set over medium-high heat. When hot, pour in egg mixture. Use a soft spatula to lift edges of omelet; tip pan to let egg flow under. When the bottom of the omelet is lightly browned and the top not entirely set (about 2 minutes), scatter on cheese/herb mixture. Top with the artichokes. Fold omelet in half, cook until just set (about 1 minute). Voilà.

INTO THE WILD

Noah gets up early and packs his knapsack with pocketknife, Band-Aid, and plum. He endures carpool, then is released into the wild.

At camp he chooses from the obvious: hike, paddle, climb. And the irresistible: dig a hole. Camp is hip to summer's meditative pleasures.

On the last night there's a campout. Noah roasts corn and gnaws it from the cob. He slouches by the fire and hums along. He sleeps under the stars and wakes to the scent of flapjacks.

He takes his time with the flapjack. It's wide as a skillet, heavy with blueberries, and scorched with regret. Summer, and its meditative pleasures, is gone.

Flapjacks
Makes about 10 (4-inch) flapjacks

Stir 2 cups Flapjack Mix (recipe follows), 1 egg, and ¾ cup water to a thick batter. Heat a heavy skillet over medium-high heat. Brush with vegetable oil. Pour in about ¼ cup batter for each flapjack. Cook in batches until bubbles pop on the surface, about 2 minutes. Flip and cook until the other side is golden brown, about 2 minutes. Nice with fresh fruit and jam.

Flapjack Mix

Makes about 4 cups

¾ cup all-purpose flour

¾ cup whole-wheat flour

¾ cup rolled oats

¾ cup toasted pecans

½ cup nonfat dry milk

¼ cup dark brown sugar

1 teaspoon fine salt

¼ teaspoon freshly
grated nutmeg

4 tablespoons (½ stick)
unsalted butter

Measure all ingredients except butter into the food processor. Process briefly to mix. Add butter. Pulse until mixture resembles rolled oats. Store in an airtight container in the refrigerator.

FRESH START

Waste is bad. It's bad for the planet and it's bad for the soul. I know this because Mom says so.

Do not recycle that cardboard tube; save it for an art project. Do not uproot that wayward seedling; transplant it. Do not throw out that tablespoon of yogurt; wrap it and freeze it and stir it into a sauce later. Perhaps years later.

Such thrifty household management is surely right. And yet, I resist. I like to bundle up yesterday's news. Clean slate, fresh start. I find perverse pleasure in straightening up, cleaning out, organizing. And the corollary: tossing.

There may be people who manage both—to waste not and clutter not. But I think there's only one: Mom.

I try. I have a closetful of cardboard tubes awaiting the craft project. I have a stash of frozen leek greens, awaiting soup duty. And when faced with old bread, I make bread salad. Not that Mom would approve. Imagine if she knew that sometimes I make day-old bread salad with (don't look, Mom!) fresh bread.

Bread Salad

Serves 4 to 6

For salad:

2 pints grape tomatoes,
   at room temperature,
   halved on the diagonal

1 cucumber, halved the
   long way and sliced
   crosswise into
   ¼-inch-thick half-moons

1 yellow or orange bell
   pepper, chopped into
   ½-inch squares

1 roasted red pepper,
   sliced into thin strips

2 tablespoons finely
   chopped red onion

1 clove garlic, finely chopped

2 tablespoons
   red wine vinegar

6 tablespoons olive oil

¼ cup thinly sliced fresh
   basil leaves

½ teaspoon kosher salt

For bread:

½ pound Italian country
   bread (or French boule),
   fresh or not, cut or torn
   into 1-inch cubes

¼ cup olive oil

2 cloves garlic, sliced

⅛ teaspoon kosher salt

1. Toss: In a large bowl, toss all salad ingredients. Let rest while preparing bread.

2. Toast: On a rimmed baking sheet, toss bread, olive oil, garlic, and salt. Slide into a 350-degree oven and toast, shaking the pan once or twice, until bread turns crisp and golden, about 15 minutes.

3 Serve: Scrape bread mixture onto tomato mixture. Toss gently.

THE STASH

Nutella once struck us as a marvel. It suggested that European children spread chocolate on bread, for breakfast. It suggested that their parents, in deference to the hazelnut, approved. It suggested that creamy, chocolate-hazelnut collusion could be ours, in a jar.

We still admire the supermarket convenience and super-smooth ways of Nutella. But the early riser who ignores the alluring swirl on the front label will note that the product tastes a lot like the fine print on the back: sugar, palm oil, hazelnuts, cocoa, milk, whey, lecithin, and vanillin. Made in Canada.

That's how we came to be staring, awestruck, at the Italian market's wall of non-Nutella nutella. We took home nocciola this and gianduja that and discovered that chocolate-hazelnut spread covers a broad spectrum: light to dark, creamy to chunky, sweet to salty, thin to thick. We also discovered that rarified territory: too much of a good thing.

Weeks later, after we had recovered, we made a homemade batch calibrated to the local palate: creamy, medium-dark, with a mild caramelized-nut crunch. Now we've got our own version of Italy in a jar.

Chocolate Hazelnut Spread

Makes 1 cup

½ cup blanched hazelnuts*

⅓ cup sugar

2 ounces bittersweet (not unsweetened) chocolate, coarsely chopped

½ cup half-and-half

1. Toast: Spread blanched hazelnuts on a rimmed baking sheet. Slide into a 350-degree oven and toast, shaking once or twice, until caramel brown and nutty scented, about 15 minutes.

2. Caramelize: Line a rimmed baking sheet with parchment paper; keep handy. Measure sugar into a small heavy skillet. Set over medium-high heat, stirring occasionally. In about 5 minutes, sugar will clump, then melt. In another minute, caramelized sugar will turn tan, then amber. Tumble in toasted nuts; stir to coat. Scrape nuts onto baking sheet; spread out. Let cool.

3. Grind: Break up nut brittle into the food processor. Grind to bits, about 1 minute. Add chocolate. Process 1 minute. Small chunks of chocolate may linger; don't fret.

4. Scald: Bring half-and-half to a boil; with food processor running, pour in half-and-half. Process till smooth (though nutty texture will remain). Scrape into a 1-cup jelly jar. Cool. Seal and chill.

*If you can't find blanched hazelnuts, do it yourself: Bring 1 quart water and 1 tablespoon baking soda to a boil in a large saucepan. Add nuts. Boil until skins loosen easily, about 5 minutes. Drain and rinse under cool water. Slip off skins. Pat dry.

WORKING LUNCH

Lunch in the home office tended toward leftovers. Lunch in the office tended toward food-truck. I dined vicariously on Bob's daily report. Pinchos skewer. Shrimp wrap. Arepas, which he described as a corncake sandwich.

I imagined corn, fried into a cake and stuffed inside a baguette. One morning, wandering a New York street fair, I came across actual arepas, staple of Colombian and Venezuelan cuisine. It was a puck of cornmeal, split and stuffed with cheese. At first I thought it was missing its sandwich. Then I realized it *was* the sandwich.

Once I got the hang of patting arepas, I discovered the crisp chewy pockets make fine housing for spicy barbecue or roasted vegetables. In fact, just about any leftover is improved by the arepas treatment—uniting in a single tasty lunch the benefits of work-at-home and work-at-work. Though it's equally delicious if you hold the work.

Arepas

Makes 16

2 cups arepas flour*

1 teaspoon kosher salt

1 teaspoon baking powder

3 cups milk, warm

2 teaspoons unsalted butter, melted

¾ cup shredded Monterey Jack cheese

Canola or vegetable oil

1. Mix: Whisk together flour, salt, and baking powder. Pour milk and butter into a large bowl. Sprinkle in flour, mixing with fingers to form a dough as soft as mashed potatoes. Work in cheese.

2. Rest: Cover with plastic wrap and let rest, 10 minutes.

3. Roll: Divide dough into 16 equal portions. Roll into balls. Flatten balls into disks, about 3 inches in diameter and ½ inch thick. With damp hands, smooth perimeter.

4. Fry: Heat a thin film of oil on a griddle or heavy skillet over medium-high heat. Pan-fry arepas, a few at a time, until crisp and brown outside and chewy inside, about 4 to 5 minutes per side. (Add more oil to the pan, as needed.) Drain on paper towels.

5. Fill: When cool enough to handle, use a small sharp knife to split the arepas, English-muffin style. Fill, sandwich style, with shredded pork, grilled vegetables, or whatever appeals.

*Arepas flour—precooked white cornmeal—is available in the Latin-American aisle of many grocery stores or at specialty markets. Brand names include Masarepa and Harina P.A.N. Don't get distracted by regular cornmeal or masa harina.

LESSONS LEARNED

My dad was good at fixing things and he got plenty of practice. Our living room was lit by a black clay lamp carved into a lattice pattern. It stood on the table next to the sofa—ground zero for the flying pillow or the flailing foot.

The lamp was often swept off its stubby clay feet, landing on the floor, in pieces. Not big pieces. Many, many small, black pieces.

Dad would fit the shards together, working the black-on-black 3-D puzzle. He set each fracture with epoxy and splinted each weak spot until it cured. Then he'd carry the lamp back to the living room, and set it on the table next to the sofa.

Dad handled all kinds of fix-its. When I dropped a blueberry tart facedown in its bakery box, he caulked the faults with whipped cream. When I tipped over a bottle of ink and my brother Ben took the blame, Dad soothed the furrowed brows.

After I left home, I still saved my repair jobs for him. The weekend baby Hannah arrived, Mom cooked and Dad glued all the chipped cups and bowls. He got the light switch to work and the wobbly chair to hold still.

Later, when Hannah cracked her china ballerina, we slipped the pointed feet into a plastic bag and waited for Dad to visit. When Noah's train uncoupled we parked it in Dad's to-do stack.

Years ago, when Dad got sick, I made a custard to chill into his old favorite— peach ice cream. Then I dropped the churn. Dad hammered the dented cooling cylinder back into shape.

When he got sick again, we all tried to mend him. The doctors tried surgery and medicine and machines. The rest of us tried to work the many-piece puzzle of his care. Mom tried everything—night and day, day after day, month after month. We tried hope. And, in our own ways, prayer. But we couldn't fix him.

Now I don't now what we'll do when things need fixing. He taught me so much: how to tell time, ride a bike, multiply fractions. He taught me patience and perseverance. He taught my children how to build pots, roast marshmallows, and catapult strawberries across the living room. But he didn't teach us how to mend a broken lamp, or cup, or heart.

Peach Ice Cream

Makes 1 quart

2 pounds ripe peaches

¾ cup sugar

1 teaspoon freshly squeezed lemon juice

1 pinch salt

1 cup plain unsweetened almond milk

½ cup heavy whipping cream

½ vanilla bean, split and scraped

4 egg yolks, briefly whisked

1. Roast: Halve or quarter peaches and pull out stones (no need to peel). Set in a small baking dish, cut-side up. Sprinkle fruit with ¼ cup sugar, the lemon juice, and the salt. Cover pan tightly with foil. Slide into a 350-degree oven and roast until fragrant and juicy, about 1 hour.

2. Thicken: Measure almond milk, cream, and remaining ½ cup sugar into a medium saucepan. Add vanilla bean and seeds. Set over medium-high heat and bring to a simmer. Pour hot cream mixture over yolks, whisking constantly. Pour back into the pan and heat, whisking constantly, until custard thickens, about 3 minutes.

3. Swirl: Remove vanilla bean. Scrape custard and roasted peaches and their juices into the blender. Swirl smooth. Press through a fine-mesh sieve into a clean bowl. Set the bowl in an ice bath (a larger bowl partially filled with ice water) and stir peach custard until no longer hot. Cover and chill completely.

4. Freeze: Churn in an ice-cream maker; pack into an airtight container. Press a piece of plastic wrap against ice cream. Cover and freeze firm.

HOW *to* SUCCEED

n New York we saw a show. Not any show. A Broadway show. A Broadway show starring the biggest star who ever starred. If you're fourteen, and a girl. That is, Daniel Radcliffe. The earnest, boyish British star of the Harry Potter franchise played the earnest, boyish American striver in *How to Succeed in Business Without Really Trying.*

We watched as young J. Pierrepont Finch worked his winning smile and cunning attitude to rise from window washer's plank to corner office. We descended onto the sidewalk thick with fangirls—two-high, dozens deep. A big guy in a uniform cleared the path from stage door to car door. Hope of glimpse seemed futile.

A day later our fangirl was still clutching her playbill. We were slurping cheese-cake soft serve. It tasted like winning, cunning New York, chilled. We stopped a cab and told the driver: stage door. Daniel Harry J. Pierrepont Radcliffe Potter Finch was still singing. The girls outside were already sighing.

Our girl, wobbly as a window-washer, tried to climb a column. The guy in the uniform pulled her down. Perhaps she flashed a winning smile. He steered her through the mob, to a spot beside the star's car. The fangirl's corner office.

The star came out, signed her program, and left. We stood in Times Square, midnight bright. Our fangirl smiled. She had succeeded, without really trying.

Cheesecake Ice Cream

Makes about 3 cups

8 ounces cream cheese

10 tablespoons sugar

1¼ cups milk

¼ cup sour cream

8 graham cracker squares

1 pinch fine salt

1½ teaspoons freshly
squeezed lemon juice

1½ teaspoons vanilla extract

1. Swirl: Drop cream cheese into the blender. Pour in sugar. Swirl very smooth. Pour in milk; blend smooth. Scrape down sides. Add remaining ingredients, including crackers. Blend thoroughly.

2. Chill: Strain through a fine-mesh sieve into a clean bowl. Chill at least 1 hour.

3. Freeze: Churn in an ice-cream maker; pack into an airtight container. Press a piece of plastic wrap against ice cream. Cover and freeze firm.

BREAKFAST KARMA

Granola scares me. Those little brown nubs seem to suggest that the long trudge, macramé session, or drum circle is imminent.

Indeed, those clumps and wisps huddled in their twist-top baggie seem to share the same worldview as the trudge, knot, or drum-induced headache. A worldview best summarized: "Good for you." Though not good.

There was a time when adults were constantly heaping granola into heavy, lopsided bowls and urging: "Try some!" A time best summarized as the 1970s. In those days granola was heavy with safflower oil and soy nuts. Chewing through a handful was a strenuous job—one best summarized: "Don't we have any M&Ms?"

By the 1980s granola went glam, cozying up with the marshmallow, the chocolate chip, and the airy unidentifiable nugget. Granola squared off into the bar, striking a Rice-Krispy-treat pose. Somehow it maintained its reputation as wholesome, if wholly unappealing.

After that I lost track. Granola still cluttered the cereal aisle, the power bar wall, the cookie bin. When my children called it "gorilla," I gave the lump an amused smirk. Otherwise, I stuck with the cold shoulder.

One evening my friend Vanina served a beautiful bowl of fruit and ice cream graced with homemade granola. I thought: "OK, a speck."

Vanina's granola wasn't oily or heavy or chewy, it wasn't pocked with soy nut or gummed up with marshmallow. It was golden, crunchy, and absolutely delicious. I pleaded for the recipe and toasted up a batch of the sweet, buttery oat-and-nut mix. I started carrying it around, pressing it on children, urging: "Try some!"

I think there's a saying about this sort of behavior. Something like: "What goes around comes around." Only better.

Good Granola

Makes about 7 cups

3½ cups quick-cook rolled oats

1 cup old-fashioned rolled oats

½ cup sliced almonds

½ cup chopped pecans

½ cup shelled pumpkin seeds

¼ pound (1 stick) unsalted butter

½ cup dark brown sugar

½ cup maple syrup

3 tablespoons water

1¼ teaspoons kosher salt

1. Mix: Stir together both kinds oats, almonds, pecans, and pumpkin seeds in a large bowl.

2. Boil: Measure butter, brown sugar, maple syrup, water, and salt into a medium saucepan. Bring to a boil (watch closely—syrup will bubble up). Pour hot syrup over oat mix. Stir gently with a wooden spoon until the dry ingredients are thoroughly coated.

3. Bake: Divide between the two rimmed baking sheets lined with parchment paper. Press firmly (this will ensure larger chunks). Slide into a 300-degree oven. Bake, rotating trays and stirring granola once or twice, until golden brown and dry (but not brittle) to the touch, about 35 minutes. Let cool. Store in an air-tight container.

PROVENANCE: *Adapted from a recipe shared by Vanina Wolf, who adapted her recipe from that of the Hotel Fauchère, in Milford, Pennsylvania. Strangely enough, the hotel is co-owned by Sean Strub, brother of my friend Gilbey Strub. Eerie, right?*

DRY YOUR OWN

Self-sufficiency is an appealing concept. Grow your own. Harvest your own. Put up your own. Feel smug.

Not that I would know. I like sow your own. I'm not so good with water your own. Terrible at weed your own. I doubt I'd get convicted of plant murder. More like plantslaughter-by-negligence.

The brief, early crop is difficult to discourage: the pea vine scampers up the fence, sprouting pods plump with peas. The radish roots settle in, fat and sassy. Anything that takes its time, takes its time at peril. Many a tomato awaiting its trellis simply fainted. Many a carrot wandering the overgrowth went missing.

Somehow the herbs, neglected in their own quadrant of the garden, managed ragged abundance. At one point basil and thyme and sage and dill and tarragon and parsley tangled together in a fragrant mass. Given a slingshot, I might have felled squab de Provence.

Then the electrician dropped by and announced he had to dig a trench. Through the herb bed.

Shears in hand, I felt like an actual murderer, cutting down my brave basil and thyme and sage and dill and tarragon and parsley. I heaped them into bundles, tied the stalks with twine, and hung them upside down in the kitchen window like ducks at the Chinese market.

I felt self-insufficient. Until I realized I'd have dried herbs handy all winter. Then I tasted just a pinch of smug.

Tarragon Chicken
Serves 2, generously

1 (2½ to 3 pound) chicken, whole

2 tablespoons duck fat*

1 bunch fresh tarragon

1 teaspoon kosher salt

½ teaspoon freshly ground black pepper

1 pound (about 9 medium) carrots

7 large (or 14 small) shallots

5 cloves garlic

1. Clean: Pull the chicken out of its packaging and the innards out of the chicken. Save or toss the innards. Plunge the chicken into a big pot of cold salted water. Let soak, 1 minute. Drain water and repeat until water is clear and chicken is clean. Pat dry with paper towels.

2. Rub: Tuck wings behind back. Rub all over with 1 tablespoon duck fat. Sprinkle with, then rub in, salt, pepper, and 2 tablespoons chopped tarragon. Fill the cavity with remaining tarragon. Cover loosely with plastic wrap or wax paper. Let rest at room temperature, 1 hour.

3. Trim: While chicken is resting, peel and trim carrots, shallots, and garlic. Keep handy.

4. Heat: Scoop remaining tablespoon of duck fat into a 10-inch cast-iron skillet. Slide pan into a cold oven; heat oven to 425 degrees. Pan and oven will heat up together.

5. Sizzle: When oven reaches temperature, carefully swirl skillet to cover the bottom with duck fat. Lower in chicken, breast-side up. All that sizzle will ensure a crisp underside. Tuck the vegetables around the chicken. Roast, shaking pan once or twice, until chicken is cooked through (juices will run clear when inner thigh is pierced), skin is golden and blistered, and vegetables have caramelized, about 1 hour. Carve. Serve chicken and vegetables with pan juices.

*Available in the meat department of many grocery stores or fancy-food markets. If you can't find duck fat, substitute unsalted butter.

'OO(.OO'

INSTANT GRATIFICATION

After the school day comes the after-school day. Now is the time for soccer practice and ballet class, for play rehearsal and voice lesson, for pottery and pitching. Each of which requires a dedicated outfit, dedicated equipment, and a dedicated adult to escort the scholar/athlete from here to there.

Parent and child return home to find that dinner, sullenly, has refused to prep and cook itself. The famished family may search the cupboards and turn up nothing but dried pasta, hard cheese, and garlic.

Inspiration enough. Simply add boiling water and the threat of insurrection and the resourceful can transform pantry staples into steaming supper. The alchemy demands mere minutes. Which is a good thing, since that's all that's left of the day.

Emergency Pasta
Serves 4 to 6

⅓ cup olive oil

1 fat pinch red pepper flakes

½ teaspoon kosher salt

4 cloves garlic, thinly sliced

1 pound spaghettini

½ cup grated Parmesan or
   Pecorino cheese

¼ cup finely chopped
   fresh parsley

1. Sizzle: In a small sauce pan or skillet, stir together oil, red pepper, salt, and garlic. Turn heat to medium and let garlic sizzle golden, stirring regularly, about 5 minutes.

2. Boil: Meanwhile, heat a large pot of salted water to boil pasta. Set a serving bowl over the pot for a few seconds to warm. Scrape garlic and oil mixture into the warm bowl. Cook pasta until tender but firm. Drain, none too thoroughly.

3. Toss: Tumble pasta into serving bowl. Toss glossy. Scatter on cheese and parsley. Toss again. Phew!

AWFULLY GOOD

The snowflake drifts dreamily from its cloud. The cornflake rustles happily in its bowl. Pie strives for flake. The rest of us consider it a snub. The flake is unreliable. Shifty. Flakey.

Especially the coconut flake. There's something unrelentingly eager, unbearably chewy about the coconut flake. It refuses to blend in. There's no melting it into sauce or beating it into fluffy batter. There's no grinding the flake into submission. Coconut flake just keeps on keeping on.

Inspiring the flakeless coconut cake: alluring coconut flavor, moist cake, smooth buttercream. Flake optional.

No doubt many a baker considers flakeless coconut a mutually exclusive condition, a set of circumstances that cancel each other out. Something along the lines of calculated error or even odds. But the two concepts can coexist in a single cake. In fact, it's awfully good.

Flakeless Coconut Cake

Makes one 8-inch layer cake

2¼ cups cake flour

1 tablespoon baking powder

½ teaspoon fine salt

¾ cup unsweetened coconut milk (whisk smooth before measuring)

½ cup milk, at room temperature

1 teaspoon vanilla extract

12 tablespoons (1½ sticks) unsalted butter, softened

1½ cups sugar

4 eggs, at room temperature

Cream Cheese Buttercream (page 248)

Sweetened flaked coconut, entirely optional

1. **Prep:** Butter three 8-inch cake pans. Line bottoms with rounds of parchment paper; butter the paper. Sift together flour, baking powder, and salt. Briefly whisk together coconut milk, milk, and vanilla.

2. **Mix:** Cream butter and sugar, using a stand mixer fitted with the paddle attachment, on high speed, scraping down sides as needed, until light and fluffy, about 3 minutes. Add eggs, one at a time, beating well after each. Scoop in one-third of the flour; mix on low just until incorporated. Pour in half the milk; mix just until incorporated. Work in remaining doses of flour, milk, flour.

3. **Bake:** Scrape batter, dividing evenly, into prepared pans. Slide onto the center shelf of a 350-degree oven and bake until a toothpick poked in the center comes out clean, about 20 to 25 minutes. Cool 10 minutes. Turn out on a rack. Peel off parchment. Cool completely.

4. **Frost:** Set one cool layer, bottom-side up, on a cake plate. Cover with buttercream. Repeat with remaining layers, covering top and sides of cake. If you actually like coconut flakes, sprinkle a few on top. Serve at room temperature.

NOTE: Alternatively, use this recipe to make 24 cupcakes. Fill cups two-thirds full; bake about 15 to 17 minutes.

TWINKLE ENVY

They have Santa and carols and presents under the tree. We have potato pancakes. I'm good with this division of revelry. Except for the lights. In the cold, dark season, they offer pretty, twinkly cheerfulness.

I, too, could string up pretty, twinkly cheerfulness. After all, it's not a tenet; it's a tradition. A tradition as old as cold and dark, as comforting as campfire.

So, while cruising Home Depot I steer my cart to the twinkle department. I park and stare: There are pastels and brights, stars and garlands, elves, and mammoth flashing reindeer, mid-leap. There's solar, LED, and "commercial grade." An elf tending his own flock of reindeer shows me around. I choose a simple white strand.

I spend the next three hours standing on my porch, trapped in 297 feet of green cord and white bulbs. There's untangling and wrapping and hooking up. Revealing lights that won't light. Followed by unwrapping, unknotting, uncorking, and searching for the scissors.

At dusk I plug in my potted plant and it glows with 150 poorly dispersed dots of commercial-grade white light. My shrub and I shrug.

Fortunately, I can quit now. While they're trying to shimmy down the chimney and fell a tree and sing in tune, I get to order Thai takeout and flick on a flick. Maybe I'll pick a DIY title from Home Depot. They must have one that explains how to hang lights.

Thai-style Crispy Duck

Serves 2

1 (1-pound) boneless duck
   breast, skin-on

1 teaspoon Chinese
   five-spice powder

1 teaspoon kosher salt

½ teaspoon freshly ground
   black pepper

2 cloves garlic, chopped

1 small chili pepper, chopped

Freshly squeezed juice
   of 1 lime

1 teaspoon sugar

1. Season: Rub duck breast all over with five-spice powder, salt, and pepper. Cover and let rest at room temperature, 1 hour.

2. Crisp: Set duck breast, skin-side down, in a cast-iron pan. Cook over medium-high heat, carefully spooning off fat several times, until skin is completely crisp, about 12 minutes. Turn and cook the other side until cooked through and 165 degrees, about 12 more minutes.

3. Sizzle: Set duck aside on a cutting board. Cover loosely with foil. Reduce heat to medium. Add garlic and chili pepper to pan and cook until fragrant and soft, 1 minute. Pour in lime juice and cook, scraping up any browned bits, 1 minute. Add sugar and stir. Remove skillet from heat.

4. Serve: Thinly slice duck breast. Fan onto two serving plates. Scrape on pan juices. Enjoy.

COLD AND HOT

Pot au feu means pot on the fire. The sort that sits on the back burner all day, bubbling. The French farm wife, puttering around her handsome, rustic kitchen, tosses in the spare turnip, sack of potatoes, marrowbone, pig knuckle, hunk of beef, string of sausages, or hen. Late in the day, her three-course meal is ready. She ladles the broth into bowls and spreads the marrow on toast. She pulls from the cauldron steaming turnip, potato, pork, beef, sausage, and hen. Ideal entertainment for the cold night and hearty appetite.

Lacking farmhouse and cauldron (not to mention handsome, rustic kitchen) we still managed pot au feu. Not one teaming with pig knuckles and marrowbones, nor one simmered all day. But a reasonable stockpot reasonably crowded with carrots and pork shoulder, a dish equal to the challenge of cold night and hearty appetite.

We liked to arrange the sharp turnips, smoky sausage, and brawny pork in bowls shaped and glazed by Noah and Hannah, the family's newest potters. The earthy homemade meal looked at home in its earthen homemade pots. Ones that had already endured trial by fire.

Pot au Feu

Serves 6

2 pounds boneless pork shoulder (aka butt), rolled and tied

2 cloves garlic

1 onion, quartered

1 bouquet garni (1 sprig thyme, 1 sprig parsley, and 1 bay leaf tied into cheesecloth)

1 tablespoon kosher salt

10 peppercorns

3 smoked sausages, such as andouille

12 slim carrots

12 small waxy potatoes (such as red or Yukon Gold), whole

3 leeks, white and pale green, sliced into 1-inch rings, soaked and drained

2 turnips, quartered

1 celery root, cut into wedges

Dijon mustard

Horseradish

Cornichons

1. Skim: Settle pork shoulder in a soup pot. Pour in cold water just to cover and bring barely to a simmer. Let simmer 15 minutes, skimming all foam.

2. Simmer: Add garlic, onion, bouquet garni, salt, and peppercorns. Simmer, covered, skimming as needed, 45 minutes.

3. Stock: Add sausages and remaining vegetables (and more water, if needed, just to cover). Simmer, covered, until meat and vegetables turn tender, about 45 minutes.

4. Serve: Discard bouquet garni. Pull out pork and slice thick slabs against the grain. Cut sausages into big chunks. Settle meat and vegetables on a platter. Ladle on about 1 cup hot broth (save the rest for making soup). Serve hot with mustard, horseradish, and pickles.

ONE BIG, HAPPY FAMILY

The first time Bob's dad brought a babka, it was gone in a flash. Papa set the white bakery box on the kitchen table, then turned to get a knife. There was a flash of fur, the gnash of teeth, silence. Theo makes quick work of his prey. We never even found the box.

The next time Papa came to visit, we were prepared. When he set the butter-stained box on the table, we closed in, shoulder-to-shoulder. We folded back the flaps to reveal something drab. Babka is round and brown.

We sliced the round, brown loaf into wedges and discovered strata of sweet white marbled with chocolate dark. We peeled apart the layers, following the veins to the center swirl where sugar grit, cinnamon flecks, and chocolate shards converge. The motherlode.

Our technique took longer than Theo's, but the result was the same: The babka was gone.

We slumped around the kitchen, waiting for Papa to visit again. We passed the time by tracing the babka family tree. The butter-and-egg enriched dough calls to mind the braided challah and the tender brioche. It's related to the syrup-soaked baba au rhum, the custard-filled savarin, and the tall kugelhopf. Babka comes from a big happy family of sweetened breads baked up bumpy, like a beehive hairdo, which is (more or less) what babka means.

We tried kneading our own rich dough twisted up with treasure. We kept adding more of the of good stuff until we'd concocted a loaf so buttery and sweet and chocolate-chocked it deserved the name babka. We didn't tell Theo. Or Papa. We still prefer delivery.

Babka

Makes 1 large bundt loaf

For the babka:

²/₃ cup warm whole milk

1 tablespoon active dry yeast

½ cup sugar

3 eggs, lightly beaten

10 tablespoons unsalted butter (1 stick plus 2 tablespoons), melted and cooled

1 teaspoon fine salt

⅛ teaspoon grated nutmeg

3½ cups flour

Ingredients cont'd

1. Proof: Pour warm milk into the bowl of a stand mixer. Stir in yeast and a pinch of the sugar. Let sit until creamy looking, about 5 minutes.

2. Knead: Attach dough hook. Mix in, in order, sugar, eggs, butter, salt, nutmeg. Sprinkle in flour ½ cup at a time. Let mixer run on medium speed, kneading a smooth soft dough, about 5 minutes.

3. Rest: Cover bowl with plastic wrap and let rest 1 hour (dough may not double). Punch down dough, let it rise again, 1 hour.

4. Chop: Meanwhile, make the filling. Break up chocolate and tumble into the food processor. Add cinnamon and sugar. Buzz to small bits. Add pecans and pulse a few times.

5. Fill: Divide dough in half. Set one piece on a floured work surface. Roll out to a ¼-inch-thick rectangle,

For the filling:

8 ounces semisweet
chocolate

1 teaspoon ground cinnamon

¼ cup sugar

½ cup pecans, toasted

For the egg wash:

1 egg beaten with
1 teaspoon water

about 20 x 10 inches. Brush one of the long edges with a 1-inch wide stripe of egg wash. Leave this stripe bare of filling. Cover the rest of the dough with half the filling. Roll lightly with the rolling pin to press in filling.

6. Roll: Roll up dough into a 20-inch-long log, starting at the long chocolate-covered edge and working your way toward the egg-wash-covered edge. Pinch to seal. Set this log aside. Repeat with remaining dough and filling.

7. Twist: Lay the two logs side by side. Twist the logs around each other (it's easiest to start in the center and work toward one end, then the other). Curl into a large (6 cup or more) bundt pan. Cover with plastic wrap and let rise, 1 hour. Or, refrigerate until babka time.

8. Bake: Slide pan into a 350-degree oven and bake until loaf looks deep brown and sounds hollow when thumped, about 40 to 45 minutes. Turn out onto a wire rack. Cool completely. Slice with a serrated knife.

IN A WORD

We like a good sticky word, one with the courage of its convictions. Like "cheese," which is straightforward and to the point. Say "cheese" and hearty Cheddar or nutty Parmesan come to mind. "Cheese" stands alone. It isn't one of those shifty words that hold two opposing views at once.

Consider "bolt." It fastens shut, clamps down, locks up. Bolt secures the sentence: "Bolt the fridge so no one steals the cheese." Of course, the same low-scoring collection of letters also means dash. As in: "That guy in the toque grabbed the cheese and bolted." A word that says both "stay" and "go" has some issues to work out.

Likewise "cleave," which chops apart and presses together. "Buckle" snaps tight or caves in. "Clip" links up or snips apart. "Bound" stays put or leaps high. "Temper" flares up or calms down. The ordinary conversation is lousy with such conflicted "antagonymns."

They are hardly better than those cranky couples that seem to be at odds but actually agree on everything. Like "ravel" and "unravel"—both handy for teasing apart a string. Or "flammable" and "inflammable," each up in flames. Or "void" and "devoid," equally empty.

They exasperate the ordinary word officer, who expects enlisted words to demonstrate clarity, brevity, and a sound work ethic.

Fortunately in this great land, rich in excess verbiage, there's always backup vocab willing to step in and sort out. When we grind winter pesto, we shun the coy "shelled" walnut, uncertain if this nut is dressed or undressed. We opt for straight and to the point: naked.

Winter Pesto Pasta

Summer pesto is all sunny basil and creamy pine nuts. In winter, switch to sturdy parsley and rich walnuts. It's decidedly different and equally delicious.

Serves 6 as a first course

1 cup naked walnuts

3 cloves garlic

¾ teaspoon kosher salt

¼ teaspoon freshly ground black pepper

2 cups loosely packed parsley leaves and tender stems

⅓ cup finely grated Parmesan cheese

½ teaspoon freshly squeezed lemon juice

⅓ cup olive oil

1 pound spaghetti

1. Toast: Spread walnuts on a rimmed baking sheet. Slide into a 350-degree oven and toast, shaking pan once or twice, until fragrant and crisp, about 6 minutes.

2. Buzz: Split garlic the long way and pull out any green shoot (the "germ"). Measure the salt and pepper into the food processor. With the machine running, drop garlic cloves down the chute, one by one, buzzing garlic to bits.

3. Thicken: Add parsley, cheese, and lemon juice. Pulse a few times. With motor running, drizzle in oil, swirling into a thick sauce. Tumble in toasted nuts. Pulse a few times, leaving pesto chunky.

4. Boil: Cook spaghetti in a large pot of boiling, salted water until tender but firm. Drain. Tumble into a serving bowl. Scrape on pesto. Toss well. Twirl while hot.

SWEET TART

Bob over-indulgenced only in exercise. That, and Pop-Tarts. It took me years to notice his Achilles' tart. That's because he was so keen on Pop-Tarts that he rarely permitted himself to eat them. But he admired them. Greatly.

When I set out to bake a homemade version he took an unprecedented interest in my work. Would it be cinnamon brown sugar? Would it be frosted? Would it be ready soon?

I folded tarts from tart pastry, pie pastry, and galette pastry in white, whole wheat, and cornmeal. I filled their pockets with cinnamon, jam, nuts, fruit, chocolate. I tried unadorned, sprinkled, heavily iced. My final tart was fun and friendly: crisp outside, sticky inside, and lightly glazed.

I offered it to my sweetheart. "It's fine," he scoffed, "if you want a handheld, rectangular jam-filled pie. But that's not a Pop-Tart®." He pronounced the silent ®.

I still thought mine was sweet. And, unlike the original, tasty.

Pop Tarts
Makes 8 tarts

1¾ cups all-purpose flour

¼ cup corn flour
(or fine cornmeal)

2 tablespoons sugar

¾ teaspoon fine salt

12 tablespoons (1½ sticks)
unsalted butter, cut up

2 eggs

5 tablespoons milk,
plus a little

½ cup raspberry or
strawberry jam

½ cup powdered sugar

1. Mix: In a large mixing bowl, whisk together all-purpose flour, corn flour, sugar, and salt. Using a pastry blender or nimble fingers, work in butter, until mixture is crumbly, with lumps ranging in size from crumbs to cornflakes.

2. Gather: Mix together eggs and ¼ cup milk. Drizzle about half the egg mixture over the flour mixture, tossing with a fork just until the dough comes together in big clumps. Divide pastry in 2, pat each half into a rectangle.

3. Roll: Dust a sheet of parchment paper with flour. Set one dough rectangle on top. Dust with flour. Roll out to about ⅛-inch thick and trim to 12 x 8 inches. Use a pizza or pastry wheel to slice into four 8 x 3-inch strips. Note: If at any time the dough is uncoopera-

tive, slide the parchment paper onto a baking sheet and the sheet into the freezer for a few minutes.

4. Fill: Brush pastry all over with remaining egg wash, as glue. Spread 1 tablespoon jam onto the lower half of each dough strip, leaving a ½-inch bare border. Fold dough in half, forming four jam-filled 4 x 3-inch rectangles. (The easiest way is to fold over the parchment paper, dough and all, then peel away the paper.) Press the edges of each tart to seal. Press again with the tines of a fork. Poke the top several times with a fork.

5. Freeze: Slide tarts into the freezer for 15 minutes. Repeat with remaining dough. (If you're working ahead, slide frozen tarts into a plastic bag and store in the freezer. Bake without defrosting, adding about 5 minutes to total baking time.)

6. Bake: Separate tarts a bit. Slide tarts (still on parchment paper, still on pan) into a 350-degree oven and bake until golden and crisp, about 25 to 30 minutes. Cool.

7. Glaze: Mix powdered sugar with 2 to 3 teaspoons milk to make a glaze. Drizzle over tarts.

AMERICAN SPRING

Occupy was a popular theme on many a street corner and park bench. I'd been trying to churn up interest in the idea in my own home, without success.

Fifty percent of our local census, 100 percent of those younger than working age, remained resistant. They did what they need to do: go to school. They did what they were cajoled to do: homework, practice, dishes. Faced with the unscheduled minute, they were stumped.

They were keen on preoccupation—staring at the computer screen or phone screen or movie screen. But engage in spontaneous, bottom-up, leaderless movement? Clueless.

I decided to launch a movement called "Occupy Yourself!" It insisted that the 99 percent of children unable to amuse themselves figure out how to do so, pronto. Without TV, text, or Twitter. No coach, no carpool, no accompanist.

For those who couldn't figure out how to operate a book, pencil, or garden trowel, I provided remedial training by way of fava beans.

Fava beans tasted of damp, eager green spring, season of uprisings. They needed to be shelled. Twice. First the thick outer pod, then the pale inner skin. It was a task that took—minimally—two colanders, two hands, and two hours. Which should have incentivized the protesters to find something—anything—to do. Solo.

Fava Bean Crostini

Makes 12 crostini

½ cup olive oil

2 cloves garlic, smashed

12 very thin slices
  French bread

2 pounds fava beans
  in the pod

Kosher salt

3 small shallots, thinly sliced

Ingredients cont'd

1. Crisp: Heat ¼ cup olive oil in a wide skillet. Add smashed garlic and let it sizzle, flavoring the oil. Add bread. Cook until golden and crisp, turning once, about 2 minutes per side. Set crisp toasts on a baking sheet.

2. Shell: Snap off the top of a fava bean pod and pull its "string" down the side. Slide a finger along this seam, opening the pod. Slide a thumb along the spongy inner pod, releasing the five or so beans, each wearing a pale jacket that looks something like

2 cloves garlic, chopped

1 teaspoon finely chopped fresh mint

1 teaspoon finely chopped fresh parsley

Freshly ground black pepper

a scuba suit tailored for a bean. Repeat with remaining pods. Pull up a chair; this takes a good long time.

3. Blanch: Bring a medium saucepan of salted water to a boil. Tumble in the fava beans. Stir. In 1 to 2 minutes the jackets will turn translucent, revealing bright green inner beans. Drain beans. Drop them into a bowl of ice water. Drain again.

4. Shell: Now it's time to slip off those jackets. Use a thumbnail to nick the jacket along its outer seam. Squeeze, popping out a bright green fava bean. Repeat with remaining beans. Find that chair. Amazingly, 2 pounds of favas in the pod yields 1 cup naked beans. Your compost will appreciate the castoffs.

5. Soften: In a medium skillet, heat remaining ¼ cup olive oil over medium heat. Add shallots and chopped garlic and cook, stirring, until fragrant but not brown, about 2 minutes. Add beans. Pour in enough water to barely cover beans, about ⅓ cup. Cook, stirring regularly, until beans turn tender, 5 to 10 minutes. Stir in mint and parsley.

6. Heat: Reheat toasts by sliding the baking sheet into a 400-degree oven for a few minutes. Spoon fava bean mixture onto each toast. Sprinkle with a little salt and pepper. Enjoy. You earned it.

OVER THE BACK FENCE

Competition was not your thing. You'd spent your formative years in a small school-house where teachers had fostered tolerance, teamwork, and a taste for tie-dye. You had earned no grades, trophies, or badges. You'd shared your feelings.

Now, at far remove from your tie-dye days, you found yourself keeping up with the Joneses. Or, more to the point, not keeping up.

It was spring, time to sprinkle the ground with seeds and hope they'd grow. Your goal was low: to let the school-age set pick pea or berry or bean. Which might foster tolerance, teamwork, and a taste for tomato.

Trowel in hand, you gazed across the fence and were met with industry. The Joneses, big and little, were busy building bunkers. Raised beds, explained Mrs. Jones. Suddenly your dirt-level dirt looked low.

Mrs. Jones took delivery of a truckload of fancy soil. Your dirt-level dirt looked dirty. Mr. Jones hauled in potted persimmon, masses of marigolds, flats of straw-berry seedlings.

You drove to the nursery and chose strawberries. Back home you dug them into the dirty dirt-level dirt. You wondered if that droopy look was how plants shared their feelings.

Later, you leaned over the fence, neighbor style. You pointed with pride to your strawberries, all six. Mrs. Jones offered a tolerant smile. She'd already put in 75. Twice.

You sighed. You noticed that feral cilantro and mint had sprung up in the herb plot, in the flower plot, and in the sidewalk cracks. You claimed no credit for such weedy excess. But you were willing to share.

Free-Range Cilantro Shrimp Wraps

Makes 8 small wraps, serves 4

1 cup mayonnaise

2 cloves garlic, degermed and finely chopped

2 tablespoons freshly squeezed lime juice

½ teaspoon kosher salt

½ teaspoon ground chipotle pepper

1 pound medium shrimp, peeled and deveined

1 cup red pepper matchsticks

1 cup cucumber matchsticks

¼ cup finely chopped fresh cilantro

¼ cup finely chopped fresh mint

Iceberg or Bibb lettuce

1. Blend: Whisk together mayo, garlic, lime juice, salt, and chipotle pepper. Scrape half this spicy mayo into a small bowl, cover, and chill.

2. Season: If you're using wooden skewers, soak them in water for 10 minutes. Thread shrimp onto 4 skewers. Brush shrimp all over with remaining spicy mayo. Cover and chill.

3. Toss: In a large bowl, toss together red pepper, cucumber, cilantro, and mint. Dress with about ¼ cup chilled spicy mayo; toss with a fork.

4. Fill: Choose 8 sturdy lettuce leaves. Set 2 on each of four plates. Divide vegetable mixture evenly onto lettuce leaves.

5. Grill: Build (or spark) a hot fire. Grill shrimp until pink, curled, and just cooked through, about 3 minutes per side.

6. Roll: Use a fork to slide shrimp off skewers and onto vegetables. Let each guest roll up lettuce, burrito style, into a fresh and tasty wrap. Serve with additional spicy mayo, if you like.

NEW IN THE NEIGHBORHOOD

Mrs. Robin moved in. I'd seen her around, flitting from tree to telephone wire. I didn't realize she was scouting real estate.

Saturday I noticed a scattering of twigs and leaves on the patio near one of the pergola posts. Sunday the post was crowned by a nest. Monday the nest was filled with Mrs. Robin.

Her spot was high enough to clear the foot traffic, low enough to offer easy-in easy-out. Wisteria provided sunscreen and privacy. Maybe other birds scoffed at her treeless nest, but I thought it was smart urban development.

Mrs. Robin and I kept an eye on each other. She worked long hours, breaking to run errands, grab a drink, or pick up a snack. Back at the nest she looked things over, then settled down, gazing out with an expression that was half preoccupied, half bored. My routine was about the same as hers, only at ground level, and required a car.

We both liked the herb garden. She poked around for berry or bug. I stopped by to snip off a bit of basil, thyme, mint, or oregano. I liked to tuck the leaves into salad or pasta or even ripe melon.

Sun-warmed cantaloupe peppered with pepper and brightened with basil was unexpectedly refreshing. I had the feeling Mrs. Robin, with her taste for the unusual, would approve.

Melon Salad

Serves 4

1 cantaloupe, perfectly ripe, chilled

1 small bunch fresh basil

Freshly ground black pepper

Olive oil

1. **Carve:** Quarter the melon, north to south. Trim away rind. Slice—thin or thick—crosswise. Fan melon slices onto four plates.

2. **Decorate:** Tuck in basil leaves, whole or torn, here and there. Weird, right? Grind on pepper, generously. Weirder, right?

3. **Serve:** Drizzle with a bit of olive oil. Strangely delicious, isn't it?

KNOW YOUR ONIONS

The story begins with "Once upon a time." The recipe begins with "Onions." Both have the same effect: to set the mood. Onions get right to work scenting the kitchen savory, flavoring the oil sweet, deepening the color and complexity of the dish as it unfurls.

Not that every opening line reads alike. The recipe may suggest a mere sweat: low heat until limp. It may insist on caramelized: low heat all the way to a deep, sticky sweet. It may specify the sauté: medium heat until golden. Or it may brave brown: medium heat until crisp—usually reserved for liver-and-onion duty. Then there's the deep-fry, best for the onion ring.

I had assumed the onion spectrum ran from pale to sticky to crisp. An assumption that, like most, proved wrong.

I was enlightened while cooking curry with friends. The recipe I'd been assigned called for onions, brown-fried. Which called for me to look perplexed. And, giving in, to read the instructions.

Brown-fry is unique—or so the cookbook claimed—to Indian cuisine. It sizzles in the zone between sauté and deep-fry. Compared with browning, the technique calls for more oil—about 2 tablespoons per cup of onions. It calls for more heat—a medium-high flame. And it calls for more attention—constant stirring until the onions turn a deep crisp/tender brown.

It's a lovely method and yielded a lovely stew. It's good to know that even "Once upon a time" can be refreshed. And refreshing.

Indian Lamb and Cashew Stew

Serves 6

¼ cup vegetable oil

2 cups finely chopped onions

2 pounds ground lamb

2 teaspoons finely chopped garlic

1 tablespoon grated fresh ginger

3 teaspoons garam masala or ground cumin

2 teaspoons ground coriander

1 teaspoon ground turmeric

¾ teaspoon ground red pepper

2 bay leaves

1½ teaspoons kosher salt

2½ cups chopped fresh tomatoes (or one 28-ounce can whole tomatoes run through the food processor)

1 (15-ounce) can chickpeas, including liquid

3 tablespoons Cashew Butter (recipe follows)

About 2 cups cooked rice

For garnish:

1 onion, quartered and thinly sliced

1 green chili, seeded and chopped

⅓ cup Roasted Cashews (recipe follows)

1. **Brown-fry:** Heat oil in a large heavy pot over medium-high heat. Add onions. Cook, stirring regularly, until caramel brown, about 25 minutes.

2. **Brown:** Meanwhile, in a wide skillet, cook meat over medium-high heat, breaking up with a wooden spoon, until no longer pink, about 12 minutes. Drain in a colander. Set aside meat.

3. **Season:** Add garlic and ginger to the onions and cook until fragrant, about 2 minutes. Add garam masala, coriander, turmeric, red pepper, bay leaves, and salt; stir 1 minute.

3. **Thicken:** Add tomatoes. Add browned lamb, chickpeas (and their liquid), and cashew butter. Simmer, covered, until thick (like chili), about 45 minutes. Stir often.

4. **Serve:** Add more salt and ground red pepper if need be. Heap rice onto one side of a serving bowl, lamb stew on the other. Garnish. Dig in.

Roasted Cashews and Cashew Butter

Makes about 3 tablespoons cashew butter and ½ cup roasted cashews

Measure ⅔ cup cashews into a small cast-iron pan. Add 1 teaspoon butter, 2 teaspoons vegetable oil, and ⅛ teaspoon kosher salt. Slide pan into a 400-degree oven and roast, shaking now and then, until deep brown and crisp all the way through, about 11 minutes. Set aside half the roasted nuts for garnish. Run the rest through the food processor or blender until mixture resembles smooth peanut butter.

PROVENANCE: *Adapted from Julie Sahni's* Classic Indian Cooking, *by way of my friend Elizabeth.*

THE UNDEAD

The zombie apocalypse struck many with fear, but I was all for it. I had seen the upside.

Consider the blender. It worked hard, blending. Grimy work. After a long day on the countertop, it needed a bath. And yet, were the kitchen human to wet a sponge and flip over her blender base, she would find a warning: "Do not immerse."

How was grime lifted from the grime-spattered blender, if not via water? What was water, adequately applied, if not immersion? Not that I was confessing to blendicide. Merely vigorous scrubbing, with water. After which, the blender died.

Services were brief, and unprintable. I shoved the thing into the deepest corner of the counter.

The dead, in my experience, tended to stay that way. And yet, the zombie infestation revealed that at times the dead came to and stalked the earth.

Weeks later I was buttering toast, regretting the whole immersion incident, when I sensed I was being watched. I looked up; two blender buttons glowed red, then blinked. Days passed. Then, mid-salad, I heard a low growl. I spun around, fork prongs flared: quiet. One evening the blender groaned, lurched, and sputtered back to life.

Thinking quickly, I tossed in some cold coffee, clamped on the lid and stood back. It spun, it swirled, and completed its entire smoothie sequence, yielding a milkshake creamy and caffeinated enough to bring anyone back to life.

Coffee Milkshake

Serves 2

1 tablespoon whole espresso beans

2 tablespoons cold coffee

2 tablespoons heavy whipping cream

1 pint coffee ice cream

1. Cool: Make sure the blender is cool. If need be, set the carafe in the freezer for a few minutes.

2. Swirl: Drop in beans, coffee, and cream. Scoop in ice cream. Cover securely. Let it rip. Pour into two tall glasses. Slurp. Feel lively.

Chocolate Malted

Serves 2

Buy 1 pint vanilla ice cream. Use the kitchen scissors to cut away the carton (saves the bother of scooping). Drop ice cream into the blender. Scrape in ⅔ cup chilled Malted Base (recipe follows). Swirl smooth.

Malted Base

Makes about 4 cups, enough for 12 malteds

6 ounces bittersweet (70 percent) chocolate, chopped

4 ounces semisweet chocolate, chopped

2 cups heavy whipping cream

1 cup whole milk

1½ cups malt powder (such as Ovaltine)

1. Scald: Tumble both types of chocolate into a medium heat-proof mixing bowl. Whisk together cream and milk in a medium saucepan. Bring to a boil; pour over chocolate. Cover and let rest 5 minutes. Whisk smooth.

2. Chill: Set bowl in an ice bath (a larger bowl of ice water) and whisk chocolate completely cool. Stir in malt. Pour into a clean glass jar. Seal and chill.

PROVENANCE: *Inspired by Mindy Segal of Chicago's Hot Chocolate restaurant.*

SCIENCE

The husband yearns for steak. He may not admit it. He may not even realize it. But telepathists concur: deep in the caveman subconscious lurks a hunger for New York strip, medium-rare.

Steak strikes me with dread. Something about its simplicity. Its machismo. Its price.

Steak seems to exist in a state of perfection raw. One ruined by the wrong temperature, the wrong timing, or the wrong wife. There's no hiding the incinerated ex-steak under a parsley leaf. It's either done right, or done with. After a few debacles, I developed a recipe for success: I stopped making steak.

This technique spared me the frustration of the undercooked steak, the over-cooked steak, or the overwrought husband. Eventually it occurred to me that my steak recipe exposed me as chicken.

I went back to the butcher. The guy in the white apron explained all the cuts, again. I gave him a confused look and he handed me something expensive, wrapped in paper.

I read about seasoning and searing and resting. I remained perplexed by the essential steak conundrum: the outside may sizzle delightfully while the inside (hidden, well, inside) remains inedible.

Finally I discovered steak telepathy. The cook might poke the steak with a curious finger, or compare the texture to that of his own fleshy sub-thumb (as chefs reputedly do). But there is an actual scientific method using actual scientific equipment to determine the goings on inside the steak. It's called a thermometer.

I gave this method a try. And achieved satisfying steak, along with the standard accompaniment: satisfied husband.

Satisfying Steak
Serves 2

2 (8- to 10-ounce) New York strip steaks, 1½-inches thick, trimmed of fat

2 tablespoons whole peppercorns

1½ teaspoons kosher salt

3 tablespoons unsalted butter

¼ cup brandy, such as Cognac

1 tablespoon Dijon mustard

½ cup chicken broth

⅓ cup heavy whipping cream

1. Season: Pat steaks dry with paper towels. Roll peppercorns into a zip-top bag. Smack with a mallet or rolling pin to coarsely crack. Sprinkle steaks with pepper on both sides. Press in pepper to help it adhere. Sprinkle both sides evenly with salt. Cover loosely with plastic wrap and let steaks come to room temperature, about 1 hour.

2. Sizzle: Heat the oven to 400 degrees. Heat a large cast-iron skillet over medium-high heat. Add half the butter. Add steaks and let sizzle without budging until the bottoms are seared dark-brown, about 4 minutes. Add remaining butter, flip steaks, and sear second side dark brown, about 4 minutes. Using tongs, tip steaks up on their sides and brown edges, a few seconds.

3. Rest: Slip steaks onto a heat-proof platter, cover loosely with foil, and slide into hot oven until done, about 4 to 6 minutes for medium-rare, 135 degrees. A meat thermometer is the most reliable gauge.

3. Thicken: Meanwhile, reduce heat under pan to medium. Carefully pour in brandy (mixture will sputter) and deglaze pan, scraping up browned bits from the bottom of the pan. Whisk in mustard, chicken broth, cream, and any juices accumulated on steak platter. Increase heat to high and whisk thick, about 4 minutes. Pour sauce onto a serving platter. Slice steaks about ¼-inch thick, across the grain. Fan slices over sauce. Serve with confidence.

A HOT MESS

The storm blew over a tree and the tree knocked out the electricity and the electricity—or lack of it—shut down the air conditioning.

I hadn't previously given air conditioning much thought. It's one of those modern amenities, like running water, that's handy, but not, say, interesting.

Lack of air conditioning, on the other hand, is appalling. Especially when it's 104. And breeze, in solidarity with AC, has walked off the job.

At 104 the scene shifts into slo-mo. Walking resembles swimming. Sitting resembles sticking. Air conditioning, and its correlate, refrigeration, seem not just handy, but ingenious.

We moved to the movie theater. We subsisted on a diet of Diet Coke and popcorn. We watched one megaflick after another. Desperation is a desperate business.

Days later, once the tree and the electricity and the air conditioning were back in business, we moved back home. We celebrated over tomato sandwiches. The tomato sandwich requires no electricity and maintains a good attitude in weather crisp or soggy. It's a blast of summer, on bread. And especially good with the AC on full blast.

Tomato Sandwich

Serves 1

Big, beautiful tomatoes, never refrigerated

Kosher salt and freshly ground black pepper

Sliced white sandwich bread

Mayonnaise

1. **Season:** Slice tomatoes into fat disks. Season with salt and pepper.

2. **Toast:** Toast bread golden.

3. **Compose:** Slather 2 slices of toast with mayo. Pile tomatoes on one. Top with the other. Munch.

SOLITUDE

Running was not my thing. There was so much jostling involved. It was the sort of hobby best pursued by the lithe and lively. I was neither nor.

Yet I had been running. There was no good explanation, only a bad one: the dog.

The dog spent his day hurtling from one window to the next, identifying the potential invader—say, the passing bunny or a falling leaf—and directing each, loudly, to back off.

Because the dog and I shared a workspace and because I was often short on aspirin, I yearned to curb his enthusiasm. And so, leash in hand, I loped.

Apparently the experienced runner strived for something more graceful. She maintained a light step and strong stride by imagining herself prancing over hot coals, by gazing into the distance, and by—get this—smiling.

An hour's slog left the dog nap-happy. And me wilted.

I'd heard running threw off healthful side-effects and right away I noticed one: With the dog off duty, it was possible to toss together a delicious wilted kale salad, gaze into the distance, and down the whole thing undisturbed. While smiling.

Wilted Kale Salad

Serves 4

1 bunch kale

2 tablespoons sesame oil

1 teaspoon flakey salt, such as Maldon

1 teaspoon sugar

1 tablespoon cider vinegar

6 scallions, white and tender green, sliced into fine matchsticks

2 carrots, shredded

3 tablespoons roasted salted peanuts, chopped

1. Prep: Fold 1 kale leaf along its center rib; cut away and discard rib. Slice leaf into thin ribbons. Repeat with remaining kale. Pile ribbons into a salad spinner. Soak in cold water. Drain. Spin dry. You should have about 6 cups greens.

2. Massage: Toss kale in a large salad bowl. Drizzle with sesame oil. Sprinkle with salt and sugar. Plunge in a clean pair of hands and rub oil, salt, and sugar into the kale until it darkens and wilts a bit, about 2 minutes.

3. Decorate: Sprinkle on vinegar. Toss. Add onions, carrots, and peanuts. Toss. Crunch undisturbed.

KITCHEN TAXONOMY

The English scholar boils down literature to seven plots. No more. Much the way the culinary scholar recognizes five sauces: béchamel, velouté, espagnole, tomato, and hollandaise. All sauce, he insists, flows from one of these "mother sauces." A compact, if incomplete, worldview, ignoring, as it does, the chutneys and pestos and salsas of the globe.

I like to think of my life as more creatively exasperating than seven plots and five sauces. But then, what character recognizes her plight, trapped in a storyline?

Lunch and literature collided one day when I heard tell of a Bolognese thickened with mascarpone. I browned and simmered and sighed in bland disappointment. I braved Marcella Hazan's six-hour Bolognese, a creamy, fine-grained endeavor I would term "grandmother sauce." Too timid. I yearned for bold, chunky, and quick.

After a week in which our family was nourished by nothing but pasta, heavily sauced, I hit on a pleasingly bold, chunky, quick combination. I thought the English scholar would call it plot 3: the quest. And the culinary scholar would call it sauce 4: tomato. I would call it success and—given the swirl of mascarpone—finished with a twist.

Quick Bolognese

Serves 4

1 tablespoon unsalted butter

1 tablespoon olive oil

½ an onion, finely chopped

1 stalk celery, finely chopped

1 clove garlic, finely chopped

¼ pound ground beef

¼ pound ground pork

Kosher salt and freshly
 ground black pepper

½ cup dry red wine

1 (28-ounce) can plum
 tomatoes in juice

½ teaspoon dried oregano

¼ teaspoon freshly
 grated nutmeg

¼ teaspoon red pepper
 flakes

2 tablespoons mascarpone

¾ pound pasta (gemelli
 twists work nicely)

Grated Parmesan cheese

1. Soften: In a wide heavy skillet, heat butter and oil over medium heat. Add onion, celery, and garlic. Cook, stirring, until soft, about 5 minutes.

2. Brown: Add beef and pork. Season with salt and pepper. Cook, breaking up meat with a wooden spoon, until no longer pink, about 5 minutes. Pour in wine. Cook, stirring, until wine has disappeared, about 5 minutes.

3. Simmer: Use the food processor, blender, or food mill to purée tomatoes and their juices. Pour into skillet. Season with oregano, nutmeg, and red pepper. Let simmer, stirring occasionally, until thickened and flavorful, about 25 minutes. Swirl in mascarpone.

4. Boil: Meanwhile, cook pasta until tender but firm. Drain. Toss with sauce. Serve with Parmesan.

DRAWING THE CHANCE CARD

Storm prep called for action: lug in the herbs, latch the windows, charge the phone. It called for supplies: candles, batteries, butter, and eggs. It called for fire, cookie dough, Monopoly.

During the first hours hunched over the board, while you snagged Mediterranean Avenue and the Water Works, the game distracted from the rush of wind and the snap of tree limbs.

Later, after you'd secured both Park Place and Boardwalk, you noted the similarities between board and bored, Monopoly and monotony. And yet, you trudged on, counting out your paces, building houses, and frequently, without benefit of trial, landing in jail.

In the final stages of house arrest, when the winds of greed whipped through the living room, you were forced to mortgage Boardwalk, close the Water Works, sell off those sturdy green houses. The storm seeped down through the roof, up through the foundation. On the board, your bank account was drained dry.

In real life you'd rolled a lucky number. Many others suffered real loss. You sawed the logs of cookie dough—a sweet and savory combination of butter and sugar, rosemary and cornmeal. The shortbread baked up tender and gritty, strange and satisfying. Like weathering the storm with most everything—except your pride—intact.

Rosemary Shortbread

Makes about 4 dozen cookies

2 cups flour

¼ cup fine cornmeal

½ teaspoon fine salt

½ pound (2 sticks) unsalted butter, softened

10 tablespoons sugar

2 egg yolks

1½ tablespoons finely chopped fresh rosemary leaves

1. Whisk: In a small bowl, whisk together flour, cornmeal, and salt.

2. Mix: In a stand mixer fitted with the paddle attachment, beat together butter and sugar. Mix in egg yolks, then rosemary. Add dry ingredients and mix just until dough holds together.

3. Chill: Roll dough into 2 logs, each about 6 inches long and 2 inches in diameter. Wrap in wax paper and chill until firm, at least 1 hour.

4. Bake: Slice logs into ¼-inch-thick disks. Settle disks on parchment-paper-lined baking sheets. Slide into a 350-degree oven and bake until golden at the edges, about 12 minutes. Cool.

5. Serve: Nice before dinner with cheese or after dinner with fruit.

PROVENANCE: *Adapted from* Ready for Dessert *by David Lebovitz.*

CRACKING THE CODE

The omelet seemed obvious: eggs cooked flat, filled, and folded. I was disappointed to discover that the simple supper I sometimes served was not an omelet. It was an *American* omelet. Nothing like a French omelet.

The difference came down to technique. Apparently one hand was supposed to shake the pan while the other one stirred. Restaurant pros focused on the details: vigorous mix, small pan, hot flame, shake and stir, roll, flip. In less than one minute.

It took practice. Many eggs. And a certain comfort with lumps. After a while, I got the hang of it. My French omelet slipped out of its pan buttery and pale. It was tender and tasty. And made me feel, at least for one minute, like a pro.

French Omelet

Serves 1

2 eggs

1 teaspoon water

1 teaspoon snipped fresh chives

Kosher salt and freshly ground black pepper

1 tablespoon Clarified Butter* (recipe follows)

1. Focus: Omelet-making takes practice. Stack up a couple cartons of eggs, find that tub of clarified butter, and gather a tableful of ravenous, bleary-eyed adolescents. That, or acquiesce to wasting a few eggs. Cheaper than culinary school, right?

2. Mix: Crack 2 eggs into a glass measuring cup. Drop in water. Poke the yolks with a fork, then mix vigorously with the fork for 30 seconds. The goal is an even, pale yellow—no swirls of yolk or white. Mix in chives and a pinch each of salt and pepper.

3. Heat: Choose an 8-inch non-stick (or well-seasoned) pan with sloped sides. Set over high heat. Scoop in butter; swirl to coat the bottom and sides of the pan.

4. Set: When butter is very hot, pour in eggs. Let set 5 seconds. Now the egg shuffle: One hand, grasping the pan handle, gently shakes the pan back and forth, keeping the omelet slip-sliding in its hot butter. The other hand, working with the side of an ordinary fork, pulls the omelet from the edge of the pan toward the center. Shake and pull until the pan is covered with fine curds, about 30 seconds.

5. Fold: Tip the handle up. The omelet will slide down the pan, then begin to climb up the far slope. Now the omelet is seated in the curve of the pan, like a football fan at ease in the La-Z-Boy. Use the fork to flip the footrest up and the headrest down, forming an oval omelet (or a cramped football fan).

6. Tip: Switch your grip, grasping the pan handle from underneath, fingers and thumb on top. Hold a plate against the edge of the pan and tip the omelet out, inverting it onto the plate.

7. **Consider:** The omelet should be pale, just cooked through, and form a football shape. You can neaten things up, tucking stray bits under, with the side of the fork. Relish. Or try again.

* Make your own following the recipe below or buy a tub of Indian ghee at the grocery store.

Clarified Butter

Removing the milkfat gives clarified butter a higher smoke point than ordinary butter. This is an easy technique.

Makes ¾ cup

½ pound (2 sticks) unsalted butter

1. **Melt:** Cube butter and toss into a microwave-safe glass measuring cup. Zap just until melted, about 3 minutes. Do not stir.

2. **Set:** Chill, about 1 hour. The layers—water below, yellow butterfat in the middle, white milk solids on top—will separate and solidify.

3. **Separate:** Scrape off white foam with a spoon. Pop out butter puck and drain liquid from the bottom of the cup. Rinse clarified butter and pat dry. Wrap in plastic. Keep refrigerated.

HOME DECORATING

Holiday traditions vary, and mine involved moving furniture. Table from downstairs to upstairs, couch from up to down. The heavier the better. Some children came home to find the house done up in twinkle. Mine found the house in disarray.

It was holiday decorating, without so much focus on décor, or decorum. It filled the need for novel. What could be more novel than a massive cherry table on the formerly empty landing? It astonished everyone.

After a few rounds of this tradition, some bruised shins, and a dog showing signs of concussion, we switched to celebrating. And that's when decorating know-how really came in handy.

Consider the ordinary glass of Champagne: fizzy, festive, fun. And yet, it could be tinted tart, astonished with orange, and decorated with single-cranberry restraint. The resulting pink drink was delightful, delicious, and dressed to the teeth. Though Champagne, like my house, may be best left unadorned.

Pink Drink

Makes 1½ cups syrup, enough for 12 cocktails

1 cup cranberries
(fresh or frozen), plus
more for garnish

1 cup water

1 cup sugar

Zest of 1 orange

Triple sec (or sub freshly
squeezed orange juice)

Champagne or sparkling
wine (or sub ginger ale)

1. Pop: In a saucepan, bring 1 cup cranberries, the water, sugar, and zest to a boil. Reduce to a simmer and cook until cranberries pop and syrup turns pink, about 10 minutes.

2. Chill: Set a fine-mesh strainer over a wide glass measuring cup. Pour cranberry mixture through, pressing with a soft spatula. Discard cooked cranberries and zest. Cool syrup. Pour into a 1-pint glass jar, cover, and chill.

3. Mix: For each cocktail, pour 1 tablespoon triple sec into a Champagne flute. Add 2 tablespoons pink syrup. Fill with Champagne. Drop in 1 cranberry, for decorative effect. Cheers.

PERSISTENT COOKIES

Cookies are small bundles of information stored on a computer's hard drive. News to me. I'd thought of cookies as small bundles of butter and flour stored in a tin and downloaded, frequently.

Apparently cookies did annoying things like traipse around the Internet, snooping. Which was why many a savvy consumer installed a cookie blocker.

Denying access to cookies, or to certain cookies, sounded like a sound idea, especially over the holidays, when cookies appeared on every platform—at work, school, gym, checkout counter, and dentist's lair. Cookies attended the party, meeting, swap, carpool, and stroll. The internal browser couldn't avoid gingerbread boy, coconut bar, or almond horn. A condition the search engine termed "persistent cookies."

Cookie-handling instructions began, "Delete all cookies previously installed." If only! Then, set the browser to accept only good cookies.

Like chocolate smooches. Which were truffles, in cookie form. They melted on contact. Each little lump was so chocolate-suffused and butter-blessed that no user could have considered it a nuisance. Frankly, any browser directed to block this cookie would have exercised artificial intelligence, and refused.

Chocolate Smooches

Makes about 5 dozen

2 cups semisweet chocolate chips

4 ounces unsweetened chocolate, chopped

6 tablespoons unsalted butter, cut up

½ cup flour

2 tablespoons unsweetened cocoa powder ("natural," not Dutch-process)

Ingredients cont'd

1. Melt: Tumble 1 cup chocolate chips, the unsweetened chocolate, and the butter into a mixing bowl. Zap just until soft; stir until melted. Let cool.

2. Sift: Sift flour, cocoa, baking powder, and salt.

3. Fluff: Use a stand mixer fitted with the paddle attachment to beat sugar, eggs, and vanilla until pale and frothy, about 2 minutes.

4. Mix: Scrape in melted chocolate mixture; mix on low. Pour in flour mixture; mix on low. Use a soft spatula to fold in remaining 1 cup chocolate chips.

¼ teaspoon baking powder

½ teaspoon fine salt

1 cup sugar

3 eggs

1½ teaspoons vanilla extract

5. Chill: Cover and chill firm, about 1 hour.

6. Scoop: Use a 1¼-inch diameter ice-cream scoop (or a heaping teaspoon and damp hands) to shape small balls. Arrange 2 inches apart on parchment-paper-lined baking sheets.

7. Bake: Slide sheets into a 350-degree oven and bake until puffed and set but still soft in the center, about 10 minutes. Cool on a rack. Share.

PROVENANCE: *From Danielle, who snipped the recipe out of* Gourmet, *which got the recipe from reader Ann Bolger. Lightly adapted.*

LIMITED TIME OFFER

ash held captive in a foreign bank account emailed me daily, begging for release. Deep discounts shouted from my mailbox. Low, low rates phoned incessantly. None of which tempted me. I was on steady terms with reality.

And yet, I was an easy mark. All a recipe had to claim was "easy" and "cassoulet" and I bit. Again.

I last fell for this scam years ago. Ever credulous, I had skipped to the store, where I snagged a sack of beans, a string of sausages, and a stack of duck legs confit. Why couldn't a three-day project be collapsed into an hour?

I had soaked and stewed. I had shredded and rendered. I had tried, and tried again. For a week. Mention cassoulet and my children still turned the color of lima beans slicked with duck fat.

Years later, I was due for another bout. I came across a compact recipe for classic cassoulet; it boasted last-minute, 50-percent-off, deal-of-the-day appeal.

Imagine my shock to find its simple steps hid a day of soaking here, a night of simmering there. After which my bean stew spooned up somewhat rare. Crisp, even. Which, in a bean, is not good.

It occurred to me that beans should be tender and that beans come pretenderized in a can. And that by applying can and opener to recipe, I might make something both cold-weather cozy and easy. If not—strictly speaking—classic.

Can-soulet

Serves 8

8 cloves garlic,
  whole and unpeeled

1 teaspoon olive oil

Kosher salt

¼ pound fresh kielbasa or
  other garlic/pork sausage

3 cups chicken broth

2 prepared duck legs, confit*

1 onion, chopped

1 teaspoon chopped fresh
  thyme leaves

4 (15-ounce) cans cannellini
  beans, drained and rinsed

¾ pound smoked chorizo
  sausage, sliced on
  the diagonal into
  elongated coins

1½ cups fresh bread crumbs

2 tablespoons butter, melted

1. Roast: Drizzle garlic with olive oil. Wrap in two layers of foil and toss the packet in a 400-degree oven until soft and fragrant, about 30 minutes. Let cool. Squeeze roasted garlic cloves from their skins. Use a fork to mash with a pinch of salt.

2. Poach: Meanwhile, settle fresh sausage in a saucepan. Pour in broth. Bring to a boil, lower heat, and simmer until cooked through, about 10 minutes. Pull out sausage; save broth. When cool enough to handle pull off casing, crumble sausage. Skim any fat from broth.

3. Shred: Pull apart duck meat, discarding skin and bone, reserving fat.

4. Wilt: In a large saucepan, heat 2 tablespoons duck fat. Add onion and thyme and stir until wilted, 10 minutes. Stir in beans, garlic mash, both types of sausage, and shredded duck. Pour in enough reserved sausage-poaching broth so that mixture looks somewhat thinner than chili. You may not need all the broth. Taste; add salt if need be. Bring to a boil.

5. Bake: Pack cassoulet into an ovenproof casserole. Toss together breadcrumbs and butter. Spread over top. Bake at 425 degrees until bubbling and thick at the sides, golden brown on top, about 45 minutes.

*Purchase duck legs confit (duck legs preserved in fat and spices) at the grocery store meat counter (just ask) or from one of the fancy food stores. D'Artagnan is a good producer.

A STORYBOOK TRIP

My Madeline and Pepito were ignorant of France. They had been raised in captivity, first in Chicago, then in Baltimore. Pepito had slingshot into his teens; time for an outing.

As Miss Clavel, I packed shapeless black robes. Who could manage Parisian style? Besides, I was there for the food.

We made up for lost time. We summited the Eiffel Tower. We gasped at the Musée d'Orsay. We applauded the Opéra. We ate.

Meals so good we remembered almost nothing. Like waking from a dream, all that remained was a feeling of sublime contentment and a whiff of creamed parsnips, roast duck, and lemon curd.

Perhaps, too, the scent of crème fraîche. Fresh cream is schooled by erudite bacteria until it develops a thick texture, deep flavor, and profound thoughts. Crème fraîche is cultured. And we were hungry for culture.

We loafed at Les Deux Magots, where long ago, in our family adaptation of the storybook, the Ambassador had asked Miss Clavel for her hand. We twisted open the windows of our hotel room and peered out at a storefront done up in wedding dress. In the early morning, a taut, young Parisian tapped her high heel on the sidewalk. Perhaps she, too, knew Deux Magots.

We gathered pebbles. Hunted macarons. Sighed. It was so short. All that remained was the scent of crème fraîche and a feeling of sublime contentment.

Crème Fraîche

Makes 1 cup

1 cup heavy whipping cream (if you can find cream that's not ultra-pasteurized, all the better)

1 tablespoon cultured buttermilk

1. Stir: Pour cream into a clean glass jar. Stir in buttermilk. Cover, with lid slightly ajar.

2. Wait: Let rest at room temperature until thick and flavorful, about 36 hours.

3. Chill: Cover. Chill. Keeps about two weeks. Good on everything.

Cranberry Bread

This recipe has nothing to do with Paris. The French don't mess with cranberries. It does, however, call for crème fraîche and it is my absolute favorite quick bread. Wrapped in a pretty kitchen towel it makes an excellent hostess gift.

Makes 1 loaf

¾ cups flour

1 teaspoon baking powder

¼ teaspoon fine salt

1 tablespoon finely grated orange zest

¼ cup freshly squeezed orange juice

½ cup crème fraîche

¼ pound (1 stick) unsalted butter, softened

¾ cup sugar

2 eggs

2 cups cranberries, coarsely chopped

1. Prep: Sift together flour, baking powder, and salt. In a separate bowl, stir together zest, juice, and crème fraîche.

2. Fluff: Using a stand mixture fitted with the paddle attachment on medium-high, beat butter and sugar fluffy, about 2 minutes. Add eggs, one at a time; beat fluffy. Scoop in one-third the flour; mix on low just until incorporated. Pour in half the juice; mix just until incorporated. Work in remaining dose of flour, juice, flour. Fold in berries.

3. Bake: Scrape into a buttered and floured 9 x 5 x 3 loaf pan. Slide into a 350-degree oven and bake until a toothpick poked in the middle comes out clean, about 90 minutes. Cool. Slice. Serve.

PROVENANCE: *Adapted from* Everyday Greens *by Annie Somerville.*

ON THE TRAIL

Hannah returned from the winter trail with a wide smile, sore feet, and a taste for gorp. "It's the perfect food," she explained. "It has everything: protein, fruit, and chocolate." Flawless logic.

She ransacked the cupboards for nuts and seeds, like a mouse expecting house guests. She scooped together great bowls of sunflower kernels, dried mango, roasted peanuts, and chocolate chips. She pursued the ideal balance of gorp's essential elements: salty, chewy, and sweet.

Just because a dish is known by the acronym for "good ol' raisins and peanuts," doesn't mean it needs raisins. My winter camper believed it was a rare dish that needed raisins. Flawless logic.

Indeed, wordy sorts claimed gorp as a "backcronym," pieced together to explain an inexplicable, but actual, word. Logical enough.

Hannah packed mason jars of the mix to fuel her hikes from kitchen to bedroom, eventually attracting an actual mouse houseguest.

She refined her recipe. Seeds, she decided, were superfluous. Worse, they sank. Mango distracted. M&Ms trumped chocolate chips; they crunched.

Her final formula balanced salty, chewy, sweet, and crunchy. It fueled the hike up a steep trail or through a long night of homework. It offered everything: protein, fruit, and chocolate. Plus the flawless logic of self-sufficiency in a jar.

Gorp

2 parts roasted salted peanuts

1 part dried sweetened cranberries

1 part chopped dried sweetened pineapple

1 part plain M&Ms

Toss everything together. For the trail, portion into easy-access plastic bags. Munch as needed.

MAGIC

Carnitas count as magic trick: Start with a blob of fatty pork shoulder. Add water. Say the magic word. And voila: an arsenal of crunchy crisp-fried pork bombs.

Magicians are supposed to keep their secrets secret, but I'm happy to tell. I shrug off other rules of the trade, like the cape, hat, and wand. I'm more the apron, bobby pin, and wooden spoon type.

Carnitas

Here's how to work the trick: Buy 2 pounds of pork shoulder. It might be called pork butt, which means shoulder. Go for a fatty piece.

A 2-pound slab (enough to serve four) resembles a big steak—about 2 inches thick and 8 inches across. You want it low and wide. Rub all over with 1 teaspoon kosher salt. Settle pork in a heavy pan with a snug fit. I use my standard cast-iron cauldron—10 inches across, 3 inches deep, with a lid—but no need to be picky.

Pour in just enough water to barely cover the meat, about 4 cups. Bring to a boil. Lumps of mud-colored foam will bob up here and there. Skim and forget. Magic is a mysterious art form. Lower to a simmer. Cover (leaving the lid just a bit askew). Wait.

Now unfurl the magic word: Patience.

It takes about 1½ hours for the meat to turn fork-tender. Use two forks to break the meat into chunks, say about 1 x 1 x 2-inches.

Continue to cook, uncovered. By now most of the water will have disappeared. The meat will render its fat, leaving pork chunks on top, lard below. Say the magic word again. Let the meat cook, meddling as little as possible, so that it fries in its own fat. After about 30 minutes, you should have a heap of brown, hot, crunchy "little meats." Something like bacon-wrapped pork roast.

Scoop out carnitas with a slotted spoon. Heap onto fresh, hot corn tortillas. Add a wedge of avocado, some shards of scallion, and a squeeze of lime. As they say in the business: Ta-da.

EARLY RISERS

The early mom gets a quiet cup of coffee. Which should be reward enough, but isn't. I usually succumb to snooze. Still, I'm impressed by early. The friend who wakes predawn to work. Or worse, work out. The quick-study who files early. Or worse, retires early. Problems I will never share.

Outside knows the same division of labor. While the hedgehog rolls over, while the onion snuggles deep in its bed, the crocus shoots up, cracks a purple grin and shouts "Ta-dah!" Morning sorts tend toward smug.

I tried. One sunny Sunday, sandwiched between weeks of slush and rain, I dragged out the grill. I peered at the herb patch, dozing under a blanket of last fall's leaves. Slacker mulch. Everyone seemed to be asleep, so I tiptoed around, trimming dried stems from the mint and lavender. I pulled back a tangle of twigs and discovered bright green curls of parsley, eager to get to work.

Who knew earnest parsley—never smug—was a morning sort? I tossed together a salmon salad bright with lemon, scallion, cilantro, and parsley and savored—late in the day—the benefits of rising early.

Salmon and Parsley Salad

Serves 4

4 sprigs fresh thyme

2 garlic cloves, split

2 cardamom pods

2 bay leaves

1 tablespoon kosher salt

1 teaspoon freshly ground black pepper

1 pound salmon fillet, deboned, skinned, grey strip removed

About 1½ cups olive oil

2 bunches fresh parsley

Ingredients cont'd

1. Poach: Choose a pot that will offer the fish a snug fit. Scatter in half the thyme, garlic, cardamom, bay leaves, salt, and pepper. Settle in fish. Pour in olive oil to completely cover. Add remaining thyme, garlic, cardamom, bay leaves, salt, and pepper. Set over very low heat until salmon turns light pink, but remains slightly rare in the center, about 40 minutes.

2. Chill: Cover—fish, spices, oil, and all—and chill overnight.

3. Toss: Coarsely chop leaves and tender stems of the parsley and cilantro. Coarsely chop nuts and seeds. In a serving bowl, toss together parsley, cilantro, nuts, seeds, and onions.

1 bunch fresh cilantro

2 scallions, white and tender green, thinly sliced

3 tablespoons roasted peanuts

3 tablespoons toasted almonds

3 tablespoons toasted pumpkin seeds

3 tablespoons toasted sunflower seeds

2 tablespoons freshly squeezed lemon juice

4. Serve: Fish fish from its oil bath. Crumble over parsley salad. Season with about 4 tablespoons of the cooking oil, the lemon juice, and a little salt. Toss gently and serve.

PROVENANCE: *Adapted from Manta Ray restaurant, Tel Aviv.*

GOOD DOG

Theo was a good bad dog. He ate anything he could get his canines around: scraps, shoes, sweaters. He once snatched two pounds of pork meant for meatballs. He sniffed gum from my purse. He chewed vitamins out of the luggage. He crunched a bottle of Advil. An expensive bottle of Advil, given the ER and the 48 hours of surveillance. Theo needed 48 hours of surveillance every day.

On his first birthday I baked him a cheesecake. I set it between his paws and snapped a shot. It shows Theo. No cake.

Theo maintained an odd social life. Trotting the neighborhood, human in tow, he crossed paths with colleagues big and small. Sometimes he'd pause for a brief tail sniff. Sometimes he'd bristle into 80 pounds of gnashing, thrashing fury. I never knew what set him off. Did those dogs whisper something snide?

Theo ran the back fence in heated laps, prepared to shred the intruder. Should someone—friend, stranger, milkman—step through the gate, Theo turned gregarious. He leapt. He licked. He laid down and offered up his pink belly. He loved overnight guests. He joined them in bed.

Bob and I thought Theo was the kids' dog. Theo thought he was my dog. When I worked, he stretched out at my feet. When I cooked, he sprawled by the stove. When I read, he wedged himself onto the couch, head on my shoulder, paw slung over my ribs. He liked the foot of the bed, but preferred the pillows.

Theo's last night, he slept head on pillow, fur on sheets, and snored. In the morning we followed our routine: Theo jumped in the way back, snapped into his snoot loop and leash. I scooted into the driver's seat, snapped into stretch pants and running shoes. We dropped the kids at school. We parked on the shoulder by the woods. I opened the door a crack. I grabbed his leash.

Then Theo saw the bus. He hurled himself out of the car, ripping the leather through my hands. I don't know if he meant to shred the intruder. Or sniff its tailpipe.

Theo seemed startled to find himself on the pavement. I looked into his pale eyes and saw this: Joy. He was delighted to see me. And then he was gone.

Now no one steals the meatballs. No one buries my boots. No one rushes the front door. Ordinary tasks are so easy. And so hard.

Meatball Muddle

Serves 4

1 onion, cut in half

2 cloves garlic

2 teaspoons dried oregano

1 tablespoon unsalted butter

1 tablespoon olive oil

1 28-ounce can tomatoes
in juice, run through
the blender

1 cup water

1 teaspoon kosher salt

½ teaspoon freshly
ground pepper

¾ cup whole milk

36 Meatballs (recipe follows)

1 pound dried tagliatelle, or,
if you're adventuresome,
homemade Tagliatelle
(recipe follows)

1. Grind: Defying conventional wisdom, let the food processor have its way with the onion, garlic, and oregano. Heat the butter and oil in a deep, wide pan. Scrape in the onion mix and cook over medium-low until soft, about 10 minutes.

2. Simmer: Add tomatoes, water, salt and pepper. Cook 10 minutes. Stir in the milk.

3. Coddle: Settle the meatballs into the sauce, one by one. To prevent meatball breakup, don't stir for a few minutes. Simmer, partially covered, about 20 minutes. You may need to add some water to keep the sauce bubbling cheerfully.

4. Boil: Cook pasta in boiling salted water (fresh pasta only needs 1 to 2 minutes). Drain, letting some water cling to noodles. Ladle on some tomato sauce (without meatballs), toss, and heap into a serving bowl. Pour on the remaining sauce and meatballs. Dig in.

Meatballs

½ pound ground pork

½ pound ground beef

1 egg

2 tablespoons freshly grated
Parmesan

1 clove garlic, finely chopped

1 teaspoon dried oregano

3 tablespoons fresh
bread crumbs

1 teaspoon kosher salt

½ teaspoon freshly ground
black pepper

1. Mix: Combine all ingredients gently, by hand.

2. Shape: Roll 36 small balls, each about 1 inch in diameter. Line them up on a baking sheet. Cover and chill.

Tagliatelle

2 cups semolina flour

1 fat pinch of salt

4 eggs

1. Mix: Heap the flour and salt in large bowl. Crack in the eggs. Plunge in clean hands and cajole. After a few minutes, when the mixture looks less like a mess and more like dough, transfer to a lightly floured work surface.

2. Knead: Take your time, 10 to 15 minutes. When the dough becomes less springy and more accommodating, when something in its tender demeanor and smooth shape makes you feel motherly, stop. Dust lightly with flour, wrap in a kitchen towel and let rest, 1 hour.

3. Roll: Get out that neglected pasta machine. Cut the dough into four sections and rewrap. Pass one section through the widest roller setting. Fold in thirds, like a letter. Pass an open end through the widest setting again. Repeat several times until dough looks perfectly smooth. Now stop down the settings, passing the dough once through each, without folding. Dough will stretch long and lovely. When it's as thin as you like, usually the second to last setting, stop. Drape over the backs of chairs or across towels, like laundry, and let dry about 15 minutes. Repeat with remaining sections.

4. Cut: Slice into wide noodles with the machine's cutting blade, a sharp knife, a pastry wheel. Don't you feel a sense of accomplishment?

PROVENANCE: *Inspired by Nigella.*

A BREATH *of* SPRING

The fledgling bird fixes her eyes on the horizon, draws a beakful of air, and jumps. The fledgling girl fixes her eyes on the horizon, draws a deep breath, and sighs. So many speed bumps.

She waited nearly sixteen years, endured thirty hours of classroom drivers' ed, and skimmed an entire booklet of road rules before braving the motor vehicle administration.

She was tested: One hour standing in line. Two hours slumped in the loud lounge. Three minutes clicking through questions. Landing her back in limbo. Finally: smile, snap, sign. And grin. She pocketed her learner's permit.

Perched behind the wheel, she peered at her toes, then pressed them to the accelerator. She edged across the empty parking lot, confronted a lamp post and, following etiquette, yielded the right of way. She stopped the car, slid down the window, and breathed.

The air smelled damp and green. It was spring, time for the pale fava bean popped from its pod, time for the tender egg cracked from its shell. Time for the fledgling to flex her wings and—within the limits of the law and under the supervision of a licensed adult driver—to fly.

Shakshouka

Shakshouka, which means (more or less) "shaken," can be as simple as eggs poached in tomato sauce. It's a popular quick meal in Israel, where it was imported by Tunisians. This version shakes up fresh spring flavors.

Serves 2

1 fat artichoke

3 tablespoons olive oil

½ teaspoon kosher salt

1 clove garlic, finely chopped

2 tablespoons chopped
fresh mint leaves

2 tablespoons chopped
fresh parsley

1 cup shredded zucchini

¾ cup blanched and shelled
fava beans (see page 358
or use fresh or frozen
baby limas)

½ cup water

2 tablespoons freshly
squeezed lemon juice

2 teaspoons harissa*

2 eggs

Freshly ground black pepper

Crusty bread

1. Trim: Slice away the prickly top half of the artichoke. Trim stem to 1 inch. Peel away dark green leaves, exposing light green leaves. Use a vegetable peeler to smooth away bumps and peel the stem. Cut artichoke in half. Scrape out the fuzzy choke. Cut each half into 4 (somewhat bent) crescents.

2. Brown: Heat oil in a medium (10-inch) skillet set over medium heat. Add artichokes and ½ teaspoon salt. Cook, turning once until beautifully browned, about 4 minutes.

3. Simmer: Reduce heat to medium low; stir in garlic, mint, and parsley. Cover and cook 1 minute. Stir in zucchini, beans, water, lemon juice, and harissa; cover and cook until vegetables are tender and most of the liquid has evaporated, about 20 minutes.

4. Poach: Scoop two wells into the vegetables. Crack an egg into each. Season with salt and pepper. Cover and cook to your liking, about 5 minutes for whites that are set and yolks that are not.

5. Serve: Scoop onto two plates and serve with bread for dipping. Enjoy.

*The spicy North African tomato and pepper condiment can often be found next to the hummus.

GOODNIGHT ROOM

Boyhood calls for supplies. Rocks, of course. Magnifying glass to study rocks. Dirt to keep rocks company. Stick collection, shell collection, stamp collection. State quarters, minus Alaska. Pocket knives. Possible fossil. Spring-loaded snake, packed into its candy tin. Juggling balls. Baseball, signed. Basketball, soggy. Glove and cleats and shin guards and helmets and goggles and high-tops and low-tops, in a heap. Trophies, ribbons, certificates. Monopoly. Legos. Pinch pots. Dog portraits. Sister photo. Guitar, unstrummed. Poker chips. Skateboard. And books. Many, many books.

One day the boy will survey his storehouse and decide: enough. Enough of rocks and sticks, of stamps and coins. He's ready to redecorate.

He starts with the books. He stacks the never-read giveaways here, the graphic-novel keepers there. In between towers the treasures: The books so bound to boyhood that he cannot let them go. Nor, he declares, can they stay.

And so we box. Goodnight, Frog. Goodnight, Toad. Goodnight Mike and your Mary Anne. Goodnight Curious George, and The Red Balloon. Goodnight, Babar. Goodnight wild things. Goodnight to that truck, always stuck. Goodnight Fox in Socks. Goodnight poems. Goodnight air. Goodnight pancake books, everywhere.

Once, the boy leaned into your pages, finding adventure, solace, and breakfast menu. Under his stare your shapes crisped into letters, your letters clumped into words, your words linked into stories. Your naughty wolves and pensive bears will accompany the boy forever. But the boy, he's already gone.

Blueberry Pancakes

Serves 4

4 tablespoons (½ stick) unsalted butter

1 egg

6 tablespoons sour cream

¾ cup milk

Zest of 1 lemon, finely grated

1¼ cups flour

¼ cup sugar

2 teaspoons baking powder

¼ teaspoon fine salt

A few grates of nutmeg

1 cup blueberries

Canola oil, for cooking

1. Whisk: Settle butter in a large bowl. Zap to melt. Cool a bit. Whisk in, in order: egg, sour cream, milk, and zest.

2. Mix: Sift flour, sugar, baking powder, salt, and nutmeg over milk mixture. Whisk briefly. Don't fret about lumps. Let batter rest 10 minutes.

3. Crisp: Set a nonstick skillet or griddle over medium-low heat. Slick with just a little oil. Scoop on batter, using a ⅓-cup measure. Dot each pancake with berries. Cook pancakes, a few at a time, until the center of each is speckled with bubbles, about 3 minutes. Flip and cook until the other side is nicely browned, 1 minute. Savor, before they're gone.

Acknowledgments

This book grew out of my work at the *Chicago Tribune*. I am grateful to Ann Marie Lipinski and Elizabeth Taylor for hiring me and for inspiring me.

My Tribune colleagues have been a pleasure to work with and learn from. At the magazine I had the good fortune to work alongside Brenda Butler, Desiree Chen, Marshall Froker, Joe Darrow, Rick Kogan, Jeff Lyon, Jessica Reaves, William Rice, Anna Seeto, Jean Rudolph Scott, Don Terry, Nancy Watkins, Katrina Wittkamp, and Michael Zajakowski. I owe special thanks to David Syrek, who first paired my writing with the charming illustrations of Alison Seiffer Spacek. I am grateful to Bill Hogan and Joan Moravek, who every week make the column look delicious.

At the Sunday section I have found sound guidance and good cheer from editors Joe Gray and Seka Palikuca. My column benefitted from the support of George DeLama and James Warren. I'm grateful to Karen Flax, Gerould Kern, Colin McMahon, Randall Weissman, and Joycelyn Winnecke, who helped me move from newsprint to bookshelf. Thanks to Monica Eng, who joined me on many a last-minute tasting mission.

I am indebted to many friends outside the Tower. This book would never have made it off my office floor without the steady encouragement and insightful editing of Alison True. I was pulled through many a quandary by the ever-able Gail Ablow. Thanks to Ellen Lupton for sharing her keen eye.

Many thanks to Kim Witherspoon, my freshman friend and grownup agent. Thanks to Allison Hunter at InkWell for her help and helpful attitude. I am deeply grateful to Jennifer Kasius at Running Press for believing in this book and for seeing it through, quirk intact.

Thanks to the readers who have read, cooked from, and commented on my work. Your words have sustained me.

Thanks to my friends who have lived through these stories with me. Thanks to Mom and Dad and Josh and Ben, with whom I have shared so many wonderful meals. Thanks most of all to Bob and Hannah and Noah. I love to cook for you.

INDEX

A

Aioli, Quickie, 303
Almond Cake, Big Fancy, 222–223
Almond Cookies, 318
Almond Tea Cake, 76
Anchovy Butter, 124
Angel-Hair Pasta, 15
Anticipatory Noodles (with scallops), 62
Aperitif, 115

APPETIZERS: *It's fine to serve nothing: works up the appetite. If you're more ambitious, consider: Crisp Asparagus Rolls (page 173), Lumpia (page 324), Cod Fritters (page 303), Fava Bean Crostini (pages 358–359), Dumpling Pillows (page 109), Walnut Pesto Crostini (page 239), or my favorite: Ricotta-Stuffed Focaccia (pages 191–192). You may not need the rest of the meal.*

Apple Tart, 95
Apricot Filling, 61
Apricot Pie, 121
Arepas, 336
Artichoke Omelet, 330
Asparagus Rolls, Crisp, 173
Aushak, 286–287

B

Babka, 353–354

BACON: *Easiest to slice if you first freeze it about 20 minutes. Some people like to wrap up sets of 2 slices of bacon and freeze them for easy access later. Some people are very organized.*

Banana Bread, 183

BBQ Sauce, Simple North Carolina, 93
Beans
    Can-soulet, 382
    Cassoulet, Two-Hour, 146
    Fava Bean Crostini, 358–359
    Greens and Beans, 87
    Papas Tacos, 293
Beef
    Après-Ski Stew, 148–149
    Bolognese, Quick, 373
    Brisket, Basic, 54
    Filet Mignon Kebob, 84
    Meatball Muddle, 391
    Pot Roast, 74
    Steak, Satisfying, 368–369
Berry Pie, 251–252
Birthday Cake, 11
Biscuits, Best-Friend, 21
Blondies, 20
Blueberry Pancakes, 396
Blueberry Preserves, 75
Bolognese, Quick, 373
Bread Salad, 333
Breads and Muffins
    Almond Tea Cake, 76
    Babka, 353–354
    Banana Bread, 183
    Bread Dough, Simple, 192
    Challah, 138–139
    Cinnamon Loaf, Standoffish, 265
    Cranberry Bread, 384
    Focaccia, Ricotta-Stuffed, 191–192
    Muffins, Dinosaur Pumpkin, 34
    Scones, Coffeehouse, 132
    Scones, Take-a-Stroll, 315
Breakfast, Swiss, 279
Brisket, Basic, 54
Broccolini, Roasted, 319

BROTH: *Technically speaking, broth is made from meat and stock is the made from bones. Whichever you've got on hand is fine. The stuff in a box at the grocery store is broth, which is why these recipes specify broth.*

Broth, Mushroom, 273
Brownies. *See also* Cakes; Cookies
    Blondies, 20
    Encouraging Brownies, 13

BRUNCH: *I always make Onion Tart (page 153). Other good ideas: Tortilla Española (page 185), Sparkling Salad (page 64), and Crab Cakes (page 111).*

BUTTER: *Best to rely on unsalted butter. It tastes better and it's easier to control the salt content of a dish.*

Butter
    Anchovy Butter, 124
    Cashew Butter, 365
    Citrus Butter, 124
    Clarified Butter, 378
    Herb Butter, 123
    Honey Butter, 327

BUTTER, CLARIFIED: *Butter with the milkfat removed can tolerate higher heat than ordinary butter. To make your own (it's easy) see page 378. Or buy a tub of Indian ghee at the grocery store.*

C

Cakes
    Almond Cake, Big Fancy, 222–223
    Almond Tea Cake, 76
    Babka, 353–354
    Birthday Cake (chocolate), 11
    Carrot Cake, Grown-up, 247–248
    Carrot Cake, Cupcakes, 247–248
    Chocolate Cake, Almost-Perfect, 210–211
    Coconut Cake, Flakeless, 348

CAST-IRON: *Skip the fancy cookware in favor of cast-iron. Good for almost everything. Wash by hand. Dry and oil right away.*

FLOUR: *Use all-purpose flour, unless otherwise specified. I like the ordinary grocery-store sort.*

FOOD PROCESSOR: *Get one. It will make your life easier. It handles lots of chopping tasks (not onion – do that by hand) and does a terrific job with keeping pie pastry cool and crumbly. In a pinch, a knife and patience (or a hand-held pastry blender) can stand in.*

FRIDAY NIGHT: *Make a roast chicken (page 41), a green salad with Lemon Vinaigrette (page 46), and Almost-Perfect Chocolate Cake (page 210). Works every time.*

G

GARLIC: *If garlic will be downed raw (as in pesto), first degerm: Split the clove the long way, pull out any green shoot (this is the "germ"). If garlic will be cooked, skip this step.*

H